THE CHARTERED INSTITUTE OF MARKETING

Introductory Certificate in Marketing

STUDY TEXT

Unit 1 What is Marketing?

Unit 2 Understanding Customer Relationships

Valid for assessments up to September 2015

The Chartered Institute of Marketing

BPP LEARNING MEDIA

First edition July 2012

ISBN 9781 4453 9156 4

e-ISBN 9781 4453 6135 2

British Library Cataloguing-in-Publication Data
A catalogue record for this book
is available from the British Library

Published by

BPP Learning Media Ltd
Aldine House, Aldine Place
142-144 Uxbridge Road
London W12 8AA

www.bpp.com/learningmedia

Printed in the United Kingdom by Polestar Wheatons

Hennock Road
Marsh Barton Industrial Estate
Exeter, Devon
EX2 8RP

Your learning materials, published by BPP Learning Media Ltd, are printed on paper obtained from traceable sustainable sources.

We are grateful to The Chartered Institute of Marketing for permission to reproduce in this text the unit syllabus.

Lead Author: Richard Bakare

A note about copyright

Dear Customer

What does the little © mean and why does it matter?

Your market-leading BPP books, course materials and e-learning materials do not write and update themselves. People write them: on their own behalf or as employees of an organisation that invests in this activity. Copyright law protects their livelihoods. It does so by creating rights over the use of the content.

Breach of copyright is a form of theft – as well as being a criminal offence in some jurisdictions, it is potentially a serious breach of professional ethics.

With current technology, things might seem a bit hazy but, basically, without the express permission of BPP Learning Media:

- Photocopying our materials is a breach of copyright
- Scanning, ripcasting or conversion of our digital materials into different file formats, uploading them to facebook or e-mailing them to your friends is a breach of copyright

You can, of course, sell your books, in the form in which you have bought them – once you have finished with them. (Is this fair to your fellow students? We update for a reason.) Please note the e-products are sold on a single user licence basis: we do not supply 'unlock' codes to people who have bought them second-hand.

And what about outside the UK? BPP Learning Media strives to make our materials available at prices students can afford by local printing arrangements, pricing policies and partnerships which are clearly listed on our website. A tiny minority ignore this and indulge in criminal activity by illegally photocopying our material or supporting organisations that do. If they act illegally and unethically in one area, can you really trust them?

Contents

Page

BPP LEARNING MEDIA

1 Studying for The Chartered Institute of Marketing (CIM) qualifications

There are a few key points to remember as you study for your CIM qualification:

(a) You are studying for a **professional** qualification. This means that you are required to use professional language and adopt a business approach in your work.

(b) You are expected to show that you have 'read widely'. Make sure that you read the quality press (and don't skip the business pages), *Marketing*, *The Marketer*, *Research* and *Marketing Week* avidly.

(c) Become aware of the marketing initiatives you come across on a daily basis, for example, when you go shopping look around and think about why the store layout is as it is; consider the messages, channel choice and timings of ads when you are watching TV. It is surprising how much you will learn just by taking an interest in the marketing world around you.

(d) Get to know the way CIM write their exam papers and assignments. They use a specific approach (the Magic Formula) which is to ensure a consistent approach when designing assessment materials. Make sure you are fully aware of this as it will help you interpret what the examiner is looking for (a full description of the Magic Formula appears later).

(e) Learn how to use Harvard referencing. This is explained in detail in our CIM Introductory Certificate Assessment Workbook.

(f) Ensure that you read very carefully all assessment details sent to you from CIM. There are strict deadlines to meet, as well as paperwork to complete for any assignment or project you do. You also need to make sure have your CIM membership card with you at the exam. Failing to meet any assessment entry deadlines or completing written work on time will mean that you will have to wait for the next round of assessment dates and will need to pay the relevant assessment fees again.

2 The Introductory Certificate Syllabus

The Introductory Certificate in Marketing is aimed at anyone who is interested in finding out more about marketing, whether they are in a job that involves marketing or not. It provides information about what marketing is and aims to develop knowledge and skills for people who are working to support others in basic marketing tasks.

The qualification contains two units:

- Unit 1 What is Marketing?
- Unit 2 Understanding Customer Relationships

CIM stipulates that each unit should take 30 guided learning hours to complete. Guided learning hours refer to time in class, using distance learning materials and completing any work set by your tutor. Guided learning hours do not include the time it will take you to complete the necessary reading for your studies. You should add an additional 30 hours for self study.

The syllabus as provided by CIM can be found below with reference to our coverage within this Study Text.

Unit characteristics – Unit 1 What is Marketing?

This unit seeks to provide the backdrop to the importance of marketing in terms of what marketing is and how it is defined. This unit focuses on the role of marketing, its cross-functional importance and its contribution to business success. It also looks at the role of marketing as a service provider within the organisation.

The unit also provides a basic understanding of the internal and external marketing environment and the marketing mix, with consideration of how these factors differ from one sector to another.

This unit provides the foundations needed for the functional and aspirational goals of the Level 3 market, whilst giving explanation to the language and terminology of marketing.

By the end of this unit, students should be able to demonstrate a sound knowledge and understanding of marketing and its contribution to organisational success

Overarching learning outcomes

By the end of this unit, students should be able to:

- Define marketing in the context of an exchange process
- Determine the importance of marketing as a cross-functional activity contributing towards business success
- Explain the importance of understanding the organisation's marketing environment and the impact it has upon an organisation's ability to satisfy customer needs and wants
- Identify each element of the marketing mix in the context of customer needs and achieving customer satisfaction
- Apply the marketing mix to a range of different organisational sectors and contexts

SECTION 1 – Understanding the role and function of marketing (weighting 15%)

		Covered in chapter(s)
1.1	Define marketing as an exchange process: ▪ Definition: Marketing is the management process responsible for identifying, anticipating and satisfying customer requirements ▪ The exchange process being the exchange between the organisation, its customers and suppliers	1
1.2	Explain the role of marketing in achieving customer satisfaction: ▪ Marketing and its involvement in analysis and planning ▪ Making customer satisfaction a business objective ▪ Ensuring marketing practices secure customer retention	1
1.3	Determine the importance of the role of marketing as a cross-functional activity within the organisation. The links with marketing and: ▪ Research and Development ▪ Human resources ▪ Production / operations / logistics ▪ Linking the role of marketing with information technology within the organisation (ie websites, intranets and extranets) ▪ Customer service provision	1
1.4	Explain the key differences between internal and external marketing and the role of marketing as an internal service provider within the organisation: ▪ Identification of internal and external customers, including their different needs and wants ▪ Marketing providing services internally including intranet services for HR, IT internal recruitment, briefings and announcements ▪ Extranet services for supporting supply chain activities	1

SECTION 2 – Understanding the marketing environment (weighting 30%)

		Covered in chapter(s)
2.1	Explain the importance of understanding the organisation's marketing environment in order to effectively manage the marketing process, and satisfy customer needs: ▪ Defining the internal, micro and external marketing (macro) environment ▪ An appreciation of controllable and uncontrollable factors	2
2.2	Explain the concept of the PESTEL model and show how each of these factors impact upon the organisation, its ability to undertake marketing activities successfully, cost-effectively and competitively, including identifying: ▪ **Political environment:** Government policy; changing governments; international environment and the impact of local government policy ▪ **Economic factors:** Interest rates; exchange rates; GNP and GDP; taxation and how it affects viability of the business ▪ **Social factors:** Increased mobility; societal marketing; representation of family; international and cultural differences and changing social values ▪ **Technological factors:** Enhanced production capability and technique; product development; enhanced and effective communications within service provision ▪ **Environmental factors:** Waste; packaging; sustainability; climate change; corporate social responsibility ▪ **Legal factors:** Consumer protection legislation (Sales of Goods Act) and Data Protection Act (1998 – upgraded 2000)	2
2.3	Identify the key characteristics of the micro-marketing environment, including an understanding of: ▪ Customers ▪ Stakeholders ▪ Competitors ▪ Suppliers ▪ Distributors ▪ Employees	2
2.4	Explain the processes that can be used for monitoring the marketing environment: ▪ Market scanning ▪ Collection of secondary data through journals, websites, etc	2

SECTION 3 – The marketing mix – 7 Ps (weighting 40%)

		Covered in chapter(s)
3.1	Explain the importance of the 7 Ps of the marketing mix as a series of tools co-ordinated to develop and delivered to meet customer needs and wants: ▪ **Product:** Core, augmented and potential product; features and benefits including the tangible nature of the product; NPD (New Product Development); product extension; product modification ▪ **Price:** Revenue generation; balance of cost versus profitability in meeting financial objectives; monitoring and responding to competitor pricing; customer expectation ▪ **Place:** Role of distribution; nature of distribution; distribution channels; maximising accessibility; changing role of logistics; differing customer needs; online and offline purchasing ▪ **Promotion:** Communicating the marketing proposition; sales; advertising; sales promotion; public relations; direct marketing; e-communications and personal selling ▪ **People:** Role of people in service delivery; reliance on people to deliver and maintain transactional marketing; role of people in customer relationships ▪ **Process:** The importance of process in enabling delivery of the customer proposition; end-to-end customer service support to enable transactions ▪ **Physical evidence:** Point at which service is delivered; physical evidence as part of the marketing proposition; environment; ambiance; corporate image	3

SECTION 4 – How marketing is applied in different organisational contexts (weighting 15%)

		Covered in chapter(s)
4.1	Explain the different ways in which customers (Business to Business) and consumers (Business to Consumer) make their buying decisions: ▪ The buying decision-making process ▪ The buying decision-making unit	4
4.2	Explain the different ways in which the marketing mix is used in different organisations to influence the buying decision-making units of each of the following: ▪ FMCGs (Fast Moving Consumer Goods) ▪ Business-to-Business organisations ▪ Service organisations ▪ Voluntary and not-for-profit organisations ▪ Internet (online) business	4

Unit characteristics – Unit 2 Understanding Customer Relationships

This unit focuses on developing an understanding of internal and external customers, and considers how a knowledge and understanding of customers can assist in designing appropriate marketing activities to engage and support customers to achieve long-term customer loyalty.

The unit also provides some insight into the practicalities of developing internal and external relationships, including consideration of networking, collaboration and co-operation in order to reduce the potential for conflict.

Developing effective tactical communications and effective customer service support is essential to harmonious relationships in both B2B and B2C organisations, and as a result the unit considers the contributions that these activities can make to developing relationships for marketing and business success.

The unit explains why organisations need to know and understand their customers and how successful relationships can be developed through effective communications and strong customer service and support.

Overarching learning outcomes

By the end of this unit, students should be able to:

- Explain the importance of understanding customers, and how marketing information aids the better development of marketing activities to achieve customer satisfaction
- Explain the value and importance of internal and external relationships of the organisation and the importance of networking, collaboration and co-operation in order to develop and maintain relationships
- Recognise the importance of internal relationships as an aid to the marketing function establishing its cross-functional presence
- Explain the different ways in which to communicate with both internal and external customers in order to develop, maintain and strengthen customer relationships
- Explain the requirements for developing effective and efficient customer service and customer care in order to maintain successful relationships

SECTION 1 – Understanding customers (weighting 20%)

		Covered in chapter(s)
1.1	Discuss the need for organisations to understand: ▪ The difference between the customer and user ▪ Differing needs and wants of the customer base ▪ Benefits of a marketing orientated approach	5
1.2	Recognise the importance of collecting information to gain a better understanding of customer needs from: ▪ Internal and external sources ▪ Secondary data sources ▪ Primary data from research ▪ Understanding some of the limitations of data collected	5
1.3	Explain how information collected from a range of sources can be stored in order to create and maintain a customer database: ▪ Control access to the database to stored information across the organisation ▪ Aid understanding of the organisation's database	5
1.4	Explain how customer information can help with: ▪ Identifying differing customer needs and wants ▪ Understanding why customers purchase ▪ Developing appropriate and effective marketing mix activities to meet those needs ▪ Identifying the factors that influence decision making	5

SECTION 2 – Building and maintaining effective internal and external customer relationships (weighting 30%)

		Covered in chapter(s)
2.1	Explain the different types and characteristics of people with which an organisation develops relationships including: ▪ Customers ▪ Users ▪ Connected stakeholders ▪ Other stakeholders ▪ Differentiating between internal and external customers	6
2.2	Describe the links between the marketing concept, a customer focus and the relationship marketing approach including: ▪ Difference between customer acquisition and retention ▪ An understanding of the benefits of retaining customers ▪ Theoretical aspects such as Pareto and Ladder of loyalty	6
2.3	Explain how marketing activities help to: ▪ Support relationships with external customers ▪ Aid customer retention and loyalty	6

		Covered in chapter(s)
2.4	Explain the importance of developing and sustaining customer, supplier and distributor relationships through: ■ Developing networking skills ■ Collaboration and co-operation between intermediaries ■ Successful negotiation between the various parties within the supply chain	6
2.5	Describe approaches used to build and develop relationships both within the marketing function and across the organisation in order to gain: ■ Internal co-operation ■ Commitment to organisational objectives ■ Internal support for marketing initiatives	6
2.6	Identify key colleagues within the organisation with whom it is important to develop relationships: ■ Other marketing team members ■ Finance ■ Research & Development ■ Human resources ■ Purchasing ■ Manufacturing	6
2.7	Identify potential areas of conflict that can occur between the functions of an organisation including: ■ The possible causes of conflict – poor, confusing, mistimed, unclear communications, different objectives, agendas and focus ■ The potential effect of conflict on individuals and the organisation	6
2.8	Describe the methods that can be used to overcome conflict between organisational functions ■ Co-operation ■ Conciliation ■ Internal arbitration	6
2.9	Discuss the need to take into account the views of others within the organisation when undertaking marketing activities including: ■ Contributing constructive ideas with colleagues to aid plans for improving marketing activities ■ Co-operating with others to follow plans ■ Keeping commitments made to others ■ Identify with others how joint efforts to follow plans can achieve improved performance	6

task 2

SECTION 3 – Communicating with internal and external customers (weighting 30%)

		Covered in chapter(s)
3.1	Explain the importance of communication as a tool to aid the development and maintenance of long-term relationships: ▪ Keeping internal and external customers up to date and informed on key issues ▪ A means of exchanging information relevant to the customer/ supplier relationships ▪ A means of gaining Attention, Interest, Desire, Action in the context of marketing	7
3.2	Explain the nature and scope of the communications cycle including: ▪ The Schramm Model ▪ Aspects of encoding the message in relation to customer needs ▪ The effect of 'noise' in the communication process	7
3.3	Explain the various business formats required for communicating both internally and externally with customers, including: ▪ Letters ▪ Memos ▪ Informal reports ▪ Emails	7
3.4	Explain the importance of good verbal and non-verbal communications: ▪ Kinetics – body language such as facial expressions, eye movements and gestures ▪ Meta – communications – the importance of silence in communications ie, actions speak louder than words ▪ Paralanguage – the use of tone	7
3.5	Identify the strengths and weakness of the following promotional activities in a range of different marketing scenarios designed to aid relationship management including: ▪ Sales promotions ▪ Public relations ▪ Intranet ▪ Extranet ▪ Internet / wed based promotion ▪ Digital technologies ▪ Personal selling from a customer perspective	7
3.6	Describe the processes involved in undertaking a range of tactical direct marketing campaigns including: ▪ E-mail campaigns ▪ E-newsletters ▪ Web pages ▪ Leaflet drops / direct marketing ▪ Sales promotional activities ▪ Tele-messaging ▪ Digital messaging	7

		Covered in chapter(s)
3.7	Discuss how customer databases can be used to support tactical marketing communications activities targeting: ■ Internal market ■ External market ■ Connected stakeholders	7
3.8	Explain the process used for effectively managing a communications budget for specific communications tasks, including apportioning costs effectively: ■ Identification of costs associated with the project ■ Allocating costs accordingly ■ Working to a set budget and planning expenditure activities ■ Using Excel spreadsheets to record and report budget information	7
3.9	Identify and explain the different methods available for monitoring and measuring the success of internal and external tactical communications campaigns: ■ Enquiry levels ■ Sales increases ■ Media evaluation ■ Satisfaction surveys	7

SECTION 4 – Providing customer service for internal and external customers (weighting 20%)

		Covered in chapter(s)
4.1	Describe the concept of customer care and customer service and its importance in different sectors including: ■ Consumer (FMCG markets) ■ Business-to-business markets ■ Not-for-profit and public sector organisations	8
4.2	Explain the relationship between customer care, customer focus, and relationship marketing: ■ Customer satisfaction being a marketing objective of a market oriented organisation ■ Customer service as an element of the marketing mix ■ The link between quality, marketing and customer service being the key to successful relationship marketing	8
4.3	Describe the different stages of a customer care programme and discuss why these programmes are important to delivering a consistent level of customer service and customer support: ■ Identify customer needs and perceptions ■ Establish a mission statement ■ Set service level standards ■ Establish a management process and communicate it to staff ■ Establish a complaints system ■ Develop control systems	8

		Covered in chapter(s)
4.4	Explain the importance of obtaining formal and informal customer feedback and identify a range of methods for collecting information including: ▪ Questionnaires ▪ Feedback cards ▪ Telephone surveys ▪ Suggestion boxes ▪ Online forums ▪ Informal methods ie discussions, questions at point of sale	8
4.5	Describe the measures that can be used to monitor the success of customer service support activities: ▪ Number of complaints ▪ Measuring / recording service standards for customer responses ▪ Level of sales growth and decline (new business from existing customers) ▪ Customer retention ▪ Existing customer data	8
4.6	Explain how an understanding of information technology and databases are essential to managing customer care and customer service activities: ▪ The importance of a database and its potential applications ▪ Data components that may be included within a customer / prospect database (including geographic, demographic, psychographic and buying pattern data) ▪ Ensuring the database is up to date ▪ Meeting the legal and ethical requirements regarding collection, storage and use of information	8
4.7	Explain the process for managing own self in a disciplined, time orderly and customer conscious way: ▪ Working to achieve your personal objectives ▪ Utilising resources effectively ▪ Completing tasks on time ▪ Seeing through what you have started and closing customer enquiries ▪ Delivering on promises ▪ Monitoring personal achievement and success	8

3 Assessment

Unit 1 is assessed by a one-hour online multiple choice exam. Unit 2 is assessed by assignment.

In order to help you revise for your exam and prepare for your assignment we have also written a Introductory Certificate in Marketing Assessment Workbook which is available either through your usual book retailer or our website www.bpp.com/learningmedia.

4 The Magic Formula

The Magic Formula is a tool used by CIM to help both examiners write exam and assignment questions, and you, to more easily interpret what you are being asked to write about. It is useful for helping you to check that you are using an appropriate balance between theory and practice for your particular level of qualification.

Contrary to the title, there is nothing mystical about the Magic Formula and simply by knowing it (or even mentioning it in an assessment) will not automatically secure a pass. What it does do, however, is to help you to check that you are presenting your answers in an appropriate format, including enough marketing theory and applying it to a real marketing context or issue.

The Magic Formula for the Introductory Certificate in Marketing is shown below.

Figure A The Magic Formula for the Introductory Certificate in Marketing

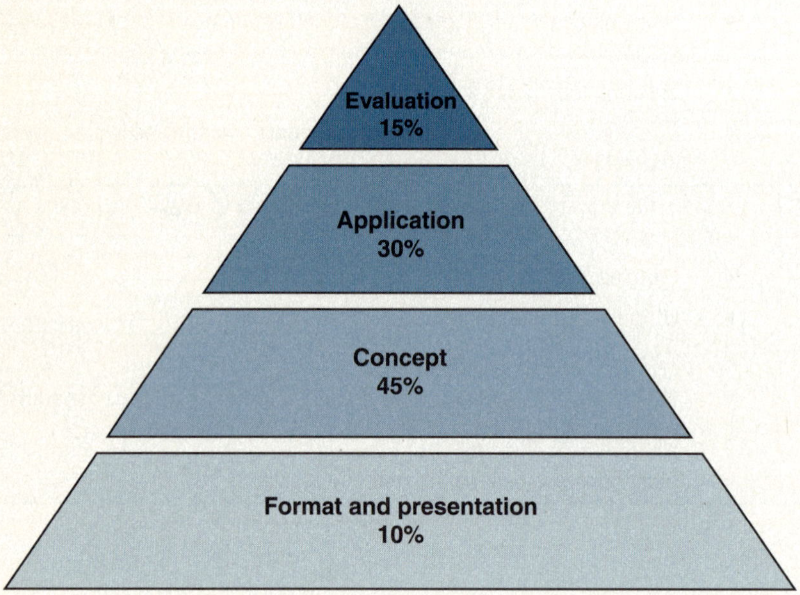

You can see from the pyramid that for the Introductory Certificate marks are awarded in the following proportions:

- **Presentation and format – 10%**

  You are expected to present your work professionally which means that assignments should **always** be typed. Attention should be paid to making your assignment look as visually appealing as possible. CIM will also stipulate the format that you should present your work in. The assessment formats you will be given will be varied and can include things like reports to write, slides to prepare, emails, memos, formal letters, press releases, discussion documents, briefing papers, agendas and newsletters.

- **Concept – 45%**

  Concept refers to your ability to state, recall and describe marketing theory. The definition of marketing is a core CIM syllabus topic. If we take this as an example, you would be expected to recognise, recall and write this definition to a word perfect standard to gain the full marks for concept.

- **Application – 30%**

  Application based marks are given for your ability to apply marketing theories to real life marketing situations. For example, a question may ask you to discuss the definition of marketing and how it is applied within your own organisation. Here you are not only using the definition but are applying it in order to consider the market orientation of the company.

- **Evaluation – 15%**

  Evaluation is the ability to asses the value or worth of something, sometimes through careful consideration of related advantages and disadvantages, or weighing up of alternatives. Results from your evaluation should enable you to discuss the importance of an issue using evidence to support your opinions.

  For example, if you were asked to evaluate whether or not your organisation adopts a marketing approach you should provide reasons and specific examples of why you think they might take this approach, as well as considering why they may not take this approach, before coming to a final conclusion.

5 A guide to the features of the Study Text

Each of the chapter features (see below) will help you to break down the content into manageable chunks and ensure that you are developing the skills required for a professional qualification.

Chapter feature	Relevance and how you should use it
Introduction	Shows why topics need to be studied and is a route guide through the chapter
Syllabus reference	Outlines the syllabus learning outcomes covered in the chapter
Chapter topic list	Study the list, each numbered topic denotes a numbered section in the chapter
Key Term	Highlights the core vocabulary you need to learn
Activity	An application-based activity for you to complete
The Real World	A short case study to illustrate marketing practice
Exam tip/Assessment tip	Key advice based on the assessment
Chapter roundups	Use this to review what you have learnt
Quick quiz	Use this to check your learning
Further reading	Further reading will give you a wider perspective on the subjects you're covering

6 Additional resources

To help you pass the Introductory Certificate in Marketing we have created a complete study package. The **Introductory Certificate Assessment Workbook** covers both units of the Introductory Certificate level. Practice questions and answers and tips on tackling assignments are included to help you succeed in your assessments.

Our A6 set of spiral bound **Passcards** are handy revision cards and are ideal to reinforce key topics for the Unit 1 exam.

7 Your personal study plan

Preparing a Study Plan (and sticking to it) is one of the key elements to learning success.

CIM has stipulated that there should be a minimum of 30 guided learning hours spent on each unit. Guided learning hours will include time spent in class, working on fully prepared distance learning materials, formal workshops and work set by your tutor. We also know that to be successful, students should spend *at least* an additional 30 hours conducting self study. This means that for the entire qualification with two units you should spend 60 hours working in a tutor guided manner and at least an additional 60 hours completing recommended reading, working on your project, and revising for the exam. This study workbook will help you to organise this 30-hour portion of self study time.

Now think about the exact amount of time you have (don't forget you will still need some leisure time!) and complete the following tables to help you keep to a schedule.

	Date	Duration in weeks
Course start		
Course finish		Total weeks of course:

Examination date	Revision to commence	Total weeks to complete revision
Assignment received	Submission date	Total weeks to complete

Content chapter coverage plan

Chapter	To be completed by	Revised or considered in relation to the assignment?
Unit 1		
1 The role and function of marketing		
2 The marketing environment		
3 The marketing mix		
4 Marketing in different organisational contexts		
Unit 2		
5 Understanding customers		
6 Building and maintaining customer relationships		
7 Communicating with customers		
8 Providing effective customer service		

Section 1:

Unit 1: What is Marketing?

CHAPTER 1

The role and function of marketing

Introduction

This chapter introduces the concept of marketing and examines the role and function of marketing. We will use CIM's definition of marketing to explore the key issue of marketing as an exchange process between the organisation, its customers and suppliers.

The second section explains the role of marketing in relation to helping to achieve customer satisfaction. We will examine the range of marketing activities and how they perform the role of putting customer satisfaction at the heart of business objectives.

The third section will explore the links between marketing and the wider organisation. When properly applied, marketing should involve cross functional activities to ensure that the organisation is working together to meet overall business aims and customer satisfaction. Key working relationships between the marketing function and other key departments will be discussed.

Finally, the fourth section will examine the concept of internal marketing and compare this to external marketing relationships. Considerations about how internal customers' needs and wants may differ to external customers will be explored along with some examples of how internal marketing works in practice.

Topic list

Syllabus reference

1.1	Define marketing as an exchange process: ▪ Definition: Marketing is the management process responsible for identifying, anticipating and satisfying customer requirements ▪ The exchange process being the exchange between the organisation, its customers and suppliers
1.2	Explain the role of marketing in achieving customer satisfaction: ▪ Marketing and its involvement in analysis and planning ▪ Making customer satisfaction a business objective ▪ Ensuring marketing practices secure customer retention
1.3	Determine the importance of the role of marketing as a cross-functional activity within the organisation. The links with marketing and: ▪ Research and Development ▪ Human resources ▪ Production / operations / logistics ▪ Linking the role of marketing with information technology within the organisation (ie websites, intranets and extranets) ▪ Customer service provision
1.4	Explain the key differences between internal and external marketing and the role of marketing as an internal service provider within the organisation: ▪ Identification of internal and external customers, including their different needs and wants ▪ Marketing providing services internally including intranet services for HR, IT internal recruitment, briefings and announcements ▪ Extranet services for supporting supply chain activities

1 What is marketing?

1.1 Definitions of marketing

Key term

Marketing is the management process responsible for identifying, anticipating and satisfying customer requirements profitably (CIM)

Although the term 'marketing' is widely misunderstood by people who have not studied business or management, it is an activity that affects most aspects of our lives. Every product you buy or use, every movie you watch at the cinema, every website you visit on the Internet and every retail outlet you walk into has been shaped in one way or the other by the forces of marketing.

Contrary to popular belief, marketing is not just another interchangeable term for selling, advertising and other forms of promotion. Some people even think that marketing is about persuading people to buy or use products that they do not really want. This is definitely not what marketing is all about.

What then is marketing? There are several key points in this definition:

(a) **Marketing is a management process.** It is something that managers do in the course of running the operations of the business on a day-to-day basis. Like other management activities, it requires the application of management skills in analysis, planning, implementation and control.

(b) **Marketing identifies customer needs.** It involves finding out who your customers are and getting to know them. This usually involves using market research to obtain more information about customers so that companies can tailor their products or services to meet their needs.

(c) **Marketing anticipates customer needs.** It involves not only monitoring customer needs and trends, but understanding them so well that suitable products and services can be developed in advance. This requires a proactive approach to understanding customer needs so that a company can achieve a competitive advantage in its industry.

(d) **Marketing satisfies customer needs.** It is about giving customers the right product or service at the right price, in the right place and at the right time. Products and services should match customer needs in terms of quality, pricing, availability and service standards.

(e) **Marketing fulfils customer requirements profitably.** Where profitability is an objective of the organisation, marketing activities should be conducted to ensure that it is achieved.

In today's dynamic and competitive business environment, marketing skills are highly valued in both the public and private sectors. What began as an extension of the sales function many years ago has now become a philosophy that has played a vital role in most recent business success stories.

THE REAL WORLD

Innocent

Writing in *Marketing Week* (29 June 2011), Lara O' Reilly reported on how successful marketing strategies have grown Innocent from three young graduates on a market stall into the largest smoothie manufacturer in Europe. The company claims its marketing campaigns are at the heart of its 20% growth in value in 2010, a trend set to continue.

Innocent work hard to build a positive relationship with their consumers and to align their business values with consumers' values. From their e-CRM activities, newsletters, and fun messages on their packaging to their commitment to sustainable business and the charitable activities of the Innocent Foundation, ethical trading and sustainability is at the heart of their ethos. Their message is one of health – social, personal, moral – and more and more consumers are buying into it. When a multi platform campaign was launched to promote a new range of fruit juice products the awareness of the range reached 47% in only two months. Innocent Marketing Director, Thomas Delabriere, commenting on this success said, 'The campaign has had a strong impact on all our brand values and has brought new buyers to the Innocent brand. As a result we've seen sales grow six fold since launch'. Promoting the purity of their product, its health benefits and the convenience of obtaining two of the recommended 'five a day' from a delicious drink shows how well Innocent understand the needs of their customer. Marketing Director Thomas Delabriere says: 'My target for this year is to grow the brand by increasing penetration again in 2011 and increasing the frequency at which people use our products.'

(*Marketing Week*, 2011)

Other definitions of marketing

The American Marketing Association's definition:

> 'Marketing is the process of planning and executing the conception, pricing, promotion, and distribution of ideas, goods, and services to create exchanges that satisfy individual and organisational objectives.' (AMA: www.marketingpower.com)

Christian Gronroos' definition:

> 'Marketing is to establish, maintain and enhance long-term customer relationships at a profit, so that the objectives of the parties involved are met. This is done by mutual exchange and fulfilment of promises.' (Gronroos, 1990)

Marketing should be considered a business philosophy as much as a function within an organisation (Baker, 1992). At its core is the notion of meeting customer needs because it is only this way that the organisation will succeed. On a practical level, think about a product or service you bought and regretted because it was either poor quality, you hadn't really wanted it in the first place, or you were unhappy with the aftercare service. It is highly unlikely that you would purchase from this company again or recommend it to others. The view that good marketers take is that a satisfied customer is a happy one who will return again. So the best starting place is to identify what customers want and then try to meet these needs.

According to Kotler (2006) marketing people are involved in marketing ten types of activity: goods, services, experiences, events, persons, places, properties, organisations, information and ideas.

1.2 Marketing and the exchange process

> **Key term**
>
> **Exchange** is getting a desired product or service from someone by offering something in return.

Kotler (2006) defined marketing as "the social process by which individuals and groups obtain what they need and want through creating and exchanging products and value with others".

This definition highlights the role of marketing in managing the exchange process. In the exchange process, the customer gets something they want (the product) and the organisation earns revenues (sales and profits).

In profit-making companies, products and services are exchanged for money. In the non-profit and public sectors, goods and services are sometimes exchanged for money (donations, taxes, etc) and sometimes also to support ideas and beliefs.

In the exchange process, the customer will not pay for something unless they perceive that they will receive a benefit. Firms cannot obtain payment, unless they offer something of value to the customer. Customers give up their 'hard earned' resources in exchange for products and services that will satisfy their needs. The level of their expectations usually depend on the importance of the purchase and how much they have to give in exchange (money).For customers, the benefits need to outweigh the sacrifice that they have made in obtaining the product or service. A proper understanding of the exchange process enables organisations to set prices and design their products or service offerings.

In order that this process can actually embed itself within the organisational culture, we must ensure that our customers become aware of the products and services that have been developed to meet their needs. Communication is, therefore, key to the continuance of the marketing process and continuous evolution of the products and services offered.

Figure 1.1 Exchange relationships

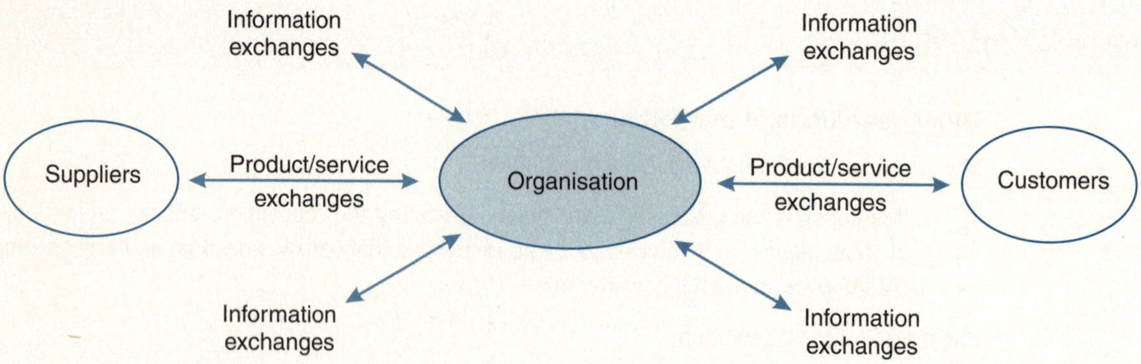

> **Exam tip**
>
> These foundation concepts are essential in order for you to properly understand the rest of the syllabus. There are also likely to be a number of questions on them in the examination.

2 Marketing and customer satisfaction

2.1 The role of marketing

Not only is marketing a philosophy (being customer-centric) but it also is a function and a 'management process', which includes:

- Identifying customer needs and wants
- Satisfying customers
- Identifying market opportunities
- Targeting the 'right' customers
- Staying ahead in dynamic markets
- Knowing and pre-empting competitors
- Using resources effectively
- Enhancing profitability

To achieve this range of activities, marketing is broken down into four manageable stages: analysis; planning; implementation and control (Kotler, 1994). The diagram below outlines these four stages and adds details about exactly what they involve and the inputs required in terms of actual marketing activities that will need to take place.

Figure 1.2 Kotler's Analysis, Planning, Implementation and Control model

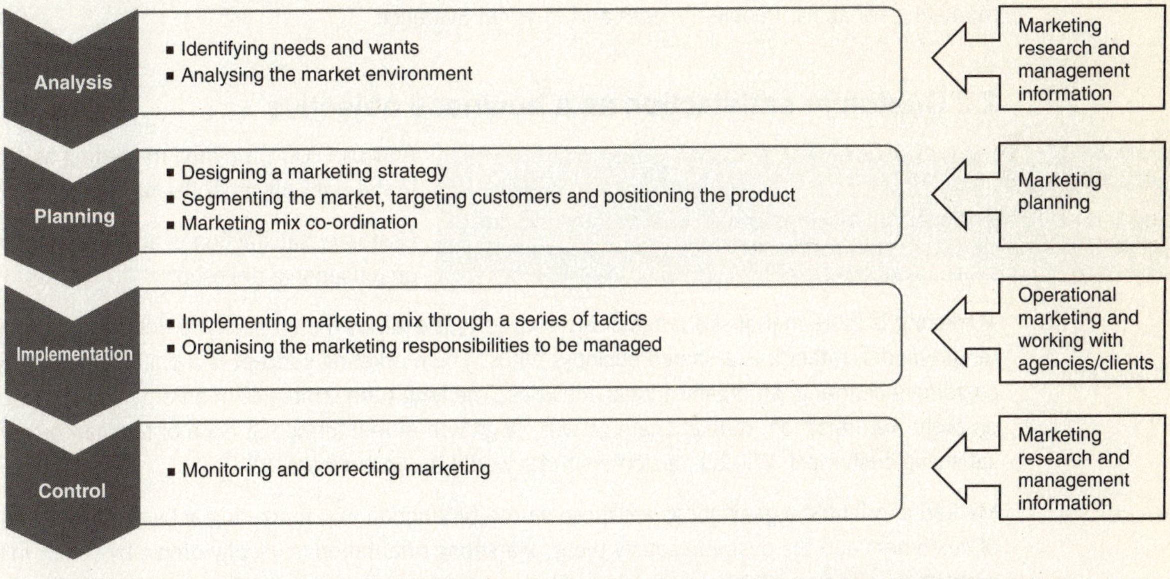

On the right hand side of the diagram you will see that the inputs which are needed at each stage include, marketing research and management information, marketing planning and actual operational marketing activities which includes day to day activities. The list of day-to-day activities will be enormous and dependent on the actual job role of the individual marketing team members but it could include anything from sales forecasting, writing press releases, booking ad space, dealing with customer complaints, monitoring a customer web forum or working with a design agency to ensure the exact colour specification for artwork.

Marketing research enables marketers to make decisions more easily and is an activity that may be ongoing in many organisations.

At the **analysis phase**, marketers concentrate on identifying customer needs and wants and deciding whether the organisation is able to satisfy these in the future. Market trends, competitor activity and factors that are outside of the organisation's control but are operating within the business environment are all analysed at this stage. The **planning phase** then tackles the design of the marketing strategy. It is imperative that this strategy is consistent with the overall business objectives and will place customer satisfaction at the centre. At this point, based on the findings from the analysis phase, the market needs to be separated into more defined groups. This is referred to as market segmentation. The organisation then selects the group which is profitable and attempts to meet their needs. This is referred to as targeting. The final stage is to position the organisation's offering to appeal to that segment of the market by implementing an appropriate marketing plan. The process is shown in the following diagram.

Figure 1.3 Positioning the organisation's offering

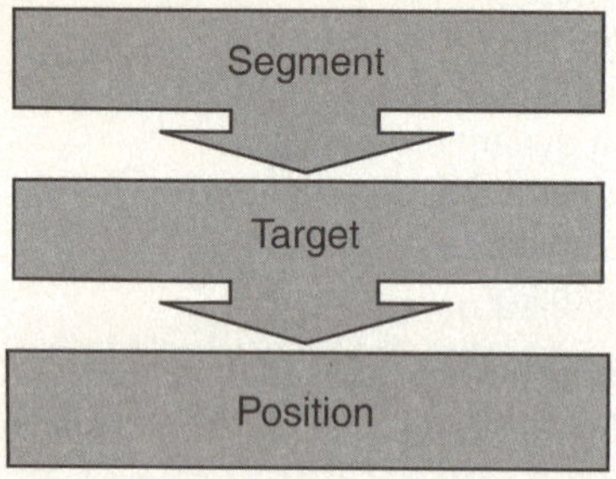

In order to put the marketing strategy into operation, marketers then compile a marketing plan which outlines the range of tactics which should be utilised. To simplify this, McGreggor (1960) summarised a 'marketing mix' to be planned, commonly known as the 4 P's which stand for: Product, Price, Place and Promotion. These four variables are at the heart of all aspects of marketing. They have been supplemented by three extra service marketing variables: People, Process and Physical Evidence.

2.2 Customer satisfaction as a business objective

> **Key term**
>
> **Customer satisfaction** is a situation where the quality of the product or service delivered meets or exceeds the customer's expectations.

Adcock (2001) defined marketing as "the right product, in the right place, at the right time, at the right price".

Customer satisfaction is at the heart of marketing as an organisational philosophy.

Marketing is more than just a range of techniques that enables the company to determine customer requirements; rather it is a shared business ethos. The marketing concept is a philosophy that places customers central to all organisational activities. The long term strategies of an organisation might be centred on profit maximisation, market share growth, or growth in real terms but none of this can be achieved without satisfying customers. Without customers there would be no business.

Marketing-oriented organisations are those whose production and marketing activities are driven by the needs of customers and the desire to satisfy them. Marketing orientation is usually driven by senior managers whose motivation is to find customer wants and fill them rather than create products and sell them.

Some organisations overlook marketing as a business philosophy. For these organisations making products assumes prime concern followed by an attempt to find customers.

2.3 Marketing product orientation

Kotler & Keller (2006) discussed the competing concepts under which organisations have conducted marketing activities.

2.3.1 The Production Concept

This is one of the oldest concepts in business and holds that customers will prefer products that are widely available and inexpensive. Senior managers of production-oriented businesses concentrate on achieving high production efficiency, low costs and mass distribution. They believe that if the products are widely available and affordable, customers will buy them.

2.3.2 The Product Concept

This concept holds that consumers will prefer those products that offer the most quality, performance, or innovative features. Senior managers in these organisations focus on making superior products and improving them over time. They believe that if the products are sophisticated and technologically superior to others, customers will buy them.

2.3.3 The Selling Concept

This concept holds that consumers and organisations, if left alone, will not automatically buy enough of the company's products. The company must undertake an aggressive selling and promotional effort to achieve its objectives. Senior managers in these organisations will focus on selling more units of the product to more people more often and for more money in order to make more profits. This concept is used most aggressively with products that customers normally do not think of buying, such as double glazing, insurance and encyclopaedia.

2.3.4 The Marketing Concept

This concept holds that the key to achieving the company's goals is to be more effective than competitors in creating, delivering and communicating superior customer value to the target market. Senior managers in these organisations focus on finding out what customers want and developing products that will meet their needs better than the competition. They believe that customers are not necessarily driven by price or the product's sophistication, but are looking for the total offering that best fits their needs and therefore the company has to define those needs and develop appropriate offerings.

The most successful companies today are those that take time to understand their customers in order to offer products and services that meet their needs better than competitors. Marketing orientation is a culture where everyone in the organisation understands and appreciates their role in delivering ultimate customer satisfaction. In the market-oriented organisation, the satisfaction of customers is seen as central to the development and maintenance of long-term profitability.

ACTIVITY 1.1

Re-read the descriptions of the different concepts and identify organisations, with which you are familiar, that seem to fit each concept.

2.4 Customer retention through effective marketing

Customer retention activities are undertaken by companies in order to reduce customer defections. Customer retention has become an important aspect of marketing in recent years because it is always more cost effective to retain customers than to win new ones.

A company's ability to retain customers is not only dependent on the quality of its products or services, but strongly related to the way it services its existing customers and its reputation in the marketplace. Customer retention is more than giving customers what they expect, it is about exceeding their expectations so that they become loyal advocates for your brand by recommending your products to others.

Customer retention can be achieved by keeping in regular contact with customers and developing a range of initiatives to encourage further orders after the initial contact has been made. Such activities usually result in further sales of the same products, sales of new offers and cross-selling into related product areas to maximise revenue from established contacts. Some companies will develop a database that classifies customers according to loyalty, purchase activity, susceptibility to future offers and age of listing to help them determine the best way of approaching future communication and offers.

Brassington & Pettitt (2006) outlined five stages in a retention and customer development programme:

1. **Welcome:** This stage applies shortly after the customer has become active. An early contact reassures the customer and assists in facilitating receptivity to further communication.
2. **Selling up:** Apart from normal repeat business, companies should encourage the customer to adopt a better or higher valued model.
3. **Selling across:** This is where an organisation tries to sell a wider range of products than those in the area originally selected.
4. **Renewal:** With products or services that involve annual or regular renewal, such as home insurance, the timing of appropriate and personalised communication around the renewal date can reinforce repeat purchases.
5. **Lapsed customers:** A continuation of communication with temporarily dormant or permanently lost customers may be appropriate for a period of time so as not to lose contact with them.

THE REAL WORLD

Starbucks

Starbucks is just one of the companies who uses a loyalty reward programme to foster long-term relationships with its customers. In 2012 it launched the My Starbucks Rewards scheme, awarding one star per purchase with a free drink for every 15 stars collected. In order to add extra value more benefits are conferred once the customer becomes a 'gold level' member after 50 visits. The data collected also allows the company to offer its more frequent customers tailored offers and promotions.

(*Marketing Week*, 2012)

3 Marketing as a cross-functional activity

In order to combine the efforts within the organisation, market-orientated companies need proper co-ordination between market needs, production decisions and financial well-being. That requires good communication between the marketing function and people responsible for development, design and manufacturing, and finance.

However, that does not mean that the marketing department can impose its will on all other departments. Relationships with other departments should be developed and managed to ensure all are working towards the same overall goal.

Although every organisation is different, common patterns appear in the structure of organisations.

- Marketing departments have often evolved from sales departments. In traditional sales or production orientated organisations, marketplace issues were the responsibility of a sales director reporting to senior management.
- When the need for a market-oriented approach became apparent, a marketing director appeared in parallel to the sales director, but each had separate functional departments.
- With fuller recognition of the marketing approach to business, sales and marketing may become a single department, with sales as a sub-group within marketing (as opposed to marketing being a sub-group within sales).

Marketing managers have to take responsibility for planning, resource allocation, monitoring and controlling the marketing effort, but it can also be claimed (and often is, by marketing managers!) that marketing involves every facet of the organisation's operations. If the philosophy of a market orientation is regarded as a prerequisite for success, the marketing department naturally becomes the main co-ordinator.

(a) **Conflicts with other departments**

Care should be taken not to understate the role of finance, production, human resources (HR) and other business functions, as this may cause resentment and lack of co-operation. To reduce the potential for conflict, senior management should ensure that departmental heads have clear instructions as to the organisation's priorities.

The table below shows the types of decision typically taken by a marketing department. However, bear in mind that in the truly market-oriented organisation, marketing is not an activity that can be pigeon-holed as the responsibility of the marketing department. All of the company's activities must be co-ordinated around the needs of the customer.

(b) **Key departments**

When we look again at the central role of marketing as satisfying customers and maintaining positive relationships with customers in the long term, there are some departments that marketing will need to work closely alongside.

The table below shows these key departments and some of the shared goals.

Table 1.1 Organisational department and their shared goals with marketing

Department	Common goals with marketing
Research and development	▪ New product development ▪ Product modifications ▪ Innovation
Human resources	▪ Staff training to encourage a positive customer focus ▪ Articulate a shared vision ▪ Communicate ideas to staff ▪ Implement internal marketing
Production, operations and logistics	▪ Ensure product quality ▪ Meet customer demand efficiently ▪ Ensure product availability ▪ Efficient delivery of product
IT	▪ Effective corporate website ▪ Implementing marketers' design of online corporate messages ▪ E-commerce functionality ▪ Supplier and key customer access to extranet and intranet

Customer service	▪ Correcting customer problems ▪ Increasing levels of customer satisfaction

4 Internal and external marketing

4.1 Internal and external customers

Customers fall into two main categories, external and internal – each having very different needs and expectations of the organisation.

4.1.1 External customers

These are individuals who have no connection with an organisation, other than that they may have purchased goods or services in the past, or are purchasing at present. They can be either the traditional customer / consumer who buys a multitude of goods and services for their own use or that of their family. This category is referred to as Business-to-Consumer market (or B2C), the business consumer who is buying on behalf of their organisation, known as Business-to-Business (B2B), or individuals selling to one another (C2C).

4.1.2 Internal customers

Internal customers are those people and departments, within your organisation, with whom you exchange the products and services (often information) you create. Consider your internal customers, and how important it is that there is good internal communication in an organisation. Consider also how the roles might sometimes be reversed, with you as the internal customer.

For example when you, as an employee, receive your pay slip from the finance department, you are the customer and expect it to be correct, to be delivered on time and the salary payment actually credited into your bank account. If there is a problem, you expect to be dealt with courteously and promptly. You do not expect to have to engage in lengthy correspondence to rectify a mistake. If you do receive information from the finance department – say, for example, about a new profit-related pay scheme – you expect it to be clearly written and well presented.

At other times, you could be the service provider to your colleagues or line manager; for instance, when you are asked to cost the production of a sales promotion item as part of a future promotional campaign. Your internal customers will expect you to have completed the task on time, accurately, and to present it clearly at the next planning meeting.

4.2 Internal marketing

> **Key term**
>
> **Internal marketing** is the application of marketing tools in order to create an organisational culture that places the customer at the centre of what the company does.

So internal marketing is about working together with colleagues and providing them with a good service so that, as a team, your organisation achieves its goals. Internal marketing employs similar tools to customer-based marketing; including internal newsletter, staff magazines, staff meetings, company intranet, team-building activities and employee awards. It starts by recognising that the exchange between the employer and the employee goes far beyond simply exchanging hours or work for money. It recognises the fact that there is considerable emotional labour involved in the workplace and that employees will be better motivated if they feel proud about the activities of the company. Internal marketing is more than just informing staff of the company's policies; staff must feel that their own needs are being met, beyond the salaries that they are paid at the end of the month.

THE REAL WORLD

The Body Shop is a good example of a company that has been successful at motivating its staff and building enthusiasm in them for the aims of the company. Body Shop's employees are not only aware of the company's aims; they regularly participate in community activities to help fulfil them.

"I just want The Body Shop to be the best, most breathlessly exciting company – and one that changes the way business is carried out. That is my vision." - Anita Roddick. Human Rights Activist. Founder of The Body Shop.

(The Body Shop, 2012)

The marketing function is also usually responsible for managing an organisation's internet presence. Marketing works with IT to provide intranet services for internal recruitment, training, briefings, HR issues and announcements to other departments within the company.

ACTIVITY 1.2

Draw a network diagram that shows the customer / supplier relationships between yourself and others in your organisation.

4.3 Supporting supply chain activities

In today's dynamic and competitive business environment, suppliers play a vital role by providing the organisation with the right quality and quantity of resources (raw materials, equipment, accessories and services) that it needs to deliver the products and services that will meet the needs of its customers.

Key term

Extranet – a collaborative network that uses intranet technology to link businesses with their suppliers, customers, and other businesses that share common goals. (Chartered Institute of Management Accountants)

An extranet helps organisations connect with their suppliers. Many organisations also use this tool as a means to obtain competitive advantage. For example, a computer manufacturer may allow customers to access the support database providing details of parts used in each computer along with known problems or errors with those parts.

This will allow the customer to diagnose faults with their computers more quickly, and also help the manufacturer provide an additional useful service, at effectively zero cost.

The current competitive business climate often requires a team of separate business partners to work together to meet the diverse, complicated, demands of today's markets. This team of partners has been referred to as a 'business ecosystem'. It has been suggested that only a truly co-operative system is suited to assemble the creative ideas necessary to develop complex new products, achieve manufacturing agility, and attain a long-term customer focus. Much of this co-operation can be achieved by applying internet technology. The fairly recent emergence of extranets may bridge the gap between intranet and Internet applications.

ACTIVITY 1.3

Outline the essential concepts that a good definition of marketing should include.

CHAPTER ROUNDUP

- Marketing is the 'management process responsible for identifying, anticipating and satisfying customer requirements profitably' (The Chartered Institute of Marketing).
- In the exchange process, the customer gets something they want (the product) and the organisation earns revenues (sales and profits).
- To achieve its objectives, marketing is broken down into four manageable stages: analysis, planning, implementation and control. Customer satisfaction is at the heart of marketing and is a situation where the quality of the product or service delivers, meets or exceeds the customer's expectations.
- A company's ability to retain customers is not only dependent on the quality of its products, but strongly related to the way it services its existing customers and its reputation in the marketplace.
- Effective marketing requires good communication between the marketing function and the people responsible for development, design, manufacturing and finance.
- In order to avoid resentment and lack of co-operation, marketing professionals should not understate the role of finance, production, HR and other business functions.
- Internal customers are those people and departments, within your organisation, with whom you exchange the products and services you create.
- Internal marketing is the application of marketing tools in order to create an organisational culture that places the customer at the centre of what the company does.
- Some companies use an extranet that is made accessible to other companies to support their supply chain activities.

FURTHER READING

Chapter 1 of:

Blythe, J. (2008) *Essentials of Marketing*. 4th edition. Harlow, Prentice Hall.

Chapters 1 and 2 of:

Brassington, F. and Pettitt, S. (2007) *Essentials of Marketing*. 2nd edition. Harlow, Prentice Hall.

REFERENCES

Adcock, D. (2001) *Marketing: Principles & Practice.* 4th edition. Harlow, Prentice Hall.

Baker, R. (2012) Starbucks launches My Reward loyalty scheme. *Marketing Week*, http://www.marketingweek.co.uk [accessed 12 June 2012].

The Body Shop (2012) About us. The Body Shop, http://www.thebodyshop.co.uk/services/aboutus.aspx [accessed 23 January 2012].

Blythe, J. (2008) *Essentials of Marketing*. 4th edition. Harlow, Prentice Hall.

Brassington, F. and Pettitt, S. (2006) *Principles of Marketing*. 4th edition. Harlow, Prentice Hall.

The Chartered Institute of Marketing (2009) *Marketing and the 7Ps*. Available online at www.cim.co.uk/filestore/resources/10minguides/7ps.pdf [accessed 12 June 2012].

Harris, D. and Botten, N. (2008) *CIM Coursebook: Introduction to Marketing*. Oxford, Butterworth Heinemann.

Jobber, D. (2007) *Principles and Practice of Marketing*. 5th edition. Maidenhead, McGraw Hill.

Kotler, P. and Keller, K. (2006) *Marketing Management.* 12th edition. New Jersey, Pearson.

Marcouse, I. *et al* (2011) *Business Studies for A Level*. 4th edition. London, Hodder Education.

O'Reilly, L. (2011) Innocent uplift the result of marketing. *Marketing Week*, http://www.marketingweek.co.uk [accessed 12 June 2012].

QUICK QUIZ

1. How does CIM define marketing?
2. What is meant by the term 'exchange'?
3. Differentiate between the production concept and the product concept.
4. What is the marketing concept?
5. Outline the five stages in retention and customer development programme as suggested by Brassington and Pettitt.
6. Who are internal customers?
7. Outline three key departments that marketing must work with in order to achieve its objectives.
8. Define internal marketing.

ACTIVITY DEBRIEFS

Activity 1.1

Production Concept: Ford (with the Model T)

Product Concept: Ferrari

Sales Concept: Insurance companies like Confused.com

Marketing Concept: Apple, Dove, L'Oréal, Microsoft,

Of course, you may have thought of many other alternatives.

Activity 1.2

This depends on your own organisation.

Activity 1.3

The essential concepts of a good marketing definition are: process, exchange, satisfaction, customers, needs and profit.

QUICK QUIZ ANSWERS

1 Marketing is the management process responsible for identifying, anticipating and satisfying customer requirements profitably.

2 Exchange is getting a desired product or service from someone by offering something in return

3 Production concept holds that customers will prefer products that are widely available and inexpensive, while the product concept holds that customers will prefer products that offer the most quality, performance or innovative features.

4 The marketing concept holds that companies should be more effective than competitors in creating, delivering and communicating superior customer value to the target market.

5 Welcome, selling up, selling across, renewal and lapsed customers.

6 People and departments within your organisation with whom you exchange the products and services you create.

7 Research and Development, Human Resources, IT, Customer Service, Finance and Production.

8 The application of marketing tools in order to create an organisational culture that places the customer at the centre of what the company does.

CHAPTER 2

The marketing environment

Introduction

This chapter explores the environment within which marketing activities are conducted. The first section explains the importance of understanding the organisation's marketing environment in order to effectively manage marketing activities.

The second section introduces the PESTEL model and explains how the political, economic, social, technological, environmental and legal factors impact upon the organisation and its ability to undertake marketing activities successfully.

The third section explores the key characteristics of an organisation's micro-environment and provide an understanding of the role of customers, stakeholders, competitors, suppliers, distributors and employees.

Finally, the fourth section examines the processes that are use by organisations for monitoring the marketing environment in order to ensure that they are kept informed about developments.

Topic list

Syllabus reference

2.1	Explain the importance of understanding the organisation's marketing environment in order to effectively manage the marketing process, and satisfy customer needs: ▪ Defining the internal, micro and external marketing (macro) environment ▪ An appreciation of controllable and uncontrollable factors
2.2	Explain the concept of the PESTEL model and show how each of these factors impact upon the organisation, its ability to undertake marketing activities successfully, cost-effectively and competitively, including identifying: ▪ **Political environment:** Government policy; changing governments; international environment and the impact of local government policy ▪ **Economic factors:** Interest rates; exchange rates; GNP and GDP; taxation and how it affects viability of the business ▪ **Social factors:** Increased mobility; societal marketing; representation of family; international and cultural differences and changing social values ▪ **Technological factors:** Enhanced production capability and technique; product development; enhanced and effective communications within service provision ▪ **Environmental factors:** Waste; packaging; sustainability; climate change; corporate social responsibility ▪ **Legal factors:** Consumer protection legislation (Sales of Goods Act) and Data Protection Act (1998 – upgraded 2000)
2.3	Identify the key characteristics of the micro-marketing environment, including an understanding of: ▪ Customers ▪ Stakeholders ▪ Competitors ▪ Suppliers ▪ Distributors ▪ Employees
2.4	Explain the processes that can be used for monitoring the marketing environment: ▪ Market scanning ▪ Collection of secondary data through journals, websites, etc

1 The importance of the marketing environment

1.1 The marketing environment

> **Key term**
>
> **Marketing environment** refers to 'the external factors which affect a company's planning and performance, and are beyond its control' (CIM, 2008)

The environment refers to those things outside any system that have some sort of effect on the way that system operates. The success of every organisation is determined not only by its own activities, but also by the actors and forces in its environment. At the very least, it must understand the needs of customer in order to make products that they will buy.

A marketing environment represents the world that the organisation exists within and the related factors which will determine its success. Obviously this is very broad and so marketers split their 'environments' into different levels in order to make it easier to understand the complex situations.

1.1.1 Levels of a marketing environment

The marketing environment is often defined into different levels. Initially internal and external environments are distinguished.

(a) The **internal environment** is the environment within the organisation. It consists of the other departments of the organisation that impact on the activities of the marketing function.

(b) The **external environment** includes all those forces and events outside the organisation which directly impact on its activities.

In the external environment, we can differentiate micro and macro environments:

(a) **Micro environment** is the closest external environment where changes and events directly impact on the organisation eg competitor activities.

(b) **Macro environment** is also external but beyond the immediate environment. This environment can have major impacts on the organisation eg political changes.

Figure 2.1 The marketing environment

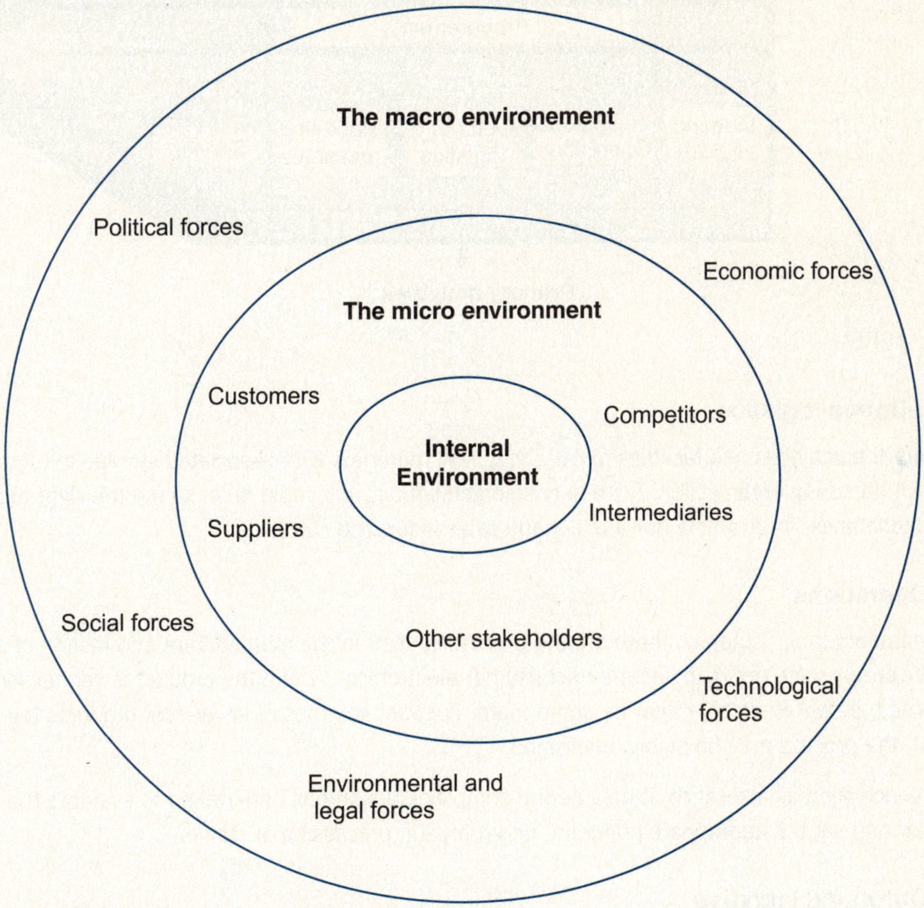

(Adapted from Palmer, A. and Hartley B., 2006)

1.2 The internal environment

The marketing-oriented organisation is effective and offers goods and services to its customers, which have appropriate market valuation and are affordable. To be profitable, the organisation needs to be efficient and to make and market products and services in the most economic way consistent with the required product quality and standard of service.

Michael Porter's value chain (*Competitive Advantage*, 1985) provides marketers with a tool to appraise the internal efficiency and effectiveness of the organisation.

The primary activities are the day-to-day activities that we need to undertake to provide goods and services to the marketplace. However, just as a car will not go forever if it is not refuelled, longer-term support activities are required to ensure that the primary activities can continue successfully. As always with business models, intelligent creative interpretation is required to apply them. The end result of well-tuned, balanced, primary and support activities adds value for the mutual benefit of the organisation and its customers. The value chain model is illustrated (Figure 2.2) and explained below.

Figure 2.2 The value chain

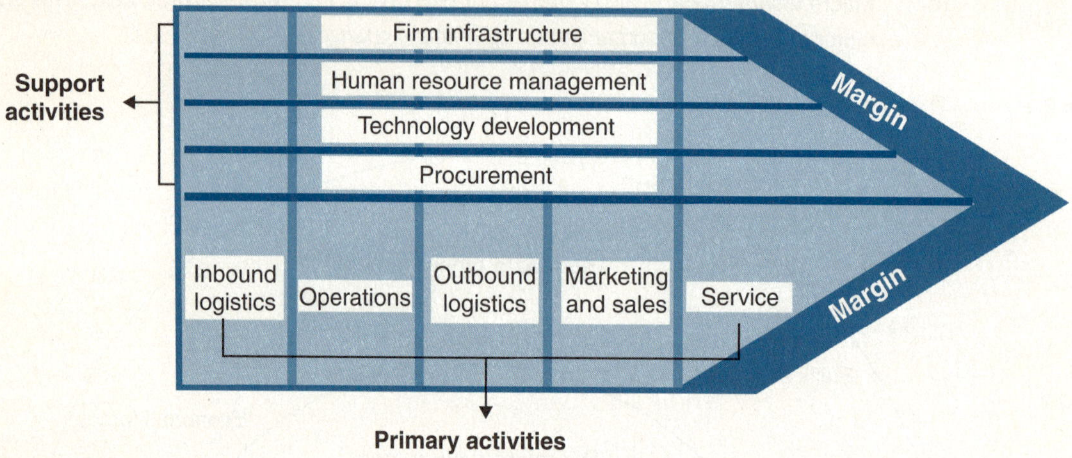

(Porter, 1985)

1.2.1 Inbound logistics

These are the activities and facilities for receiving raw materials with associated storage and quality procedures for a manufacturing organisation. For a service organisation, this could be ensuring the right number and type of telephone lines, for example, for a telephone-sales insurance company.

1.2.2 Operations

For a manufacturing company, these are the processes used in the manufacture and testing of a product. Typical examples are the manufacture of consumer electronics. Where the product is very expensive and customised, batch assembly might be appropriate. For vast volumes of lower-cost products (eg personal stereos), the process may be highly automated.

For a service such as insurance, it may be the complex calculations undertaken to evaluate the risk for a new customer and set the appropriate premium, or simply the processing of claims.

1.2.3 Outbound logistics

For the manufacturing organisation, this is the packaging and the physical distribution of the product. This aspect of the value chain clearly links up with the P = Place (physical distribution) of the marketing mix (see Chapter 3). Different approaches may be appropriate for the same product under different outlet conditions. For a service such as insurance, the outbound logistics involves the efficient delivery of documentation to the client.

1.2.4 Marketing and sales

For the manufacturing company, the cycle is: customer's order, the product is manufactured or taken out of stock, delivered to the client and, most importantly, payment is made! The sales cycle involves a number of functions. Sales plans drive the production schedule and stocking requirements. For a supermarket, the sales system can be considered as the checkout. Remember this is not just the laser reader and payment system (electronic point of sale – EPOS), but also involves efficient and friendly operation by a person. The best information and communications systems will not provide a quality experience if run by an unfriendly or poorly trained operator.

1.2.5 Service

Here we have to take care how we define service. This is not the overall efficiency of the value chain but should be taken to cover value-added service for the product or service. As an example, for a car manufacturer this might include maintenance servicing (and spare parts) and financial services such as insurance and a loan to buy the vehicle. For an insurance company, it might involve providing emergency advice (eg where to find a plumber at midnight when a pipe bursts).

1.2.6 Firm infrastructure

This covers very general aspects of the business, such as reputation, image and tangible assets. Companies need to ensure they have the relevant approach to their operations and markets. Thus, low-cost airlines are ruthless in cost-cutting with a very basic 'no frills' strategy.

Their proposition to the market is that no one will get you there more cheaply and their value chain is tuned to move people at the lowest possible cost to selected low-cost destinations (often at less fashionable or less convenient airports). The leading airlines provide a 'value-for-money service' with a different proposition: to fly people round the world in comfort. This implies a complex interconnecting system of hub and long-haul routes to be operated with comparatively lavish facilities such as 'club' lounges and operating from major airports such as Heathrow.

If the organisation's buildings are dilapidated and machinery outdated then poor products and services will be produced, often expensively.

1.2.7 Human resource management

No organisation can be better than the people in it. Even with the most effective equipment and the best facilities, customers will not be happy if front-line staff are not well trained and empathetic. Roles and responsibilities must be effectively defined by job descriptions and organisational structures. The nature of people (eg recruitment processes and procedures), their skills (eg effective training) and motivation (eg appropriate reward systems) are key. This aspect also interacts with the marketing mix in the element P = People.

1.2.8 Technology development

To remain a market leader, attention must be paid to developing the product (new product development), the manufacturing operations and logistics (the first three elements of the value chain primary activities), sales (eg internet sales systems) and marketing (eg new methods of market research). Any element of the value chain can be improved and needs development for a successful organisation.

Information and communications systems have been added to the traditional value chain model, as an appropriate framework is vital for most companies, and for some e-based organisations it almost *is* the whole organisation. In knowledge-based industries, the ability to lever knowledge and skills internationally with the internet, intranets and others is vital. For the modern company, it is just as bad for the computer to crash as for there to be a total power-out. In both cases, all operations come to a shuddering halt.

1.2.9 Procurement

Procurement, the purchase of the inputs to the value chain, is vital. For a supermarket, the greatest percentage of costs is the price it pays for the items on the shelves. Getting the right products at the right price is vital.

Procurement not only covers the purchase of the materials for manufacture, but also covers all inputs to the operation. In marketing, it is vital to get the best prices for printing and media space to make the most out of a limited budget.

1.2.10 Controllable and uncontrollable environmental factors

An organisation exists within society as a whole: changes in the external environment will form the basis for building marketing plans. Careful monitoring of the external environment will help an organisation to identify opportunities and threats and be proactive rather than reactive in the face of change.

The organisation will have different levels of control of the various forces within its marketing environment. It is likely that there will be more control of the internal environment and less control over the external environment.

As long as marketing has the full support of top management, it should be able to influence the activities of the other departments within the organisation. It is also possible for the organisation to influence the actions of customers, stakeholders, suppliers, distributors and employees by properly understanding their needs and establishing good relationships with them. Competitors are a lot more difficult or impossible to control as their needs are usually contrary to the objectives of the organisation.

The external macro-environment is usually quite dynamic and often not susceptible to direct control by the organisation. The best that marketers can do in most situations is to influence some elements of it and to take appropriate actions in order to exploit the opportunities and avoid the threats that macro-environmental changes present.

THE REAL WORLD

Wikipedia protest at US anti piracy legislation

In January 2012 Wikipedia and other news site Reddit took their online content offline for 24 hours as a protest against the Protect Intellectual Property Act (PIPA) in the United States. Their reason: the 'destructive legislation" could "fatally damage the free and open internet' and 'severely limit people's access to online information'. The Act intended to support the film and music industries was potentially very detrimental to user-generated news sites and other online content providers.

(*The Guardian*, 2012)

In recent years it has been possible for very large firms to influence the macro-environment by lobbying parliament, or even affecting the national culture directly. Social media firms like *Facebook* and *Twitter* have influenced the socio-cultural environment significantly by changing the way that we communicate and network.

However, in most cases, marketers will be best advised to carefully monitor the developments in both micro and macro environments and adjust their actions to enable them to best meet the needs of all stakeholders.

2 The PESTEL model

2.1 The PESTEL model – overview

Key term

PESTEL Model: PESTEL is an acronym for Political, Economic, Social, Technological, Environmental and Legal. It is a model for analysing the different macro-environmental forces affecting an organisation's activities.

The PESTEL model is designed to provide senior managers with an analytical tool to identify different macro-environmental factors that may affect business strategies, and to assess how these different factors may influence business performance now and in the future. The six types of environmental influences identified by the model are Political, Economic, Social, Technological, Environmental and Legal. Although these factors may seem independent, they have a tendency to affect each other. For example, the development of social media (like *Facebook* and *Twitter*) is a technological development that has affected both the social and political environments.

Marketing managers use the PESTEL model to analyse the major factors in the macro-environment that can affect marketing strategies and to assess the nature of their impact. For the organisation to take advantage of opportunities and minimise the impact of threats, managers must identify the main drivers of change and properly assess their impact on the industry in which the firm operates.

Major changes in the macro-environment can, at times, take place quickly (for example, the 9/11 attacks in the United States). With rapid changes, it is vital to analyse the impact of the event on the organisation. Slow changes such as shifts in population demographics are also important, since if the organisation is not alert, the change can become so advanced before its impact is detected that major problems arise; even survival may become questionable.

For travel agencies, the advent of the internet as a means of booking holidays was a major development, which could be clearly identified. The change in social attitudes to holidays from 'package' to *'à la carte'* has been more incremental. However, failure to respond to either would impact on the profitability of the business and service to the customers.

Table 2.1 General overview of selected key PESTEL issues

PESTEL element	Selected key issues
Political	Government policy, changing governments, international environment, local government policy, stability, attitudes to industry, attitudes to competition, climate for 'free trade', attitudes to foreign investors
Economic	Business cycle, inflation rates, interest rates, disposable income, wealth distribution, consumer spending patterns, credit availability, employment levels, exchange rates, taxation, GNP, GDP
Social / Cultural	Demographics, society, culture, increased mobility, societal marketing, representation of family, changing social values
Technological	Inventions, discoveries, information and communication technology, enhanced production capability and technique, product development
Environmental	Consumer pressure, volatile organic compounds (VOC), Persistent Organic Pollutants (POP), climate change, waste, packaging, genetic engineering issues, environmental fate, laws, sustainable development, life cycle analysis, corporate social responsibility
Legal	Monopolies and mergers, competition, consumer protection legislation, health and safety, consumer safety (eg strict liability), employment law, environmental law, regulations (eg labelling), codes of conduct, self-regulation

2.2 Political factors

Politics involves governing a country or region and administering its internal and external affairs. The political environment involves the interaction between the government and organisations and is reputed to be one of the most unpredictable for marketing managers. Political office holders make and change laws that significantly impact the activities of business organisations and can potentially determine their success or failure.

Political systems within UK markets can be categorised into central, regional, local and European Union:

- Central government consists of Parliament, the Cabinet, ministers, civil servants and political advisers, not all of whom are elected.
- Regional government eg Scottish Parliament, National Assembly for Wales, Northern Ireland Assembly and Greater London Authority

- Local government eg County, Town and District Councils are responsible for social services, education and local services
- The European Union co-ordinates business law throughout the member states in order to ensure a fair competitive environment.

The government overall will influence organisations in a number of ways as shown in the following diagram.

Figure 2.3 Government influences on an organisation

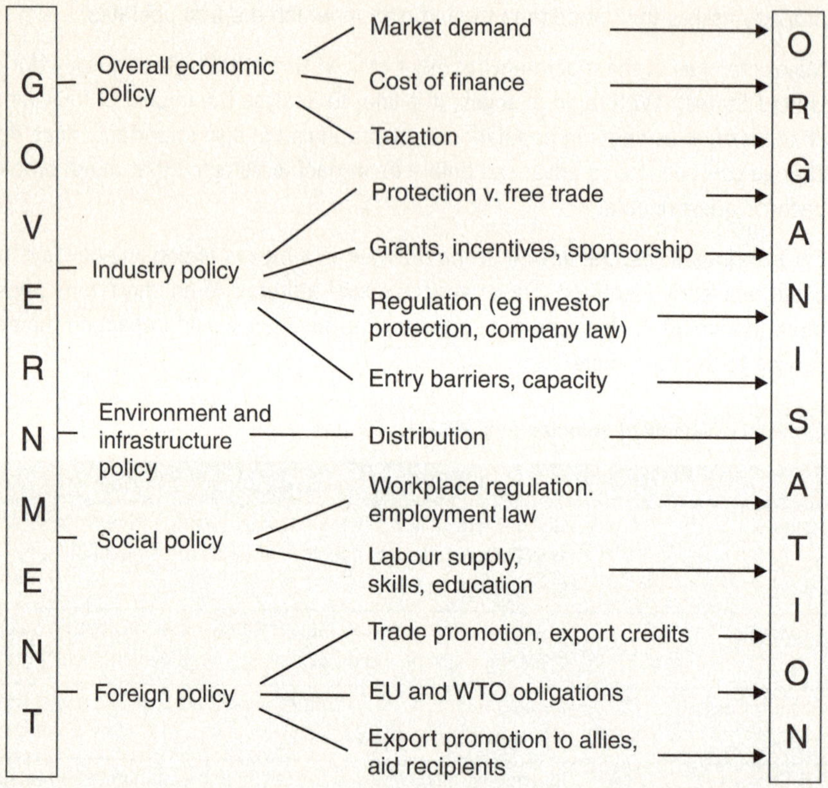

There are a number of facets to 'political' issues. Politics and politicians shape laws, and many organisations see the lobbying of politicians as a key part of their strategic plans. This is not restricted to commercial organisations; social marketing groups have become most active in this area, as seen in the successful campaigning for smoking bans and the current targeting of junk food by the healthy living groups.

2.2.1 Government policy

Policies are principles or rules designed to guide decisions in order to achieve rational outcomes. Government policy normally refers to the specific ideas of the ruling government that describes the courses of action it intends to take in order to change certain situations. They act as a foundation for making decisions on the specific steps to be taken to solve political problems. The government uses policy to tackle a wide range of issues; including taxation, immigration, healthcare, education, defence, foreign relations and the economy. Usually, laws will be changed by governments so that when they create a policy it can be made to affect specific groups of people or everyone in the society.

Government policy is such a broad area and can affect all of the other categories in a PESTEL analysis. Governments will influence the economic factors in a country by deciding taxation rates for individuals and companies, societal factors by education and training policy, technological factors by policies which encourage research and technology transfer, environmental factors by recycling policy and taxation of landfill charges, legal factors by their policy of the sale of goods and credit agreements.

2.2.2 Changing governments

The different political parties in a country would normally represent different shades of opinion on the way in which the country should be run and the policies that should be implemented by the government. Thus, a change of government would in most cases represent a movement away from one set of policies towards another. The change in general laws as a result of a change in government can create significant opportunities or threats that the marketing function must respond to in order contribute effectively to the objectives of the organisation. Clearly, a change of government when there are privatisation or nationalisation policies (depending on their political colour) has an impact on the macro-environment. In the UK, Conservative governments tend to try to interfere as little as possible with the workings of business (*laissez-faire* approach), while Labour governments are more likely to be suspicious that businesses may act in their shareholders' interests rather than those of their customers. In the relatively recent past opening times of shops, the weights and measures that products can be sold in and the times at which alcohol can be sold have all been changed by governments and these changes had an impact on many individual organisations.

2.2.3 International politics

There are a number of political bodies that rest above national governments. In Europe this is through the European Union, in North America via the North American Free Trade Agreement (NAFTA), in the Pacific Basin via the ASEAN Free Trade Area (AFTA) and through similar pacts in Latin America such as the MERCOSUR customs union. Although these are often considered to be co-operative trade bodies they are, increasingly, political in their outlook and behaviour. Globally, we can add the World Trade Organisation to this list of organisations and, as business becomes increasingly more international this body regularly finds itself mediating between the national interests of large companies and industries. The activities of the European Union in ensuring free trade and fair competition across the boundaries of member states create many opportunities and threats that marketers must identify and respond to.

2.2.4 Local government

Organisations also need to consider not only the national political issues but also regional and local ones. Local governments are responsible for implementing and enforcing laws made at the national level. In the UK, local authorities have responsibility for housing, waste management, waste collection, council tax collection, education, libraries, social services, transport, planning, consumer protection and licensing. Often the expansion plans of a supermarket are dependent on winning local political debates in order to gain the required planning permissions. In some cases local authorities have invested significant time and resources in trying to encourage new industrial and commercial investment in their regions in order to create jobs and stimulate the local economy. Trading Standards Officers employed by local authorities are also the usually the first to investigate claims of shady or illegal business practices in their areas. With the power to prosecute retailers and prevent further sales of offending goods, they play an important role in ensuring consumer safety and maintaining quality and fair trading standards.

ACTIVITY 2.1

List as many types of businesses as you can which will have been affected by the government decision to ban smoking in public places from July 2007.

2.3 Economic factors

Developments within the economy – which are likely to have an impact on businesses either directly, or as a result of their impact on consumer spending – are critical to business. The economic environment is basically about the level of demand within the economy and usually determine how easy or difficult it will be for both domestic and overseas customers to afford the company's products or services. Key aspects of the economic environment include inflation, unemployment, economic growth, consumer income, interest rates and currency fluctuations (in international trade).

Some key economic indicators and factors exist of which businesses should be aware. These are shown in the table below. The table shows at the most simplistic level why these are relevant to marketers:

Table 2.2 Economic factors and why they are relevant to business

Economic factor	Relevant because...
Interest rates The price of money	▪ Impact borrowing power of businesses and consumers with higher interest rates making loans more expensive ▪ Impact on household disposable income as a result of mortgage rates and interest earned on savings ▪ Saving levels are an indicator of consumer confidence in their job security and value of assets. When confidence is low, saving is more likely.
Exchange rates The price of a currency expressed in terms of another country's currency	▪ The relative price of imported goods is affected ▪ How expensive and thus appealing domestic goods are to foreign countries (export)
Gross National Product The sum of all incomes as a result of economic activity plus the net property income from abroad	▪ The level of wealth or income within a country including monies earned overseas ▪ Indicates the general level of wealth within a nation ▪ Demonstrates the likely purchasing power within a country and the economic position
Taxation Government income through direct taxation of incomes and indirect taxation of products and services	▪ Impacts the spending power in particular market segments ▪ Can impact consumer confidence and thus spending ▪ Impacts business policies and employment strategy ▪ Some businesses in specialised areas may have a larger tax burden eg wine importers
Inflation An increase in prices	▪ Increasing prices which reduces purchasing power ▪ Once inflation increases, expectation inflation occurs. Regardless of whether the inflationary factors still exist, inflation is expected which leads to increase in wages and prices to protect future income levels

2.3.1 Interest rates

Interest rates will affect the organisation in different ways. As they rise it will impact upon consumers' ability to spend, or borrow to spend, and may reduce demand for products or services on offer. Such a rise will also impact upon the organisation in terms of its own borrowings, this will affect the profitability and may prevent marketing departments obtaining the investment that they need to carry through their plans. However, for companies in the financial services industry a rise in interest rates may encourage potential customers to save rather than spend making it easier to market their services.

2.3.2 Exchange rates

Exchange rates between currencies occur because of the perceived value, or purchasing power, of the currency of a two different countries, or in the case of the EU, groups of countries.

The stronger an economy the higher will be the value of its currency against that of a weaker one. Interest rates will also have an effect on exchange rates since, as interest rates rise in one country, those with money to save will tend to deposit in that country since it will earn more interest and is perceived to be safer because of the strength of the currency.

For the marketing manager a currency needs to have value, but that value should not be so high that people prefer to shop in other countries.

2.3.3 Wealth

Economics is much more marketing orientated than some sources would indicate. The value of a house is what people are prepared to pay. This is a consumer issue involving social attitudes and values. When people see that house prices are rising, they can cash in on this (in 2007, the majority of mortgages were not new but re-mortgages) to spend on consumer durables and that longed-for world cruise. When credit is widely available, it is as much how people feel (consumer confidence) as what they have actually got (disposable income) that drives the high street. If they do not have it they can borrow it.

2.3.4 Taxation and the viability of the business

Taxation affects business in several different ways.

- Many goods and services are purchased out of consumer disposable income. An increase in direct taxation (ie income tax) will reduce levels of disposable income, and may thus reduce demand.
- If goods and services are subjected to indirect taxation (eg value added tax) demand may fall as customers perceive price increases.
- The level of corporation tax may affect the number of business start-ups, or the growth rates of existing businesses. Higher levels of corporation tax act as a disincentive to earn increased profits.

2.4 Social / cultural factors

According to Blythe (2008) socio-cultural factors are "those areas that involve the shared beliefs and attitudes of the population". People learn to conduct themselves in particular ways as a result of feedback from the rest of the society. Behaviour and attitudes that are perceived as inappropriate or offensive are quickly modified, and people usually develop expectations about how others should behave. This environment is extremely important to marketers because it has a direct effect on the understanding of customers and what motivates them. The socio-cultural environment helps marketers to understand the way in which customer attitudes and opinions are formed and how they are evolving over time. The socio-cultural environment includes culture, demography, consumerism, social responsibility and ethics.

2.4.1 Increased mobility

Population shifts can affect the nature of society. Both Europe and North America have become much more multicultural societies, reflecting the global movements of population in the twentieth century. This affects the demand for products and services and this, in turn, generates demand for special communication channels. With broadband technology, TV can now not only be a medium of mass advertising around a soap opera but also become highly targeted for special social groups.

2.4.2 Social marketing

Societal marketing considers the needs of society and consumers wider interests (Jobber, 2007). For example, the long-term needs of society and consumers may be at odds with the short-term profit motives for some organisations. Organisations that forsake their own short-term profitable opportunities for the sake of social wellbeing are not necessarily doing this for short-term positive PR but are considering the longer-term societal needs by adopting societal marketing principles. This technique has been used extensively in international health programmes, especially for contraceptives and oral rehydration therapy (ORT), and is being used with more frequency in the United States for such diverse topics as drug abuse, heart disease and organ donation.

2.4.3 Representation of family

The traditional representation of family, as a heterosexual life partnership where the male is the 'breadwinner' and the female is the 'homemaker' is no longer as valid as it used to be. The nature of the family unit in the UK and many other countries has changed significantly during the past few decades. Despite this fact, many marketing campaigns continue the myth that such family units are still the norm. Modern marketing must recognise that there is an increasing diversity in structure of the family unit, and must plan campaigns accordingly. This is especially important for marketers of consumer products who now have to design and offer products for a range of family unit sizes rather than just the traditional British family of a man, a woman and 2.5 children.

THE REAL WORLD

Demographic changes

James Doward in an article in *The Observer* (Sunday 27 March 2011) comments how the typical composition of a UK household has changed in the ten years since the last census. More households now consist of pensioners, single parents or parents with adult-age children still living at home than two adults and 2.5 children. Single parent families now comprise 17% of all families.

The census also showed a movement in population with more affluent families moving out of London into the neighbouring counties in search of a better quality of life.

(*The Observer*, 2011)

2.4.4 International and cultural differences

General cultural knowledge includes implicit theories about the world we live in that are largely shared by the members of our society. But in addition to this shared set of ideas, we also have personal knowledge that can conflict with accepted, culturally derived practices. For example, a boy growing up in China may generally accept the importance of his relationships with others, and therefore seek to keep harmony with family members. But more personal knowledge – such as being exposed to pictures of American cultural icons like 50 Cent or Eminem – may lead him to wear clothes that his parents don't like.

Notions about cultural differences are often the basis for international marketing communications as well as global brand management strategies. Indeed, the perceived importance of cultural issues has been increasing, fuelled by new technologies that allow marketers to reach consumers across country boundaries. Marketers are spending increasing amounts of time and effort trying to understand subtle cultural differences.

2.4.5 Changing social values

Key term

Social values are principles and standards within a group of people that are regarded by members of that group as being worthy, important or significant.

Social values are a major determinant of the products and services that consumers buy. They are known to change over time and these gradual changes can have a significant impact on marketing activities. Recent changes to social values include:

- Changing attitudes to debt, consumer credit and financial stability.
- Changing attitudes towards 'conspicuous consumption' and waste.
- The growing importance of 'fashion' among age groups that were historically not perceived as fashion-conscious.
- Increasing health consciousness and increased awareness of the risks of smoking.

ACTIVITY 2.2

Think of other social trends that are likely to affect marketing activities.

2.5 Technological factors

The nature and rate of change in technology affects the way an organisation undertakes its business. Technological change has been more apparent and ever faster in recent years, most notably in computing and telecommunications (or ICT), but also in the biological sciences. This creates new product potential, faster working, improved internal and external communications – as well as new marketing tools.

The rate of change has been growing ever faster. Product development times are getting quicker and many more products are reaching the market in less time. This has significantly shortened the typical product life cycle, especially for electronics and related products. This has created serious problems for firms because as more and more products are being developed the chances of any one product succeeding are reduced. In some industries, as many as six out of seven new products fail. Even when a new product succeeds, its life cycle is likely to be relatively short. The ever higher quality demanded by today's customers has also meant that companies are having to spend more on developing products but have less time to recoup their investment.

Understanding technology from the perspective of what the organisation can use it for is essential. However, it is also important to think about it from the perspective of how your customers and the rest of society are responding to technological developments. Changes in technology are likely to lead to significant cultural and lifestyle changes which in turn will eventually impact other PESTEL factors and impact your market.

During the past few decades, marketers have witnessed significant developments in production capabilities and techniques, product development, communications and materials, components and products.

▸ Exam tip

Often students think only about the IT aspect of technology and forget other scientific developments that can help to improve packaging, ingredients, manufacturing processes and so on. Don't forget that at one time the development of the wheel was a major technological advancement and the world did exist (albeit at a slower pace) before computers!

2.5.1 Production capabilities and techniques

▸ Key term

Just-in-time methods of production involve developing: a production system which is driven by demand for finished products whereby each component on a production line is produced only when needed for the next stage. (Chartered Institute of Management Accountants, Official Terminology)

Over the past twenty years a new form of manufacturing has evolved: the computer-aided design and manufacturing operation (CAD/CAM) which is aligned to new methods of production such as cellular manufacture (small divisions within a factory having responsibility for output quality and costs). CAD and CAM are also the keys to flexible manufacturing as they enable computerised machines to perform a variety of functions. When CAD and CAM are integrated it is possible to achieve computer-integrated manufacturing (CIM) whereby a system directs data flow while also directing the processing and movements of material.

These IT developments may be allied to production techniques imported from Japan including just-in-time manufacturing.

2.5.2 Product development

The use of large, powerful databases and sophisticated computer modelling packages has radically changed the process of product development. It is now possible to model the appearance and performance of new products without manufacturing models and prototypes.

One such impact of this type of technology has been to shorten the lead time on new car models from the 1970s average of 30 months to a current norm of 26 weeks (MIRA).

2.5.3 Enhanced communications

Of all the aspects of the technological environment, none has changed as rapidly as communications technology. Mobile phones, the internet, cable television and media messaging mean that we can now contact pretty much anyone, pretty much anytime.

This leads to huge challenges for marketers, for example: word of mouth on new products can grow exponentially. Viral marketing means that a weak product can be 'found out' in a matter of hours, while a strong product can 'stock out' in the same period. On the internet, your nearest rival is only 'one click' away. Customers are now less loyal, to both products and retailers, than they have ever been. Price comparison takes seconds, feature comparison a few seconds more.

2.5.4 Materials, components and products

According to Brassington & Pettitt (2006), consumers tend to take products, and the materials and components used to produce them for granted as long as they work and live up to the marketer's promises. Recent technological developments have increased the benefits that consumers derive from these products and also raised expectations about what a product should be. Recent technological developments in these areas include low calorie sweeteners, unleaded petrol, microchips, synthetics in clothing packaging made with lightweight, recycled and recyclable materials.

2.6 Environmental factors

Environmental issues have become increasingly important as the stark truth confronts society that gross consumption of finite resources cannot continue forever and that, in the long term, sustainable production and distribution is the only way forward for society as a whole. Issues relating to the natural environment have already had a considerable impact on marketing policies and this influence is expected to increase in the future. In the past there has been a tendency to regard marketing, and business activities in general, as incompatible with 'green' principles, but it is now recognised that the two can be complementary.

Much of the concern about companies' social responsibilities focuses on their attitude towards environmental concerns of the public. The environment has come to people's attention for a number of reasons.

(a) The entry into decision-making or political roles of the generation which grew up in the 1960s, where ecological issues began to be aired for the first time, has affected the political climate. Global environmental concerns now feature heavily within politics.

(b) The growth in prosperity after World War II has encouraged people to feel that quality of life, as opposed to material production and consumption, is no longer a luxury.

(c) Expansion of media coverage (eg of famines) and wider discussion of long-term environmental trends (eg the impact of global warming on the weather) has fuelled public anxiety. This has been particularly true in relation to third world issues such as rain forest destruction and drought. The concert Live 8 held throughout the world in the summer of 2007 and similar initiatives work not only to raise immediate cash but to increase the profile of the cause through PR and media support.

(d) Some notable disasters (eg Chernobyl, oil slicks caused by the Exxon Valdez accident, the Gulf War and the Deepwater Horizon BP oil spill) have provoked public attention.

(e) Greater scientific knowledge is available about the effect of productive activity on the environment. For example, it has only recently been possible to measure the hole in the ozone layer and assess its causes.

(f) Longer-term cultural shifts against the ideals of science and rationality have encouraged the idealisation of a 'natural' way of life. (Appeals to nature are common in advertising.)

The areas which seem to cause most concern and are therefore essential for marketers to consider are packaging, waste, sustainability and climate change.

2.6.1 Waste and packaging

Consumers are becoming increasingly aware of the issue of waste, both in the production process and as a result of 'excessive' packaging. Domestic waste management systems are reaching breaking point in many countries, and there is a global trade in recyclable waste. The issue of waste management and recyclability is now a major component of packaging design – packaging is no longer just designed to protect and promote the product. Many products have been criticised either for unnecessary packaging or for using materials which are not environmentally friendly. In the 1980s and early 1990s when consumer concern about cluroflurocarbons (CFCs) intensified many aerosol-based products such as hairspray, deodorant and polishes changed to non-aerosol based. Cosmetics frequently use more packaging than strictly necessary, apparently because consumers subconsciously like to see a larger box for the amount of money that they spend. This was a strategy that the Body Shop initially entered into the market trying to combat by encouraging consumers to return their old bottles to be refilled. It is not just grocery and other FMCG items where packaging is a problem. Printer ink cartridges, for example, are also frequently returned for refilling or recycling.

Sensible disposal of packaging and the ability to recycle should also be considered. For decades snack foods have shown logos or have requested in writing that consumers dispose of their packaging in a bin. Nowadays they are likely to contain information about the type of recycling bin to use, whether this is glass, plastic or cardboard. There are a number of pressure groups such as Waste Watch who advocate the need to reduce the amount of waste we are creating in the first instance, re-use any waste for another purpose and recycle wherever possible. Waste comes in many forms and is not only an environmental but an economic issue for organisations. Waste Watch estimate that 4.5% of annual turnover is lost each year in avoidable waste. As the global trend continues towards becoming more ecologically aware and less wasteful, organisations will be defined by their actions in this area. Internally, staff will become aware of their own and the organisation's efforts, suppliers may be selected according to their green credentials and consumers will become increasingly aware of the companies who are becoming less wasteful.

2.6.2 Sustainability

Sustainability involves developing strategies so that the company only uses resources at a rate which allows them to be replenished (in order to ensure that they will continue to be available). At the same time emissions of waste are confined to levels which do not exceed the capacity of the environment to absorb them. In relation to the development of the world's resources, policies based on sustainability seek to:

- Pursue equity in the distribution of resources
- Maintain the integrity of the world's ecosystems
- Increase the capacity of human populations for self-reliance

Companies must consider the impact of a product over its total lifespan: raw materials (eg steel, wood), manufacture (eg pollution issues), distribution (eg energy use), consumer use (eg energy efficient deep freezer) and disposal (eg recycling targets). This is important, as it is not acceptable to abdicate responsibility. Therefore, a garden centre selling hardwood garden furniture needs to be assured that sustainable and legal logging has produced the wood. A car manufacturer may no longer consider that its environmental responsibilities have ended with the sale of the car, but must build into the vehicle the capacity for it to be recycled, and provide facilities for this.

2.6.3 Climate change

Climate change is the variation in the Earth's global climate or in regional climates over time. It involves changes in the variability or average state of the atmosphere over durations ranging from decades to millions of years. These changes can be caused by dynamic process on Earth, external forces including variations in sunlight intensity, and more recently by human activities.

In recent usage, especially in the context of environmental policy, the term 'climate change' often refers to changes in modern climate (or global warming). Current studies indicate that greenhouse gases are the primary cause of global warming. Greenhouse gases are also important in understanding Earth's climate history. According to these studies, the greenhouse effect, which is the warming produced as greenhouse gases trap heat, plays a key role in regulating Earth's temperature.

The biggest factor of present concern is the increase in CO_2 levels due to emissions from fossil fuel combustion, followed by aerosols (particulate matter in the atmosphere), which exert a cooling effect, and cement manufacture. Other factors, including land use, ozone depletion, animal agriculture and deforestation, also affect climate.

Climate change is high on the agenda for governments and despite conflicting reports and disparate views about the extent and effects of climate change, it will remain one of the key priority areas for the foreseeable future. Scientists predict that warming of the earth's atmosphere will lead to food shortages, disease, extreme weather and oceans rising.

2.6.4 Corporate social responsibility

CSR has been defined as having four dimensions: economic, legal, ethical and philanthropic.

As such society can:

- require business to discharge its economic and legal duties
- expect business to fulfil its ethical duties
- desire business to meet its philanthropic responsibilities.

CSR has also been defined as:

> 'the continuing commitment to business to behave ethically and contribute to economic development while improving the quality of life of the workforce and their families as well as of the local community and society at large' (World Business Council for Sustainable Development)

CSR suggests that companies should not only consider their customers and their profitability, but also the well-being of the wider communities, local and global, within which they exist. Apart from being environmentally sensitive and offering ethically considerate products, consumers now expect companies to be 'good citizens' of the community. Increasing customers are being more attracted to companies that are not just interested in meeting customer needs, but also committed to putting something back into the society.

2.7 Legal factors

The legal environment consists of legislation (made by Act of Parliament), case law (precedents developed by the courts) and quasi-laws, such as government-sponsored codes of conduct and rules developed by trade associations. European Union countries also face increasing legislation from the European Commission.

The law affects everything we do in marketing. Every aspect of the marketing mix has legal issues that need consideration. When researching, we may well have to take account of data protection legislation. Lack of knowledge is no defence. Therefore, it is vital that a marketer is aware of which aspects of a marketing plan may be affected by laws and seeks professional advice where uncertainty prevails. This is particularly important when implementing marketing plans developed for one country in another, where a different legal system prevails. A competition that is an instant hit in one country may be illegal elsewhere. Apart from legal constraints, there may be voluntary codes of conduct imposed by the industry. Thus, much of advertising regulation may not be imposed by government law but by industry codes of conduct enforced within the industry by the industry. Consumer protection and data protection are major areas of UK legislation.

2.7.1 Consumer protection

Consumer protection is linked to the idea of consumer rights (that consumers have various rights as consumers), and to the formation of consumer organisations that help consumers make better choices in the marketplace. Consumer protection legislation is designed to ensure that consumers are treated fairly by the companies from which they buy. They cover issues such as whether a product does what it claims to do, whether products are correctly labelled and measured out, levels of safety required from products and the rights of consumers after purchase for refunds or exchanges of defective products. The laws exist to ensure that no firm can gain an unfair competitive advantage by taking short-cuts in how their products are made and supplied. The Unfair Trading Regulations 2008 is a major piece of legislation that marketers must be familiar with.

The Unfair Trading Regulations 2008 ban traders in all sectors from using unfair commercial practices towards consumers. They set out broad rules outlining when commercial practices are unfair. These rules fall into four main categories:

(a) A general ban on conduct below a level which may be expected towards consumers (honest market practice / good faith). This is intended to act as a 'safety net' protection for all consumers.

(b) Misleading practices, like false or deceptive messages, or leaving out important information.

(c) Aggressive sales techniques that use harassment, coercion or undue influence on consumers. For a practice to be unfair under the rules, they must harm, or be likely to harm, the economic interests of the average consumer. For example, when a shopper makes a purchasing decision he or she would not have made had he or she been given accurate information or not put under unfair pressure to do so.

(d) In addition, the regulations ban 31 specific practices outright.

Consumer protection issues are dealt with when complaints are made to the Director-General of Fair Trading. The Office of Fair Trading will then investigate, impose an injunction or take the matter to litigation. The Office of Fair Trading also acts as the UK's official consumer and competition watchdog, with a remit to make markets work well for consumers.

At a local level complaints are dealt with by Trading Standards departments.

2.7.2 Data protection

Data protection legislation protects the rights of individuals about whom personal data is held by organisations (data users). It is underpinned by The Data Protection Act (1998) which came into force on 1st March 2000.

Especially with the advent of computer records systems, fears have arisen with regard to:

- Access to personal information by unauthorised parties
- The likelihood that an individual could be harmed by the existence of data which was inaccurate, misleading or sensitive (eg medical details)
- The possibility that personal information could be used for purposes other than those for which it was requested and disclosed.

The Data Protection Act 1998 (and the related Employment Practices Code) address these concerns. The legislation is an attempt to protect:

- Individuals (not corporate bodies)
- In regard to the gathering, storage and use of personal data (information about a living individual, including facts and expressions of opinion)

- which are processed (mechanically or manually) so that records can be systematically used to access data about the individual
- by data controllers: organisations or individuals who control the contents and use of files of personal data.

Data controllers and computer bureaux have to register with the Data Protection Commissioner. They must limit their use of personal data to the uses registered, and must abide by Data Protection Principles.

DATA PROTECTION PRINCIPLES

1 The information to be contained in personal data shall be obtained, and personal data shall be processed, fairly and lawfully. (In particular, information must not be obtained by deception.)

2 Personal data shall be held only for one or more specified (registered) and lawful purposes.

3 Personal data shall be adequate, relevant and not excessive in relation to its purpose or purposes.

4 Personal data shall be accurate and, where necessary, kept up to date. ('Accurate' means correct and not misleading as to any matter of fact. An opinion cannot be challenged.)

5 Personal data shall not be kept for longer than is necessary for its purpose or purposes.

6 An individual shall be entitled:

(i) to be informed by any data controller whether he/she holds personal data of which that individual is the subject

(ii) to be informed of the purpose or purposes for which personal data is held

(iii) to have access to any such data held by a data controller and

(iv) where appropriate, to have such data corrected or erased.

7 Appropriate security measures shall be taken against unauthorised access to, or alteration, disclosure or destruction of, personal data and against accidental loss or destruction of personal data. The prime responsibility for creating and putting into practice a security policy rests with the data controller.

8 Data may not be exported outside the European Economic Area, except to countries where the rights of data subjects can be adequately protected.

ACTIVITY 2.3

Outline other UK consumer protection legislation that marketers have to comply with.

Exam tip

It is well worth trying to remember the eight principles of The Data Protection Act because they are a topic which examiners like to test in online multiple choice examinations.

3 The micro-environment

The micro-environment comprises all those individuals and organisations that affect the operations of a business on a day-to-day basis.

The following groups influence how successful a business is:

- Customers
- Suppliers
- Distributors
- Competitors
- Employees
- Stakeholders

Figure 2.4 The micro-marketing environment

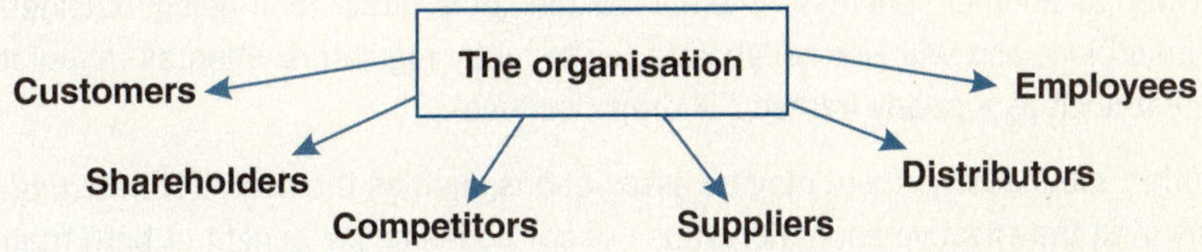

3.1 Customers

> **Key term**
>
> **Customer** – a person or company who purchases goods or services (not necessarily the end consumer). (CIM)

The marketplace consists of the buyers and users of the organisation's products and services, and the immediate microenvironment in which the purchase and use take place. Customers are clearly of vital importance to the organisation because without them the company would cease to exist. The nature of these customers will differ according to the type of organisation you are. A charity for example, will have a number of customers some of whom you may not automatically think of as a customer. Those who provide donations and those who actually are in receipt of the charity's work will be customers. Those in receipt of the charitable work will be the primary customer. The charity exists in the first place to meet their needs. The people who donate to the charity will also have needs and expectations to be met by the charity. For example, they may want to be confident that their money is being put to good use. Buyers can exert power over the organisation. Viewing the situation from the point of view of a hotel in a ski resort, it can be seen that in the high season, rooms are expensive as demand is high (low buyer power). However, out-of-season prices can be lower as customers can shop around (high buyer power). In general, from the viewpoint of the brand manufacturer of consumer goods, the power of the buyers is twofold. If the supermarkets do not stock the product then the customers are not able to buy it. If the customers select another brand as better value for money, the situation is just as bad. To address these two influences, brand manufacturers use marketing strategies directed at both the retail channels (push strategy) and the consumers (pull strategy).

3.2 Stakeholders

> **Key term**
>
> **Stakeholder** – a person or organisation that has an interest in the strategy of the organisation. Stakeholders normally include shareholders, customers, staff and the local community. (Chartered Institute of Management Accountants)

As such we can consider them to be people and organisations who have a say in:

- What you are to do
- What resources you have
- What you should achieve.

They are affected by, and feel they have a right to benefit or be pleased by, what you do. It is essential to satisfy or at least manage all the legitimate stakeholder expectations. It is no use marketing a toy to parents only for them to find their child does not play with it. Equally, it does not help if the parents do not buy the toy in the first place.

Most organisations operate within a framework of law and rules, which are enforced by regulators. For a manufacturer of shampoo, safety in manufacture and in consumer use is subject to regulatory control. The marketing claims made for the product (eg 'antidandruff' shampoo) will fall under the jurisdiction of the Advertising Standards Authority.

The activity of a firm will be scrutinised by pressure groups with their own specific agenda. In Europe, animal testing of personal care products has been discontinued; however, international companies who operate under different standards in their home market may also come under pressure in Europe. In the fashion sector of the market, consumer pressure groups may consider marketing claims extravagant and products over-priced. A key PR activity is to lobby regulators and address the issues raised by the pressure groups.

In today's just-in-time (JIT) environment, close relationships are vital with suppliers who are increasingly being viewed as another sphere of 'internal' stakeholders rather than being 'outsiders'. Firms both compete in the marketplace and will also collaborate (eg to lobby regulators when all manufacturers are faced with a common threat such as a poorly framed EU draft directive).

Within the industry, there may be associations such as the Article Numbering Association (industry forum for ensuring the effective and efficient use of bar codes to the benefit of both manufacturers and retailers of consumer products).

The media are a significant influence on the brand. Celebrity endorsement in the editorials of the glossy fashion press can be a very positive influence. Adverse reports in the consumer or environmental pages of a paper can have a negative effect. The trade press can be important in maintaining credibility with B2B customers and in attracting the most able staff to join the organisation.

3.3 Competitors

> **Key term**
>
> **Competitors** – companies that sell products or services in the same market place as one another. (CIM)

'In-segment' competition is what most people would call 'normal' competition: the battle between close competitors such as Tesco and ASDA. There are other companies that compete but not in such a direct way: Boots competes with ASDA in the personal care sector but not in clothing. However, it should be remembered that a large, distant competitor could have a significant impact on a small organisation. The supermarkets' move into bookselling has become a major threat to independent and specialist bookshops. By creaming off the sales of the latest blockbuster, the remaining sales of specialist books may not provide enough revenue to keep the small outlet above breakeven sales volumes.

3.4 Suppliers

Suppliers are organisations or individuals that provide inputs (materials, labour, services) to the organisation.

Suppliers are important because they will help the organisation to create the product or service to meet their customers' needs. The reputation of suppliers is also important. Suppliers will differ in their importance to the organisation. This will depend on how important their product is to the business, how many suppliers there are within the industry and whether the company would be able to switch suppliers easily or not. If you think about a stationery supplier for example, it probably wouldn't be that difficult to switch if a better price, superior products or better service levels were available elsewhere. A specialist supplier of a particular flavouring to be used within a confectionery product where consumer taste tests had shown that this is the preferred flavour, would be quite difficult to supplant.

3.5 Distributors

Distributors are organisations or individuals that help to get the outputs of the organisation (products, services) to the end customer.

Distributors are organisations which buy a manufacturer's goods and sell them to customers. Car dealers for example are distributors as are the major grocery retailers such as Tesco. Where products are sold is important in making sure that they are available to customers and in ensuring that the correct level of customer service and advice is available. Major cosmetics houses, for example, will only allow certain department stores and high street retailers to sell their brands because they wish to protect their reputations as high quality products. Personal sales assistants at beauty counters are required to advise customers and to ensure that they select the exact product to best meet their needs. The nature of the distribution channel will have an effect on the perception of the brand and is something that many organisations have fought to control over the years.

3.6 Employees

Internal stakeholders are vital and staff motivation and commitment are characteristics of successful organisations. Internal stakeholders can be segmented by features such as job level or job function. In internal marketing initiatives, such as during the management of change, attitude segmentation variables (eg positive, negative and apathetic) may be useful.

Employees are the lifeblood of any organisation. At the end of the day, the organisation is only as good as the people working for it. Customer facing staff can make or break a relationship with customers but equally those who work in the background are important to the long term success of the organisation. Whether an employee is the managing director or the person watering the plants they have a role to play and need to appreciate the importance of their role. The roles, responsibilities, concerns, views, ideas and contributions of employees are an important aspect in understanding your micro-environment.

4 Monitoring the marketing environment

Key term

Marketing information – any information used or required to support marketing decisions – often drawn from a computerised 'Marketing Information System' (CIM)

To fully appreciate what is going on within both the macro-and micro-environments, marketers need to continuously be aware of changes. The problem with management is that there is too much data and not enough good relevant information.

The Marketing Information System (MkIS) is not just a range of computer programs. People are needed to collect certain data. You can machine-read a bar code but not a customer complaint. Having collected the data, the system must evaluate the degree of confidence one might place in it (eg there may be some reservations about a sample scheme with market research). The data needs to be analysed and interpreted to generate relevant useful information.

There are a number of issues to be considered when formulating an appropriate MkIS for a given situation:

- What data needs to be collected?
- How can it be collected efficiently?
- What use is to be made of the information?

The macro-environment and micro-environment need to be monitored, as does the efficiency of our own value chain and those of our competitors, including the relevant marketing mix issues. Market research may be conducted on an ongoing basis to track market trends (eg TV viewing habits) or for specific issues (to evaluate if falling sales are due to changes in customer perception of the brand). The research may be quantitative (how many people take part in an activity) or qualitative (how do consumers feel about the product). If appropriate secondary desk sources do not exist, more expensive primary research will have to be commissioned.

4.1 Market scanning

Marketing intelligence is a critical source of data for the organisation. Competitors' websites and annual reports are useful sources. Mystery shopping in the competitors' and one's own outlets can provide useful data for a retail organisation. The trade press provides a continual flow of industry 'gossip': who is moving to a new company, new investment plans and product launches, and the like. On a practical note, nobody except the commissioning company takes as much interest in marketing trials as the competition!

Specific research is needed to support a unique project such as a product launch. However, knowing how the market is moving (eg whether a new product launch is required) needs a continuous flow of data and information. A key activity is not only monitoring changes with customers, but also competitors' activities. New launches and new advertising campaigns will impact on the business, and if the organisation were to wait six months to see what happens, it will be too late to act.

Specialist trade magazines may be expensive but they do contain the industry gossip: who has moved from one company to another (watching competitor recruitment gives you an idea of what skills they are strengthening for future projects) and other key news such as product launches and capital plans. For new products in technology-rich areas, patent abstracts are useful. Company websites, annual reports, advertisements and other publications are all useful sources of information. One of the key reasons for attending a trade conference is to gain competitor and market intelligence.

Every visit to a customer is a chance to gain intelligence. For example, an organisation uses a given company to provide photocopiers; the organisation becomes dissatisfied with the existing supplier and decides to trial a competitor company. The technician from the original supplier arrives to repair the existing photocopiers and notices the competitor's machine. He then informs his boss, and a representative arrives the next day to see if there are any problems.

A major technical activity for many organisations is the reverse-engineering of products. A company produces a new DVD drive or a new washing powder. The first thing for the competitor is to obtain samples, get them into the laboratory and strip them down to see how they have been built. This is, in part, to check the strength of the competition (market leaders) and to (where legal) copy with a counter-type (a typical activity for a supermarket's own brand). This can also be applied to services, with researchers acting as 'mystery travellers' on an airline, for example.

4.2 Collection of secondary data

Secondary data is marketing research data that already exists, and was collected for a purpose other than the current research process.

Vast amounts of internal data are collected by EPOS systems and loyalty cards. This can give accurate profiles of consumers (the purchase of cat food and pet litter may indicate that you are a ripe candidate for a pet insurance mailshot). Apart from computer data systems (accounts, and so on), care must be taken to capture 'soft' data such as customer complaints and sales visit reports which are not so easily converted into simple numbers but provide vital evidence of not only 'how much?' but 'why?'

Desk research involves collecting data from internal and external sources. The sources of secondary data for marketing will vary according to the needs of the organisation.

(a) Records inside the firm, gathered by another department or section for its own purposes.

- Data about sales volumes, analysed by sales area, salesman, quantity, price, profitability, distribution outlet, customer etc
- Customer database interrogation
- Data about marketing itself, such as promotion and brand data
- Employee satisfaction surveys and appraisals

- Competitor assessments
- All cost and management accounting data
- Marketing Information Systems, which model and analyse marketing data to support decisions

(b) Published information from external sources

- Publications of market research agencies, such as the AC Nielsen
- Government statistics
- Publications of trade associations (often a valuable source of under-used information within all kinds of industries)
- Professional journals

(c) The government: a major source of information about industry, population and social trends. See the website of the Office for National Statistics (www.statistic.gov.uk) where you can freely view and download economic and social data. For national equivalents (outside the UK), go to: www.wto.org.

(d) Non-government sources, including:

- The national press for example, (*Financial Times*) and financial and professional magazines (*Marketing, The Economist* an so on) and journals (and their websites)
- Companies and other organisations specialising in the provision of business information (eg Reuters, LexisNexis, Datamonitor) on a subscription basis, and specialist research organisations who analyse certain markets and publish and sell the results (eg Mintel, Euromonitor)
- Professional institutions (eg Chartered Institute of Marketing, Chartered Management Institute, Institute of Practitioners in Advertising)
- Trade sources such as the Association of British Insurers (ABI), or the Society of Motor Manufacturers and Trades (SMMT)

It is often useful to note not only the physical value but also some appropriate ratio. When comparing the sales from two differently sized shops in the same organisation, it may be appropriate to calculate the sales per square metre.

CHAPTER ROUNDUP

- The marketing environment represents the world that the organisation exists within and the related factors which determine its success.
- The internal environment consists of the other departments within the organisation.
- The external micro-environment consists of individuals and organisations that affect the operations of the business on a day-to-day basis.
- The external macro-environment consists of actors and forces in the general environment that affects all businesses.
- PESTEL is a model for analysing the macro-environmental forces that affects an organisation's activities.
- PESTEL is an acronym for Political, Economic, Social, Technological, Environmental and Legal.
- Political factors include government policy, changing governments, international politics and local government.
- Economic factors include interest rates, exchange rates, wealth and taxation.
- Social factors include increased mobility, social marketing, representation of family, international and cultural differences and changing social values.
- Technological factors include production capabilities and techniques, product development and enhanced communications.
- Environmental factors include waste and packaging, sustainability, climate change and corporate social responsibility.
- Legal factors include consumer protection and data protection.
- The micro-environment consists of customers, competitors, suppliers, distributors, employees and stakeholders.
- Market scanning and collection of secondary data are used by marketing managers to keep abreast of developments in their industry.

FURTHER READING

Chapter 2 of both of the following:

Blythe, J. (2008) *Essentials of Marketing*. 4th edition. Harlow, Prentice Hall.

Brassington, F. and Pettitt, S. (2007) *Essentials of Marketing*. 2nd edition. Harlow, Prentice Hall.

REFERENCES

Blythe, J. (2008) *Essentials of Marketing*. 4th edition. Harlow, Prentice Hall.

Brassington, F. and Pettitt, S. (2006) *Principles of Marketing*. 4th edition. Prentice Hall, Harlow.

Davies, L. (2012), Wikipedia begins blackout in protest against US anti-piracy laws. *The Guardian*, www.guardian.co.uk [accessed 18 January 2012].

Doward, J. (2011) Census 2011: The typical family is not what it used to be. *The Observer*, 27 March 2011.

Harris, D. and Botten, N. (2008) *CIM Coursebook: Introduction to Marketing*. Oxford, Butterworth Heinemann.

Jobber, D. (2007) *Principle and Practice of Marketing*. 5th edition. Maidenhead, McGraw-Hill.

Kotler, P. and Keller, K. (2006) *Marketing Management*. 12th edition. New Jersey, Pearson.

Marcouse, I. *et al* (2011) *Business Studies for A Level*. 4th edition. London, Hodder Education.

Anon (2008) *The Consumer Protection from Unfair Trading Regulations: A Basic Guide for Business.* Office of Fair Trading.

Palmer, A. and Hartley, B. (2006) *The Business Environment*. 5th edition. Maidenhead, McGraw-Hill.

Porter, M. (1985) *Competitive Advantage*. New York, Free Press.

QUICK QUIZ

1. What are the different levels of a marketing environment?
2. What does PESTEL stand for?
3. Outline the primary activities in Porter's Value Chain.
4. What are government policies?
5. Outline five factors in a company's economic environment
6. What is 'corporate social responsibility'?
7. Outline three sources of secondary data.
8. Define the term 'stakeholders'.
9. What are the six groups in an organisation's micro-environment?
10. In what way does a supplier differ from a distributor?

ACTIVITY DEBRIEFS

Activity 2.1

You should have a large list of industries which have been directly impacted by the government's decision to ban smoking in public places in the UK. Although the tobacco industry, pubs, restaurants and clubs are the most obvious businesses to be impacted by this ban, you should have identified a much larger range of industries. Smoking cessation products such as nicotine patches; shed, shelter, awning and patio heater manufacturers are some of those to benefit from the ban. Dry cleaners conversely have reported an adverse effect on sales, as customers do not need to remove the smell of tobacco from their clothing.

Activity 2.2

Demographic changes, changes in working patterns, lifestyle changes, increased availability of technical information about products and services, and so on.

Activity 2.3

Consumer Credit Act, Sale of Goods Act, Trade Descriptions Act, Weight & Measures Act, Medicines Act, and so on.

QUICK QUIZ ANSWERS

1 Internal, external micro-environment and external macro-environment.

2 Political, Economic, Social, Technological, Environmental and Legal.

3 Inbound logistics, operations, outbound logistics, marketing & sales and services.

4 Principles or rules designed to guide decisions in order to achieve rational outcomes.

5 Interest rates, exchange rates, GNP, taxation, inflation and business cycle.

6 CSR suggests that companies should not only consider their customers and their profitability, but also the well-being of the wider communities within which they exist.

7 Internal data, published information and the government.

8 Anyone that has an interest in the success of the organisations.

9 Customers, stakeholders, distributors, suppliers, competitors and employees.

10 Suppliers provide inputs (materials, labour, services) to the company, while distributors help to get the outputs to the customer.

CHAPTER 3

The marketing mix

Introduction

This chapter examines a central marketing concept: the marketing mix. Essentially the marketing mix is the toolbox that marketers have to enable them to build products to meet the needs of different customers.

To make it easier to remember, the marketing mix is also known as the 7 Ps. Each P stands for a component (or tool) of the marketing mix, they are: Product, Price, Place, Promotion, People, Process and Physical evidence.

This chapter takes each of the 7 Ps in turn and considers why each is important and how it can be used to meet customer needs and wants.

Topic list

Syllabus reference

3.1	Explain the importance of the 7 Ps of the marketing mix as a series of tools co-ordinated to develop and delivered to meet customer needs and wants: ▪ **Product:** Core, augmented and potential product; features and benefits including the tangible nature of the product; NPD (New Product Development); product extension; product modification ▪ **Price:** Revenue generation; balance of cost versus profitability in meeting financial objectives; monitoring and responding to competitor pricing; customer expectation ▪ **Place:** Role of distribution; nature of distribution; distribution channels; maximising accessibility; changing role of logistics; differing customer needs; online and offline purchasing ▪ **Promotion:** Communicating the marketing proposition; sales; advertising; sales promotion; public relations; direct marketing; e-communications and personal selling ▪ **People:** Role of people in service delivery; reliance on people to deliver and maintain transactional marketing; role of people in customer relationships ▪ **Process:** The importance of process in enabling delivery of the customer proposition; end-to-end customer service support to enable transactions ▪ **Physical evidence:** Point at which service is delivered; physical evidence as part of the marketing proposition; environment; ambiance; corporate image

1 The importance of the marketing mix

1.1 Overview

> **Key term**
>
> The **marketing mix** refers to a combination of activities used by an organisation to achieve its objectives by marketing its products or services effective to a specific target group of customers. It is also known as the 4 Ps – Product, Price, Promotion and Place, or the 7 Ps – the 4 Ps with the addition of Process, Physical Evidence and People.

According to The Chartered Institute of Marketing (2009), successful marketing depends on addressing a number of key issues; including: what a company is going to produce; how much it is going to charge; how it is going to deliver its products or services to the customer; and how it is going to tell its customers about them. The marketing mix is basically the toolbox that marketers have to enable them to build products and meet the needs of different customers.

The original marketing mix had just four elements; Product, Price, Place and Promotion. You will find that some marketing textbooks still refer to the 4 Ps, as they commonly became known. As services marketing began to develop it was recognised that the original 4 Ps did not fully explain all the issues that a services marketer needed to consider. The marketing mix was extended to 7 Ps in order to better reflect the needs of services marketing. Some texts refer to the 7 Ps as the extended marketing mix.

The newest additional Ps are a bit of a stretch on the P theme. People mainly refers to employees. Process refers to the way that services are delivered using user-friendly systems for buying and selling. Physical evidence refers to intangible aspects such as the look and feel of the organisation and brand through things like their buildings, livery, uniforms, letterhead and so on. It is useful to remember them by their P acronyms because they are more memorable.

THE REAL WORLD

Manchester United

How do the 4 Ps relate to the marketing activities of UK football club, Manchester United?

Product: Football, memorabilia, shirts, television rights, books, TV rights (Also consider the excitement of a game, the chance to celebrate success, friendship and feeling of belonging through association with other fans - this feeling of membership is all part of the offering.)

Place: Home ground, other venues, website, other global sales outlets

Promotion: Joint activities with sponsors, televised games, products such as club-branded keyrings, books, shirts, website

Price: Reputation and strength of support enables club to charge high price for season ticket to watch home league games.

(*The Times* 100 Business Case Studies, 2012)

The manager must address these fundamentals areas, so that all 'the Ps' combine to emphasise marketing as a total system of co-ordinating organisational activity focused on satisfying customer needs. For the majority of private sector organisations the aim of marketing is, generally speaking, synonymous with the overall purpose of maximising financial returns. There are clearly a wide variety of possible combinations of marketing variables which management can select. Inevitably some combinations will earn greater financial returns than others. The crucial combination of factors comprising the marketing mix is therefore of high significance.

> "Like a recipe, one ingredient of the mix will not substitute for another, and each ingredient must be added in the right quantities at the right time if the mix is to prove successful in achieving customer satisfaction" (Blythe, 2008).

1.2 Re-mixing the mix

The 'design' of the marketing mix will normally be decided on the basis of management intuition and judgement, together with information provided by marketing research. Altering one component of the mix impacts upon most, if not all, of the others. For instance, the quality of advertising may need to be raised if the selling price of products is increased.

A manufacturer may also need a marketing mix for the end consumer, and an additional mix for the customer to whom they actually sell the product. Each mix will change as the marketing environment changes.

2 Product

2.1 What is a Product?

Key term

A **product** is 'a physical good, service, idea, person or place that is capable of offering tangible and intangible attributes that individuals or organisations regard as so necessary, worthwhile or satisfying that they are prepared to exchange money; patronage or some other unit of value in order to acquire it' (Brassington & Pettitt, 2006)

A product is a 'package' of benefits that satisfies a set of wants that consumers have. When you buy a set of wine glasses, for example, you are buying them because you want to drink wine and you prefer not to do so straight from the bottle. You may also want to impress your dinner guests with your taste, and choose to do so by possessing a particularly fine set of wine glasses.

The package of benefits includes:

(a) A physical aspect, which relates to the components, materials and specifications (colour, size etc) of the product: for example, a size 12 pullover made of 100% pure wool in a natural colour

(b) A functional aspect, which is a statement of how a product performs and for what purpose it is likely to be bought: the wool pullover may give warmth and comfort

(c) A symbolic aspect, which represents the qualities the product suggests to, or confers upon, the buyer: the '100% pure wool' label may represent quality, status or ecology (as a natural rather than synthetic product).

Product embraces:

- Product quality and durability
- Product design
- Brand name
- Logo
- Packaging
- The product range
- After-sales service
- Optional extras
- Guarantees and warranties.

For service rather than product-based organisations, this category includes the nature of the service including its key features.

Product in this context also includes associated services. Marketing a product involves product design, concept testing and product launch.

The starting point should of course not be with the product, but instead with the customer.

By understanding their needs and wants an appropriate product or service can be developed to fulfil these desires. Potential customers need to be satisfied with an organisation's product or service or they are unlikely to buy it. This means that the product or service must fulfil their need and should clearly be of a quality that suits its purpose. This final sentence has two implications for the organisation:

- It needs systems to monitor customer perceptions of the product or service
- Product quality must meet the 'fitness for purpose' test.

2.2 Features and benefits

It is worth noting a key marketing concept: that the customer does not buy a product, but seeks to satisfy a need or a want. This is important for the organisation to understand so that it can concentrate on marketing the benefits of its product rather than its features. A product's features are it tangible and intangible characteristics; while its benefits are what it can do for the customer. For example, a BMW sports car has a sleekly designed body, removable roof, sporty interior and other nice features, but what the customer really wants is to get from A to B in style.

Useful questions from a marketing point of view include:

- Are customers satisfied with existing products and services?
- Do these products or services fulfil their future needs?
- How are competitors addressing themselves to the same questions?
- Can competitors' products satisfy customers' future needs?

ACTIVITY 3.1

As customers buy the benefits of a product not its features, identify a recent purchase you have made and consider both its features and benefits.

2.3 Core, augmented and potential product

The total product represents both the tangible and intangible elements of what is offered to the customer and can be broken down into bundles of benefits that mean different things to different buyers.

Figure 3.1 Anatomy of a product

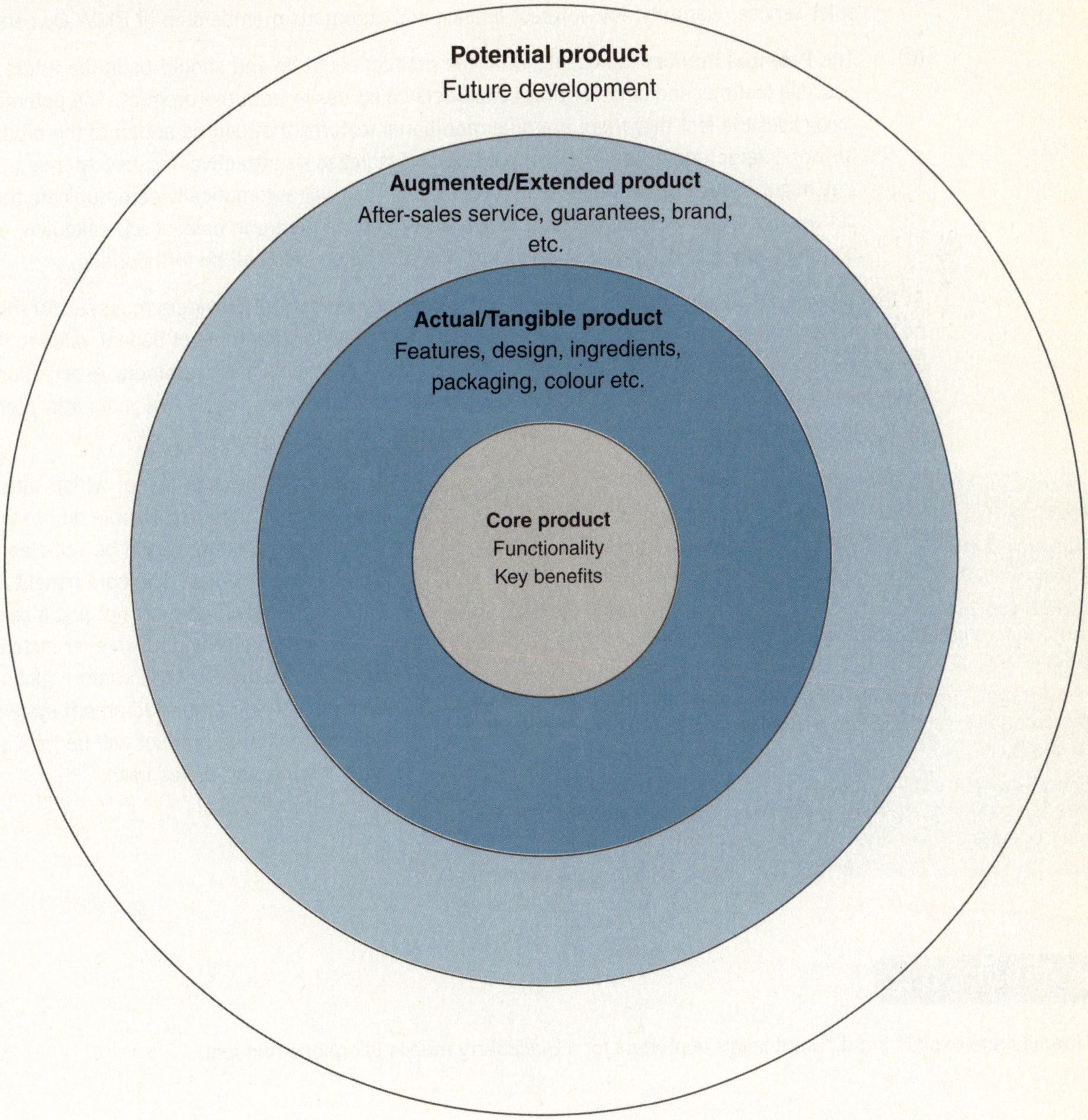

(a) The **Core Product** is the key benefit that the consumer derives from the purchase of it and the reason for its existence. It represents the minimum features that consumers will expect the product to have and the main reason why they purchase it. The core benefit of a product can be functional (as in a hairdryer) or psychological (as in an expensive designer perfume or anti-ageing cream). The core benefit of a BMW Z3 is its ability to take the customer from A to B in style and the core benefit of a mobile phone is its ability to make and receive calls, send and receive text messages and access the internet.

(b) The **Actual or Tangible Product** comprises the features of the product which are easy for consumers to identify. This includes: ingredients, design, quality level and packaging. It is the means by which marketers can clearly represent and communicate the core benefits of the products. In a BMW Z3, this will include the sexy design, leather seats, convertible roof, electronic gadgets, BMW logo and attractive choice of colours.

(c) In the **Augmented or Extended Product** are additional factors and benefits that differentiate the products from the competition. Although they do not form an intrinsic part of the actual or physical product, they are added to increase the product's attractiveness to the customer. For a BMW Z3 this will include after-sales service, warranty, low-interest finance and automatic membership of BMW Owners' Club.

(d) The **Potential Product** represents what the product could be and should be in the future. It is all the possible features and benefits that consumers could desire from the product. The potential product recognises the fact that there are other additional features that can be added to the product over time to further differentiate it from the competition and increase its attractiveness to customers. For a BMW Z3, this might include an on-board computer system that will automatically communicate the location of the car and the exact mechanical fault to the BMW Service Centre in case of a breakdown, as well as communicating to the driver in regard to how and when help will be forthcoming.

At the lower levels, customers are provided with what they expect; all providers must supply this or they gain no business at all. To gain a competitive edge, one must provide something of benefit value to the customer above and beyond the expected benefit set. This target is not static since customers' expectations grow; what delighted them five years ago is now taken for granted (eg in business hotels five years ago internet access in all rooms would have been an 'extra', now it is expected).

▶ **Key term**

Core product: the benefits that all products would have in a particular group – all cars, for example, are forms of transport.

Actual product: those features which are required to achieve the basic core product benefits – a car, for example, will have an engine, wheels and so on.

Augmented product: those features and benefits that start to set one product apart from another – an extended warranty on a car, for example.

Potential product: how the product could develop and satisfy future needs and wants, eg new fuel systems that are totally environmentally friendly.

The ultimate product is that which satisfies the dream needs of the customer. People do not want detergents; the ultimate product would be self-cleaning clothes that never needed ironing. The core benefit of a car is travel but people expect comfort not just a seat on a chassis. Today, cars are providing an ever-increasing number of electronic features (cruise control, global positioning systems and in-car entertainment systems). The ultimate potential product will be the car that provides total comfort and drives itself.

ACTIVITY 3.2

Identify and explain the different levels of product for a Blackberry mobile telephone handset.

2.4 New product development

New product development is important for maintaining customer satisfaction through change; refreshing or extending the product range; and adapting to environmental opportunities and threats. These will all contribute towards the success of a company's long-term business strategy.

New products may be genuinely innovative, but 'newness' may also mean 'adapted', 'repackaged' or 'introduced' in a new market.

What is a new product?

- One that opens up an entirely new market
- One that replaces an existing product
- One that broadens significantly the market for an existing product

An old product can be new if:

- It is introduced to a new market
- It is packaged in a different way
- A different marketing approach is used
- A mix variable is changed – for example, a new price is set, or a new distribution channel is used

Companies typically see new product development as the first stage in generating and commercialising new products within the overall strategic process of product life cycle management used to maintain or grow their market share.

Figure 3.2 The new product development process

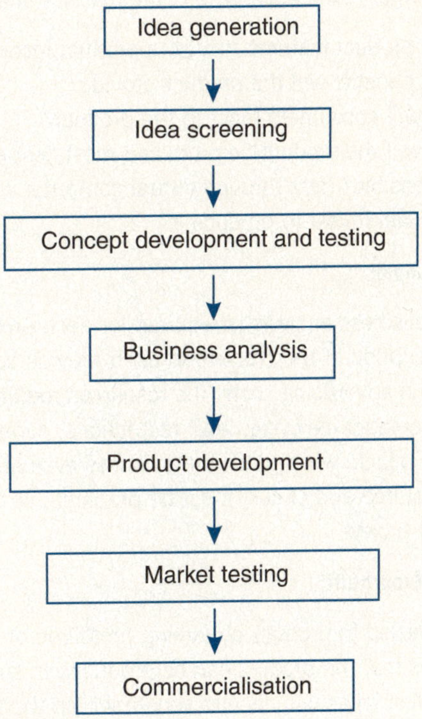

2.4.1 The new product development process

The process of NPD is outlined as follows;

1 **Idea generation**

Every new product starts as an idea in the mind of someone. Ideas for new products can be obtained from customers (through user innovation), designers, the research and development (R&D) department, competitors, focus groups, employees, salespeople, corporate spies, trade shows, or through a policy of open innovation. Formal idea generation techniques can be used, such as attribute listing, forced relationships, brainstorming, morphological analysis and problem analysis.

2 **Idea screening**

This stage involves an initial scan of the ideas generated in order to eliminate those that are unlikely to develop into successful products. The object is to eliminate unsound concepts prior to devoting resources to them.

The screeners must ask at least three questions:

- Will the customer in the target market benefit from the product?
- Is it technically feasible to manufacture the product?
- Will the product be profitable when manufactured and delivered to the customer at the target price?

3 **Concept development and testing**

This involves developing a model or image of the product that will be presented to customers, production technicians and others that can contribute to the development of the idea. In high technology industries, researchers and engineers will make a prototype that potential customers can assess and provide the company with constructive feedback. In the car manufacturing industry, the major companies produce concept cars which are displayed at motor shows in major markets in order to gauge public response to new styling, to create buzz about a new model line, or to just test new technology.

This stage helps the firm to answer the following questions:

Who is the target market and who is the decision-maker in the buying process?

- What product features must the product incorporate?
- What benefits will the product provide?
- How will consumers react to the product?
- How will the product be produced most cost-effectively?
- Is it feasible? (test through virtual computer aided rendering, and rapid prototyping)
- What will it cost to produce it?

4 **Business analysis**

A thorough business analysis is required for each product idea, projecting future sales and revenues, giving a description of the product so as to provide costs of production, providing estimates of sales promotion and advertising costs, the resources required, profits and return on investment. Other factors such as the product life cycle, legal restrictions, competitors' reactions (among others), must also be evaluated. Products which pass the business evaluation will be developed. A timetable and a budget of resources required and of cost must be prepared, so that management control can be applied to the development project.

5 **Product development**

Money is invested to produce a working prototype of the product, which can be tried by customers. This stage ensures that the product can be produced in sufficient quantities at the right price. The form which the product test takes will depend very much on the type of product concerned. The test should replicate reality as closely as possible.

- If the product is used in the home, a sample of respondents should be given the product to use at home
- If the product is chosen from amongst competitors in a retail outlet (as with chocolate bars), then the product test needs to rate response against competitive products

- If inherent product quality is an important attribute of the product, then a 'blind' test could be used
- An industrial product could be used for a trial period by a customer in a realistic setting

The marketing mix for the product will need to be planned at this stage.

6 **Market testing**

The purpose of test marketing is to obtain information about how consumers react to the product. Will they buy it, and if so, will they buy it again? With this information an estimate of total market demand for the product can be made.

A market test involves implementing marketing plans in selected areas which are thought to be 'representative' of the total market. In the selected areas, the firm will attempt to distribute the product through the same types of sales outlets it plans to use in the full market launch, and also to use the intended advertising and promotion plans.

7 **Commercialisation**

If the market research is positive and the test marketing stage has been successful then the product will go for full launch. The company needs to consider a number of factors: the timing of the launch, how the product will be launched, where the product will be launched and whether it will be a national or region by region roll-out?

These steps may be iterated as needed. Some may be eliminated. To reduce the time that the NPD process takes, many companies tackle several steps at once (referred to as concurrent engineering or time to market). Most industry leaders see new product development as a proactive process where resources are allocated to identify market changes and seize upon product opportunities before they occur (in contrast to a reactive strategy in which nothing is done until problems arise or a competitor introduces an innovation). Some industry leaders see new product development as an ongoing process (referred to as continuous development) in which the entire organisation is always looking for opportunities.

2.4.2 Product extension

Product extension involves adding new products to add to the company's existing lines. This is a strategy commonly used towards the end of a product's life cycle, with the aim of extending the product's life so further (high margin) sales can be made, and any remaining stocks cleared. Product extension may also fill any 'gap' between the tail end of one product's life and the successful launch and growth of its successor.

Product extension is common in the car industry, where a 'special edition' is often launched shortly before a car model is discontinued. This allows the manufacturer to use up any remaining components, and to earn a high margin on what is becoming an obsolete product.

One such example was Ford's 'Crusader' variant at the end of the life cycle of the Cortina.

THE REAL WORLD

CityAM

One successful example of product extension is the free newspaper City's AM launch into the recruitment market. Its readership – professionals in the banking, finance, legal and IT sectors – supported the creation of CityAMCareers, an online forum for recruiters and those seeking new employment opportunities. The site is given further exposure by a weekly printed careers section.

2.4.3 Product modification

Product modification is any significant change made to the attributes, usually in order to make it more attractive to prospective customers. It involves an adjustment to the size, shape, colour, style, price, performance, packaging or other aspect of the product.

There are several general categories of new products. Some are new to the market (eg DVD players into the home movie market), some are new to the company (eg Game consoles for Sony), some are completely novel and create totally new markets (eg the airline industry). When viewed against a different criterion, some new product concepts are merely minor modifications of existing products while some are completely innovative to the company.

3 Price

3.1 What is Price?

> **Key term**
>
> **Price** can be defined as a measure of the value exchanged by the buyer for the value offered by the seller.

Pricing decisions are important to the firm. This may be stating the obvious, but it is worth making it clear that pricing is very important as it is the only element of the marketing mix which generates income, revenue and profits, rather than creating costs.

All profit organisations, and many non-profit ones, face the task of pricing their products or services. Price can go by many names: fares, fees, rent, assessments among others.

Price was once the single most important decision made by the sales department. In those production-oriented times, price was viewed as the major factor in satisfying customer needs, and a price change was the usual reaction to competitor activity.

Today, though, marketing managers view price as just one of the factors involved in customer satisfaction. In fact, it is sometimes suggested that marketing aims to make price relatively unimportant to the consumers' decision making process. There is certainly some truth in this view. The other elements of the marketing mix are concerned with adding value to the product and tailoring it to the consumers' needs, to ensure that the choice between two products is not simply based on their different prices.

However, the role of price in the marketing mix is still significant, and should not be underestimated. It contributes towards the organisation's business and financial objectives in the following ways.

- Pricing is the only element of the mix which generates revenue rather than creating costs.
- It also has an important role as a competitive tool to differentiate a product and organisation, and thereby exploit market opportunities.
- Pricing must be consistent with other elements of the marketing mix, since it contributes to the overall image created for the product.

3.2 Influences on pricing decisions

Pricing decisions are affected by a range of factors, both internal (to the organisation) and external (in the competitive environment).

Table 3.1 Influences on pricing decisions

Internal factors	External factors
▪ Marketing objectives: profit maximisation; market share leadership; brand targeting and positioning ▪ Marketing mix strategy: factoring in the cost/ price implications of quality, distribution, brand differentiation ▪ Costs: at least setting the lowest viable price at which the company can afford to sell the product ▪ Price-setting methodologies: negotiated by sales force; set by management ▪ Product portfolio strategies: launch / new-product incentive pricing; 'loss leaders' to support the product range	▪ Competition: the extent of competition in the market; whether there is non-price competition; competitor pricing and promotions. ▪ Demand: the sensitivity of customer demand for the product to change in price (elasticity of demand) in the given market. ▪ Customer perceptions of price and what it means for quality and value ▪ Suppliers and intermediaries: impacting on costs; reacting to price decisions to protect their own margins. ▪ PEST factors: economic factors determining affordability; government price watchdogs; social responsibility dictating affordability; changing perceptions of 'value'; technology lowering costs

3.3 Pricing strategies

In practice, all these factors should be considered to some degree. In addition, an appropriate blending of the other factors of the marketing mix will also help establish the price. There are a number of methodologies that can help determine selling price.

- **Competitive** – setting a price by reference to the prices of competitive products
- **Cost plus** – adding a mark-up to costs of production which may incorporate desired return on investment
- **Market based** (or perceived value) – setting a price based on the value of the product in the perception of the customer
- **Penetration** – setting a low selling price in order to gain market share
- **Predatory** – setting a low selling price in order to damage competition
- **Premium** – achieving a 'high' price due to differentiation of the product
- **Price skimming** – setting a high price in order to maximise short-term profitability (eg the introduction of a novel product)
- **Selective** – setting different prices for the same product in different markets
- **Selective: category** – cosmetic modifications to allow variations to take place
- **Selective: consumer** – modifying the price to take account of certain groups (eg junior or OAP)
- **Selective: peak** – setting a price which varies according to level of demand (eg happy hours, premium rate calls, etc.)

3.4 Customer expectations

Customers usually have an idea of the correct price for a product. Customers' feelings about a product or service are reflected in what they are prepared to pay, so getting pricing 'right' is crucial.

The importance of price to the customer depends on several factors:

(a) The quality of the product: products perceived to have a higher quality can carry a high premium.

(b) How much consumers want the product: What a consumer is willing to pay will depend on the importance of the product to the individual.

(c) Consumers' income: Most consumers will only buy products within their income range. Consumers with more disposable income are less concerned with price than those with less disposable income. Uncertainty about the future can have the same effect as lower income.

3.5 Competition

Prices may be set on the basis of what competitors are charging, rather than on the basis of cost or demand. This sometimes results in 'going rate' pricing. Some form of average level of price becomes the norm, including standard price differentials between brands. In such situations, marketers must continually monitor the prices charged by competitors so that their products remain attractive to consumers. The petrol retail industry is a good example of a sector where going rate pricing is used.

3.5.1 Price as a competitive tool

In established industries dominated by a few major firms, it is generally accepted that a price initiative by one firm will be countered by a price reaction by competitors. Consequently, in industries such as breakfast cereals (dominated in Britain by Kellogg's, Nabisco and Quaker) or canned soups (Heinz, Crosse & Blackwell and Campbell's) a certain price stability might be expected without too many competitive price initiatives. A firm may respond to competitor price cuts in a number of ways.

(a) Maintain existing prices, if the expectation is that only a small market share would be lost, so that it is more profitable to keep prices at their existing level. Eventually, the rival firm may drop out of the market or be forced to raise its prices.

(b) Maintain prices but respond with a non-price counter-attack. This is a more positive response, because the firm will be securing or justifying its price differential with enhanced product quality, improved back-up services or other augmented features.

(c) Reduce prices, to protect the firm's market share. The main beneficiary from the price reduction will be the consumer.

(d) Raise prices and respond with a non-price counter-attack. The extra revenue from the higher prices might be used to finance the promotion of product improvements, which in turn would justify the price rise to customers.

4 Place

4.1 What is Place?

Key term

Place is concerned with the selection of distribution channels used to deliver goods to the consumer. The 'place' element of the marketing mix is really concerned with the processes by which the product reaches the consumer in a convenient way. Other terms for 'place' include distribution, delivery systems or channels.

The importance of place within the marketing mix should not be underestimated. If you get it right for your market it can be a crucial source of competitive advantage. Marketing effort will be futile if the product is not actually in the right place at the right time so that the customer has the choice of buying your product, not your competitors'.

Getting 'place' right in marketing terms means effective distribution: getting the right products into the right places at the right time. The movement of goods from production to consumption points is key. Place therefore refers to:

- Distribution channels
- Distribution coverage
- The types of transportation vehicle
- Locations of sales outlets, the arrangements of sales areas

- Stock levels
- Warehouse locations.

Research indicates that delivery performance is one of the main criteria for businesses choosing a particular supplier.

Questions from a marketing point of view include:

- Is the place of purchase convenient to customers and does it fulfil their needs?
- Is the means of distribution appropriate?
- Is the product available in the right quantities?

The choice of a particular distribution policy, such as whether or not to use wholesalers or retailers, may result in the company delegating at least part of its marketing function to others.

In setting up a channel of distribution, the supplier has to take several factors into account.

- Customers
- Nature of the goods or services
- Distributor characteristics
- Competitors' channel choice
- The costs associated with available channels
- The supplier's own characteristics

4.2 Physical distribution

Physical distribution refers to the method used by firms to get physical products to a point where it is most convenient for consumers to obtain them. The objective of any physical distribution method is to get the product from where it is made to the customer effectively and efficiently. The product must be delivered in good condition, fit the consumer's need for convenience, value for money, choice or whatever other need is important to the target market. Physical distribution covers issues such as transportation methods, wholesaling, high street retailing, direct mail marketing and electronic commerce.

4.2.1 Distribution channels

Distribution channels facilitate the movement the movement of products from the point of production to the final consumer. Few products are delivered directly from producer to consumer, but instead tend to pass through the hands of wholesalers, retailers, agents, factors and other channel members. For example, it is unlikely to be efficient for a company that imports canned fruits to deliver directly to every small retailer in the country. It is completely inconceivable for them to deliver directly to every customer in the country. The importer will deliver in bulk to wholesalers, who will then break the delivery into smaller units for distribution to small retailers.

According to Blythe (2008), the functions of channel members are:

- Sorting out: separating out heterogeneous deliveries into homogenous ones
- Accumulation: aggregating small production batches into amounts big enough to be worth shipping
- Allocation: breaking down large shipments into smaller amounts
- Assorting: combining collections of products that will appeal to groups of buyers.

Some products such as fresh foodstuff clearly benefit from short distribution channels. In the countryside it is often possible to buy produce directly from the farm. Alternatively, the farm may deliver daily to the supermarket. A specialist foreign car might, however, need to be imported, here the distribution is relatively lengthy and may take time.

The precise method of distribution chosen will vary depending upon the nature of the product and the degree of market exposure required. The greater the market an organisation wishes to access the longer and more complicated the distribution channel.

Figure 3.3 shows some patterns of distribution for consumer goods. The blocks represent stages where stock is held. This may be short term in a distribution centre or longer term for a distributor of imported goods. The arrows represent the physical transport process: in general, taking goods from the stock area, loading the goods, transportation, unloading the goods and storage.

Figure 3.3 Some channel models

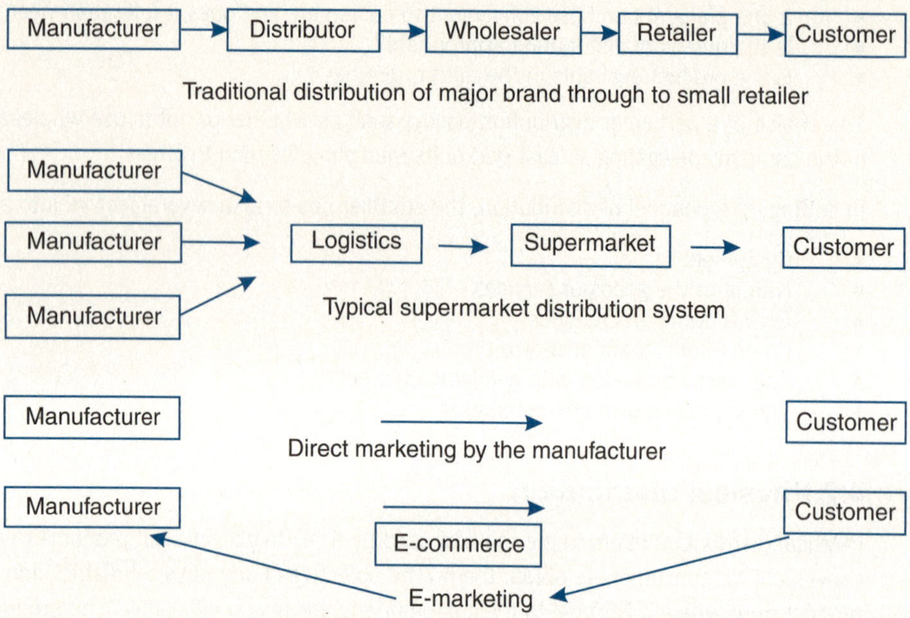

The top distribution layer represents the distribution of an imported product sold through small retail outlets. The next shows the situation typical for a supermarket: manufacturers deliver products to a logistics centre; the assorted products for a given store are loaded into a vehicle (a supermarket may have over 10,000 lines but 10,000 vehicles do not arrive each day at every branch) and are delivered to the store. The supermarket system provides a vast array of products at reduced distribution cost. The small independent retailer has a huge mountain to climb to provide sufficient increased customer value to offset their increased costs (hence the death of the village shop / post office).

For appropriate goods (eg Dell's computers), the manufacturer can supply the goods direct. Here e-commerce can be seen as nothing totally new, it augments postal and telephone ordering. However, it is much more convenient and 'alive' for the customer, and the transaction costs are much lower. The manufacturer does not need a distribution system; this can be contracted out to one of the specialist operators (eg DHL, UPS,or others). However, this does not provide the customer with a wide range of products, just those made by one manufacturer.

4.2.2 Maximising accessibility

One of the main aims for a marketer is to maximise the opportunities for customers to be able to purchase goods and services. The nature of the product will determine what this actually means in practice. For grocery products this will include trying to gain listings in as many grocery retailers as possible, such as supermarkets, convenience stores and online grocery retailers. The marketer will also try to gain the best on-shelf positions within these retailers in order to be highly visible and maximise the opportunities from this distributor.

4.2.3 Responding to different customer needs

Marketers must consider the differing needs of customers in designing the channel of distribution and selecting channel members. The distribution method used and the services available must be in line with the needs of the target market:

- If users need personalised service, you can use a local dealer network or retailer to provide that service.
- If your customers prefer to buy online, you can create an e-commerce website and sell direct; you can also sell through other online retailers or distributors that can offer your product on their own sites.
- You can develop your own specialised sales team to prospect and close deals directly with customers.

Wholesalers, retailers and other channel members already have the infrastructure and relationships to get the products to customers. Understanding the needs of channel members and marketing effectively to them will maximise revenue for everyone involved in the distribution process.

4.3 The changing role of logistics

> **Key term**
>
> **Logistics** 'is an all embracing concept that focuses on the physical movement and transformation of goods all the way from the source of supply to the point of consumption' (Brassington & Pettitt, 2006)

In recent years companies have moved away from just managing the physical delivery of finished goods to effective and efficient management of the movement and storage of materials, parts and finished goods from suppliers, through the firm and on to final consumers. This change in perspective has helped companies to improve customer service, minimise stock levels at all levels in the distribution chain and reduce cost for all members in the chain. Thus effective logistic management has become a major source of competitive advantage for companies that are using it to reduce costs and increase the standards of customer service. Computer manufacturers (like Dell) can customise their products at the last minute to match new orders or the market they are supplying to. In book distribution, major publishers use external logistic centres in order to enable rapid selection, packing, transport, invoicing and collection using one provider.

4.4 Online and offline purchasing

Online purchasing is a form of electronic commerce whereby consumers directly buy goods or services from a supplier or service provider over the internet without an intermediary service.

A central 'dot-com' e-commerce company (like Lastminute.com) takes the order and, in an ideal world, does not play any part in the manufacture, storage or transport of the goods (eg an e-travel company does not own hotels or airlines). Here there is maximum customer satisfaction (armchair shopping with a wide assortment of goods) and efficient delivery with minimum transaction costs.

Part of the problem of the 'dot-com' bubble was people were blinded by the glitz of the capabilities of the new communications channel and forgot the basics: that bargain PlayStation is no use if it arrives three days after the birthday and is damaged. Even if part-time marketers conduct much of the distribution, it is essential to customer satisfaction and it must form an integrated element of the marketing mix.

5 Promotion

5.1 What is Promotion?

> **Key term**
>
> **Promotion** covers all marketing activities that are focused on letting customers know about a product or service and persuading them to buy it.

Promotion includes the tools available to communicate with customers (and potential customers) about a product or service. In recent years the term 'marketing communications' has been used to more fully represent the role of the promotional P of the marketing mix. Overall, the role of promotion is to raise awareness of goods and services and elicit a response from the target market. A clear focus on customers and communication is central to modern marketing. Increasingly organisations attempt to understand customers and design communications to effectively and efficiently meet their needs. Once the organisation has determined what they believe the customers see as the main benefits of their product or service these aspects are focused upon when promotion takes place.

Promotion can take many forms and generally operates at one of three levels:

- Non-personal and mass, typically aimed at a market segment at large
- Personal and direct, typically one-way communication with a potential customer (eg by sending a letter)
- Personal and interactive, involving some one-to-one dialogue between the salesperson and the potential customer.

In order to be most effective, the promotional tools selected should:

- Project the image of the organisation which the marketer wishes to reflect
- Communicate a message which will raise awareness, increase sales, evoke an attitude, instil familiarity, build a relationship with customers (or a combination of all or some of these)
- Illicit some form of behavioural or attitude change in those the organisation is targeting.

Generally, the most successful marketing communications involve utilising a number of different communications methods commonly known as the promotional mix in a co-ordinated manner.

5.2 The promotion mix

The basic promotional mix consists of advertising, sales promotion, personal selling and PR, but more promotional methods are appearing all the time, particularly with the development of information and communication technologies. The following diagram indicates the extensive range of tools that can be used to communicate with a customer or potential customer.

Figure 3.4 The marketing communications mix

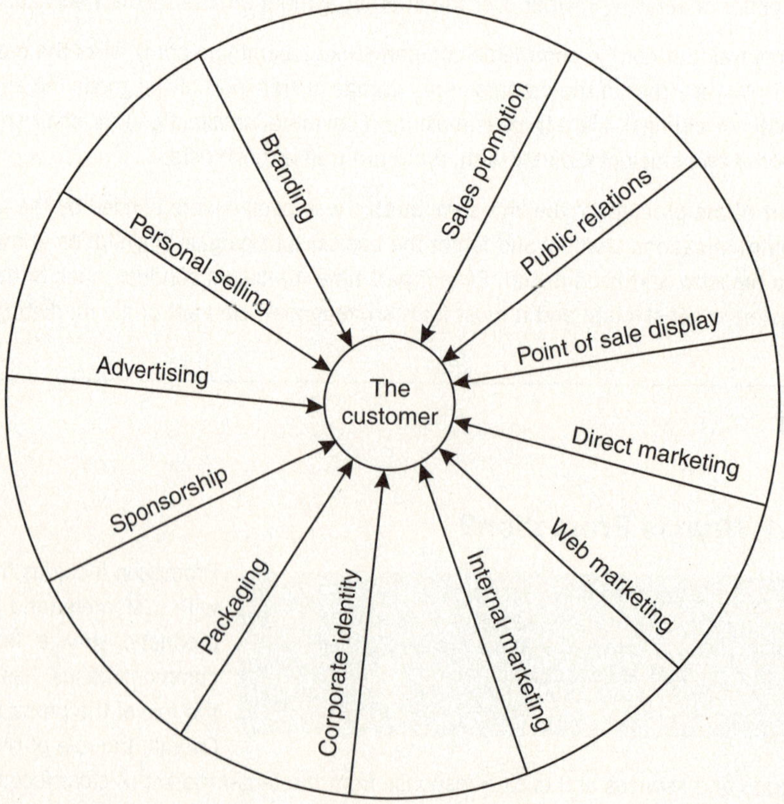

Just as promotional tools need to be blended to form a promotional or communication mix, so promotion itself needs to be blended with the other Ps comprising the marketing mix. For instance, a reduction in promotional activity may be possible if a wider range or larger number of sales outlets is developed. (This implies a heavier mix of place at the expense of promotion.)

The traditional 'push' marketing policy is concerned with transferring goods out to wholesalers and retailers who then have the task of selling them to ultimate final customers.

The emphasis of a 'push' policy is therefore on getting dealers to accept goods. A 'pull' policy by comparison is one of influencing final consumer attitudes so that a consumer demand is created which dealers are obliged to satisfy. A 'pull' policy usually involves heavy expenditure on advertising, but holds the potential of stimulating a much higher demand.

For example, producers of convenience food and alcohol advertise their products nationally rather than relying on supermarkets to promote these products.

5.3 Advertising

> **Key term**
>
> **Advertising** is 'any paid form of non-personal presentation and promotion of ideas, goods or services by an identifiable sponsor'. (American Marketing Association)

Blythe (2008) outlined the following purposes of advertising:

- To help the salesforce to open sales
- To stimulate demand for the product category
- To promote specific brands
- To counteract competitors' promotional activities
- To suggest new ways to use the product
- To remind consumers about the product
- To reinforce consumers' good feelings about the products
- To support the value of the company's shares.

Advertising can take many forms and uses a number of media including online media, press, broadcast (TV, radio etc) billboards, leaflet drops and point of sale displays. Increasingly sophisticated methods of advertising are opening up to marketers. Often the most inventive forms of advertising are also the most interesting and evoke a massive public response – there are whole books dedicated to effective campaigns. The increased use of online media and particularly social networking in recent years has meant that many campaigns are launched online first and are circulated via social networks.

It is estimated that within Western Europe every adult has up to 3000 'advertising encounters' every day. With so much expenditure on advertising it is perhaps surprising that there is any controversy over whether a company advertises or not. Although most marketers agree that advertising has a role to play, some believe that it is an ineffective way of getting customers to purchase products. Two polar opposite positions can be identified as follows:

(a) Advertising is ineffective and a waste of money, only adding to company (and hence eventually customer) costs. Brands such as Body Shop and Pizza Express do not see a need to use advertising in their promotional campaigns relying instead on other sources of information in order to form positive attitudes towards their products. In any case, some might think that advertising demeans a particular product or company. In some cases advertising may seem unethical.

(b) Advertising is so powerful and effective as to be essential. Consumers, it could be argued, will rarely purchase unadvertised brands so by not advertising a company will be at a serious disadvantage compared to competitors. The results of advertising campaigns have been undeniably successful including for brands such as Orange, Walkers Crisps, Tango and French Connection.

Lancaster and Withey (2005) conclude that some brands may be strong enough to sell on their own merits only if they are long-established and have strong brand-loyal users. For advertising to be successful it needs to be:

- Well planned and executed
- Part of an effective promotional mix
- Effective as a communication tool
- Consistent with the values and mission of the organisation.

THE REAL WORLD

The Lynx effect

Unilever made a bold brand extension move when it launched Lynx for women after 27 years of promoting Lynx as exclusively for men. Known for their provocative campaigns, the latest advertisements focus on the 'Lynx effect' for both sexes. In the first of the teaser videos a female police officer and a male robber are seen running towards each other – such is the attraction of the deodorant they are both wearing. Unilever have invested in a £7.2 million multiplatform marketing campaign to support the launch with the strapline 'Nothing will ever be the same again'.

(*Marketing Week*, 2012)

5.4 Sales promotion

The Institute of Sales Promotion (ISP) defines sales promotion as 'a range of tactical marketing techniques, designed within a strategic marketing framework, to add value to a product or service, in order to achieve a specific sales and marketing objective'. These may include discounting, coupons, guarantees, free gifts, competitions, vouchers, demonstrations, bonus commission and sponsorship.

Sales promotion activity is typically aimed at increasing short-term sales volume, by encouraging first time, repeat or multiple purchase within a stated time frame ('offer closes on such-and-such a date'). It seeks to do this by adding value to the product or service: consumers are offered something extra – or the chance to obtain something extra – if they purchase, purchase more or purchase again.

The key issue with promotion is that it is an invitation and incentive to act now; everyday low prices is not a promotion. This is a pricing strategy and should be considered as an element of the pricing aspect of the marketing mix. However, a two for one (BOGOF) promotion for a post-holiday, slow sales period is a promotional activity. There are a whole range of options including competitions and gifts. Sales promotion efforts are key in inducing trial of a new product, for example, using various forms of sampling to consumers.

In the B2B sector, promotion still has its part to play. Competitions can be used to motivate sales staff as distributors. When introducing a new computer product, free training could be offered.

The following diagram shows commonly used consumer sales promotion tools.

Figure 3.5 Consumer sales promotion tools

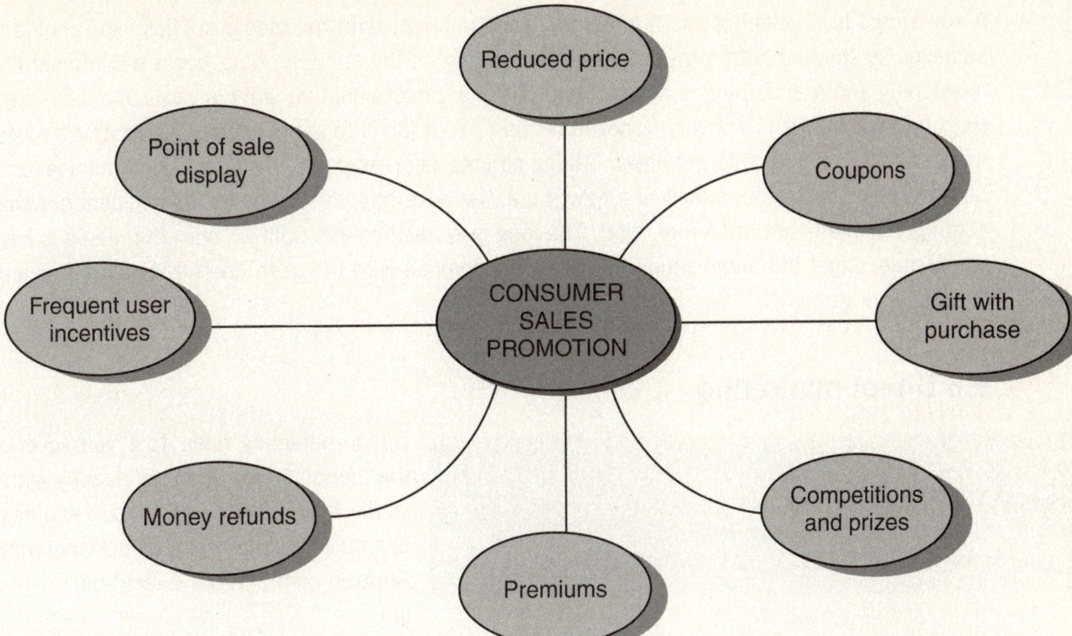

5.5 Public relations

> **Key term**
>
> **Public relations** – the function or activity that aims to establish and protect the reputation of a company or brand, and to create mutual understanding between the organisation and the segments of the public with whom it needs to communicate. (CIM)

The Institute of Public Relations has defined public relations as 'the planned and sustained effort to establish and maintain goodwill and mutual understanding between an organisation and its publics'.

This is an important discipline, because although it may not directly stimulate sales, the organisation's image is an important factor in whether it attracts and retains employees, whether consumers buy its products / services, whether the community supports or resists its presence and activities and whether the media reports positively on its operations.

An organisation can be either reactive or proactive in its management of relationships with the public.

(a) **Reactive public relations** is primarily concerned with the communication of what has happened and responding to factors affecting the organisation. It is primarily defensive.

(b) In contrast, **proactive public relations** practitioners have a much wider role and thus have a far greater influence on overall organisational strategy. The scope of the PR function is much wider, encompassing communications activities in their entirety.

Typical PR activities involve maintaining strong media and press relations, managing events and ensuring consistent corporate communications messages are maintained.

Some of the communications needed by an organisation are not best conducted by mass media. Therefore, for the management of political publics (eg planning application for a supermarket) it may be appropriate to have briefing sessions for local key decision-makers (eg local politicians).

Many organisations may not have a formal marketing department but will have a communications and public relations function (eg the police). In this context, a key responsibility will be agreeing, maintaining (here internal marketing may be key) and enforcing the corporate-communications manual. Often event management will be the responsibility of PR specialists. The opening of new facilities or a product launch are activities that most marketers become involved with sometime in their careers.

A key aspect is developing and maintaining good relations with the media publics / stakeholders. This is not achieved by sending out a press release commenting on the annual report, but is a continual process of developing and maintaining contacts. Here personal professional integrity is vital. One definition of PR is, 'the truth told well'. This is the very opposite of 'spin'. Your job is to get over the organisation's message; the media's responsibility is to get news. Taking airlines as an example, their press communications may one day be good news about the launch of a new route, the next, the worst of news, an accident or safety scare. PR contingency plans are, therefore, vital. The long-term relationship built up with the media is key to this. If the experience is that the organisation has been 'economical with the truth' then it should be no surprise that trust will be lacking.

5.6 Direct marketing

> **Key term**
>
> **Direct marketing** – all activities which make it possible to offer goods or services or to transmit other messages to a segment of the population by post, telephone, e-mail or other direct means. (CIM)

Direct marketing refers to a 'zero level channel' where the manufacturer interacts directly with the customer. Under these conditions 'place' becomes cyberspace. Examples include the web-based company Amazon.com and the direct booking of air travel on line.

5.6.1 Features of direct marketing

It is worth studying these definitions and noting some key words and phrases.

- **Response**. Direct marketing is about getting people to respond by post, telephone, e-mail or web form to invitations and offers.
- **Interactive**. The process is two-way, involving the supplier and the customer.
- **Relationship**. Direct marketing is in many instances part of an on-going process of communicating with and selling to the same customer.
- **Recording and analysis**. Response data are collected and analysed so that the most cost-effective procedures may be arrived at.

Direct marketing helps create and develop direct one-to-one relationships between the company and each of its prospects and customers. This is a form of direct supply, because it removes all channel intermediaries apart from the advertising medium and the delivery medium: there are no resellers. This allows the company to retain control over where and how its products are promoted, and to reach and develop business contacts efficiently.

5.6.2 Tools of direct marketing

Direct marketing is one of the fastest growing sectors of promotional activity. It now embraces a range of techniques, some traditional – and some based upon new technologies.

(a) **Direct mail (DM)**: a personally addressed 'written offering' (letter and/or sales literature) with some form of response mechanism, sent to existing customers from an in-house database or mailing list.

(b) **E-mail**: messages sent via the internet from an e-mail database of customers. E-mails can offer routine information, updates and information about new product

(c) **Mobile phone text messaging (SMS)**. Messages can be sent via mobile phone to a captive audience, catching them wherever they are. This form of marketing is still in its infancy, but with the proliferation of mobile phone usage it is likely to be very significant, at least in terms of numbers reached. It is also becoming increasingly sophisticated, with '3G' (third-generation) mobile phone technology. SMS marketing is governed by the Mobile Marketing Association in the UK.

(d) **Mail order**. Mail order brochures typically contain a selection of items also available in a shop or trade outlet, which can be ordered via an order form included with the brochure and delivered to the customer.

(e) **Catalogue marketing** is similar to mail order, but involves a complete catalogue of the products of the firm, which typically would not have retail outlets at all. Electronic catalogues can also be downloaded on the internet.

(f) **Call centres** and telemarketing. A call centre is a telephone service responding to or making telephone calls. This is a cost-effective way of providing a professionally trained response to customer callers and enquirers, for the purposes of sales, customer service, customer care or a contact point for direct response advertising.

Even in the e-commerce age, direct mail is still a major tool. The first and most important issue is to obtain 'clean' contact address lists. These can come from an organisation's data retrieval form, an effective in-house MkIS (eg profiles constructed from purchases using a loyalty card) or from purchased lists (eg lists bought from learned societies for professionals interested in specific areas such as analytical instruments). In this area, there are significant conformance issues, and the legal issues regarding data protection are quite restrictive (the interpretation of data protection legislation is an evolving area and the law is different in different countries).

5.7 E-communications

E-marketing has been the most significant development in marketing communications in recent years although it merely is a new medium which has become available, the same 'rules' of marketing and communications still apply – albeit at a possibly faster pace.

Key issues for e-communications include:

- The ability to optimise the visits to websites (search engine optimisation)
- The need to be more than an online brochure with the opportunity for real interaction with customers
- A consideration of the role of the networking opportunities online and the increased propensity for customers to review every aspect of a good or service and self broadcast this – the role of word of mouth has therefore become intensified

E-communications have not changed the laws of marketing. It does not matter whether the order comes by e-mail or snail mail if you get the product to the customer late and damaged.

E-commerce is a very powerful addition to the integrated communications mix and just as jet travel made long-haul holidays affordable in price and feasible in travel time, it has created entirely new business opportunities. The key is to understand what is different about e-communications and how the differences can be exploited by an organisation and, more importantly, by other stakeholders (pressure groups have been quick on the uptake).

In an integrated mix, traditional communications methods can be used to point people to the website. In addition, many sites have paid search engines like Google, Yahoo or Alta Vista to pull their address up in the first 10 or 20 responses to a general search. Product information on a pack should point to the appropriate part of the website as well as the helpline. Calls are expensive; the more the customers can do for themselves, the lower the associated transaction costs.

Developments in communication technology, specifically cable, satellite and digital technologies have provided a platform for another form of home shopping via the television.

Advantages over web-based selling include complete user familiarity with the equipment (the TV) and the ability to extensively demonstrate / advertise the products visually on a dedicated channel.

5.8 Personal selling

Personal selling is the presentation of products and persuasive communication to potential clients by sales staff employed by the supplying organisation. It is the most direct and longest established means of promotion within the promotional mix.

It encompasses a wide variety of tasks including prospecting, information gathering and communicating as well as actually selling.

Personal selling, or salesforce activity, must be undertaken within the context of the organisation's overall marketing strategy. For example, if the organisation pursues a 'pull' strategy, relying on massive consumer advertising to draw customers to ask for the brands, then the role of the salesforce may primarily be servicing, ensuring that retailers carry sufficient stock, allocate adequate shelf space for display and co-operate in sales promotion programmes.

Conversely, with a 'push' strategy, the organisation will rely primarily on the salesforce to persuade marketing intermediaries to buy the product. The following model demonstrates the tasks involved with personal selling.

Figure 3.6 Elements and tasks of personal selling

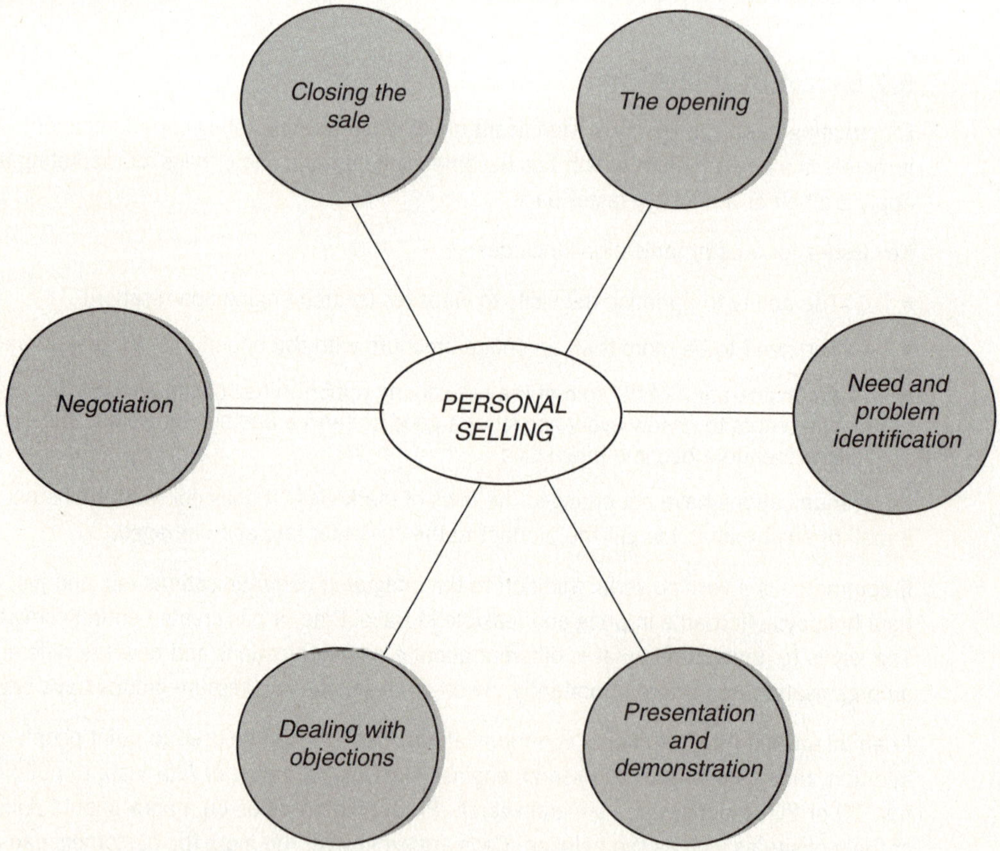

> **▸ Exam tip**
>
> The examiners for this qualification have specifically stated that they will test on the extended marketing mix (7 Ps) and **not** the original marketing mix (4 Ps).

6 People

6.1 What is People?

The higher the level of customer contact involved in the delivery of a product or service, the more crucial is the role of people. In many cases the delivery and the physical presence of the staff involved are completely inseparable. This is why the term 'people' was specifically added in order to reflect services marketing more fully.

In some cases, the physical presence of people actually performing the job is a vital aspect of customer satisfaction. Think of counter staff in a bank, or waiting staff in a restaurant, or builders who leave your house tidier than they found it. The people involved are performing or 'producing' the service, selling the service and also liaising with the customer to promote the service, gather information and respond to customer needs.

Organisations need to take measures to institute a customer orientation in all sectors of activity. People issues will include the following.

- Appearance
- Attitude
- Commitment (including quality / customer)
- Behaviour
- Professionalism
- Skills / competence
- Discretion / confidentiality
- Integrity / ethics

Managers must promote values of customer service in order to create a culture of customer service. This may entail any or all of the following.

- Job design to give people the authority they need to meet customer needs
- Careful policies of recruitment and selection
- Programmes of training and development to ensure that staff have both technical competence and 'people skills'
- Standardised rules and practices, to ensure consistent basic levels of service
- Effective programmes of staff motivation and reward, creating commitment to the organisation, quality and customers
- Effective communication of quality, service and customer care values

For members of the organisation who are not in customer-facing roles their value to the overall marketing proposition should not be underestimated. In order to provide a high quality offering, a customer centric view needs to be at the centre of every functional department.

6.2 Service delivery

People include both staff and customers. An organisation's people come into contact with customers and can have a massive impact on customer satisfaction levels. In the customers' eyes, staff are generally inseparable from the total service. This implies the need for well trained, motivated staff mindful of the adage 'the customer is always right'. It is important therefore that every member of staff contribute to the marketing philosophy and support the firm's external marketing activities.

As organisations introduce streamlined hierarchies and more flexible working practices, marketing offers the opportunity for their employees to operate in interdisciplinary teams furthering an overall marketing philosophy. Corporate investment in their most valuable asset, employees, through training and development supports the processes of creating and defending competitive advantages gained from successful marketing.

In terms of customers, good research should reveal vital, personal, cultural, social and psychological profiles of potential customers. This data can be exploited when applying other aspects of the marketing mix.

6.3 Customer relationships

Relationship marketing is a form of marketing developed from direct response marketing campaigns conducted in the 1960s and 1980s. It emphasises customer retention and continual satisfaction rather than individual transactions and per-case customer resolution. Relationship marketing differs from other forms of marketing in that it targets an audience with more directly suited information on products or services which suit retained customer's interests, as opposed to direct or 'intrusion' marketing, which focuses upon acquisition of new clients by targeting majority demographics based upon prospective client lists.

Relationship marketing is founded on the bedrock that people buy the service that is provided by other people. The effectiveness and efficiency of this process depends on relationships. Companies do not have relationships, people in companies do business and have relationships with other people in other companies. For effective service delivery, relationships must be good not only between the front-line staff and the customer, but also with all the internal stakeholders in the organisation supporting the front-line contact for all the part-time marketers. Many companies often state, 'People are our most valuable asset'.

7 Process

7.1 What is Process?

> **Key term**
>
> **Process** refers to the series of actions or activities required to get the value proposition to the customer

The term 'process' within the marketing mix is concerned with the delivery process of the customer proposition – in other words, what processes and procedures are in place to get the value proposition to the customer. You may think that this sounds very much like 'place' but it does not refer to this exactly (although in some examples there will be overlap) rather it refers to policies and procedures along with the customer service elements.

If you think about the processes associated with a trip to the dentist. The dentist will have a particular method for you to book your appointment – there may be an online booking facility for example, telephone bookings or practice of making your next check up appointment at each visit. Your practice may have a procedure or routine that you also go through when you arrive at the surgery, for example, there may be a specific queuing system in place and some method of dealing with latecomers. The complete process of delivering a quality service is sometimes referred to as end-to end customer service and encompasses every aspect of the service encounter from start to finish.

7.2 Delivering the customer proposition

The customer value proposition consists of the sum total of benefits which a vendor promises that a customer will receive in return for the customer's associated payment (or other value transfer). In simple words:

value proposition = what the customer gets for what the customer pays

Accordingly, a customer can evaluate a company's value proposition on two broad dimensions with multiple subsets:

- **Relative performance:** what the customer gets from the company relative to a competitor's offering
- **Price:** which consists of the payment the customer makes to acquire the product or service, plus the access cost

The company's marketing and sales efforts offer customers a value proposition; its delivery and customer-service processes then (hopefully) fulfil that value proposition.

7.3 End-to-end service support

The delivery of a service typically involves six factors:

1. The accountable service provider and its service suppliers (eg the people)
2. Equipment used to provide the service (eg vehicles, cash registers)
3. The physical facilities (eg buildings, parking, waiting rooms)
4. The consumer requesting service
5. Other customers at the service delivery location
6. Customer contact.

The service encounter is defined as all activities involved in the service delivery process. Some service managers use the term 'moment of truth' to indicate that defining point in a specific service encounter where interactions are most intense. However, service is a process that extends from the initial contact with the customer through to the customer's 'death' (in marketing terms, when they cease to be a customer for whatever reason).

ACTIVITY 3.3

Outline the different activities involved in the service delivery process for a customer flying to Rome on a UK low cost airline.

8 Physical evidence

8.1 What is physical evidence?

Physical evidence refers to "the tangible elements that support the service delivery, and offer clues about the positioning of the service product or give the customer something solid to take away with them to symbolise the intangible benefits they have received" (Brassington & Pettitt, 2006).

Because of the intangible nature of services, prospective customers have little evidence to evaluate in trying to make objective judgements on whether to choose one provider or the other. In marketing, physical evidence represents the tangible aspects of intangible service products that constitute the means through which customers can judge the quality of the service.

You receive monthly bank statements – but all they are, really, is reassurance in tangible form that the bank still has your money. The following are other examples of items of physical evidence that the marketer can use in the marketing mix.

Table 3.2 Physical evidence

Environment of service delivery	Facilities	Tangible evidence of purchase
▪ Colours ▪ Layout ▪ Staff uniforms ▪ Noise levels ▪ Smells ▪ Ambience ▪ Website design	▪ Vehicles / aeroplanes ▪ Equipment / tools	▪ Labels and other printed information ▪ Tickets, vouchers and purchase confirmations ▪ Logos and other visible evidence of brand identity ▪ Packaging

8.2 Environment and ambiance

Services are intangible; physical evidence provides something tangible enabling people to 'feel' the quality of the service. How many people come into a shop? How long do they spend in the shop? What they buy is affected by the ambience and physical layout of the store. Lighting, heating, sound, colour and even smell (remember your last trip to the bakery) all contribute. This can be large-scale, such as the construction of a shopping mall, to the physical display of goods (there is no sharp dividing line between environment and point of sale for a shop). Airlines, theatres and museums all take care with their physical environment. Appropriate environments and even music can speed up recovery rates in hospitals.

8.3 Corporate image

A corporate image refers to how a corporation is perceived. It is a generally accepted image of what a company 'stands for' The creation of a corporate image is an exercise in perception management. The image is created primarily by marketing experts, who use public relations and other forms of promotion to suggest a mental picture to the public. Typically, a corporate image is designed to be appealing to the public, so that the company can spark an interest among consumers, generate brand equity, and thus facilitate product sales.

A corporation's image is not solely created by the company: other contributors to a company's image could include news media, journalists, labour unions, environmental organisations, and other NGOs.

ACTIVITY 3.4

Identify the relevance of the marketing mix for Argos.

CHAPTER ROUNDUP

- The marketing mix refers to a combination of activities used by an organisation to achieve it's objectives by marketing its products or services effective to a specific target group of customers. It is also known as the 4 Ps – Product, Price, Promotion and Place, or the 7 Ps – the 4 Ps with the addition of Process, Physical Evidence and People.
- A product is a 'package' of benefits that satisfies a set of wants that consumers have.
- The total product represents both the tangible and intangible elements of what is offered to the customer and can be broken down into bundles of benefits that mean different things to different buyers.
- Price can be defined as a measure of the value exchanged by the buyer for the value offered by the seller. It is the only element of the marketing mix which generates income, revenue and profits, rather than creating costs.
- The 'place' element of the marketing mix is really concerned with the processes by which the product reaches the consumer in a convenient way.
- The role of promotion is to raise awareness of goods and services and elicit a response from the target market.
- The higher the level of customer contact involved in the delivery of a product or service, the more crucial is the role of people.
- The term 'process' within the marketing mix is concerned with the delivery process of the customer proposition – in other words, what processes and procedures are in place to get the value proposition to the customer.
- In marketing, physical evidence represents the tangible aspects of intangible service products that constitute the means through which customers can judge the quality of the service.

FURTHER READING

Chapters 6–9 and 11 of:

Blythe, J. (2008) *Essentials of Marketing*. 4th edition. Harlow, Prentice Hall.

Chapters 6–11 and 13 of:

Brassington, F. and Pettitt, S. (2007) *Essentials of Marketing*. 2nd edition. Harlow, Prentice Hall.

REFERENCES

Argos (2012) About Us. Argos, www.argos.co.uk/static/StaticDisplay/includeName/AboutArgos.htm [accessed 11 June 2012].

Baker, R. (2012) Lynx unveils deodorant launch for women. Marketing Week, www.marketingweek.co.uk [accessed 12 June 2012].

Blythe, J. (2008) *Essentials of Marketing*. 4th edition. Harlow, Prentice Hall.

Brassington, F. and Pettitt, S. (2006) *Principles of Marketing*. 4th edition. Harlow, Prentice Hall.

Harris, D. and Botten, N. (2008) *CIM Coursebook: Introduction to Marketing*. Oxford, Butterworth Heinemann.

Kotler, P. and Keller, K. (2006) *Marketing Management*. 12th edition. New Jersey, Pearson.

Lancaster, G. and Withey, F. (2007) *CIM Coursebook: Marketing Fundamentals* 07/08. Oxford, Butterworth, Heinemann.

Marcouse, I. *et al* (2011) *Business Studies for A Level*. 4th edition. London, Hodder Education.

The Times 100 Business Case Studies (2012) Re-focussing a company's culture and marketing mix: An Argos case study. *The Times*, http://businesscasestudies.co.uk/argos/re-focussing-a-companys-culture-and-marketing-mix/extended-marketing-mix.html [accessed 11 June 2012].

The Times 100 Business Case Studies (2012) The marketing mix of Manchester United. *The Times*, http://businesscasestudies.co.uk/business-theory/marketing/marketing-mix-price-place-promotion-product.html [accessed 5 June 2012].

Withey, F. and Lancaster, G. (2006) *Marketing Fundamentals* CIM Coursebook 05/06. Oxford, Butterworth, Heinemann.

QUICK QUIZ

1. What are the 7 Ps of marketing?
2. What is a product?
3. Outline the four levels of a product.
4. What are the seven stages of new product development?
5. State five pricing strategies that can be used by marketers.
6. What factors do companies have to consider in setting up a channel of distribution?
7. What is promotion?
8. Outline eight components of the promotion mix.
9. What is physical evidence?
10. Define personal selling.

ACTIVITY DEBRIEFS

Activity 3.1

This depends on the recent purchase you have chosen.

Activity 3.2

Core product: The handset's ability to make and receive calls, send and receive emails, maintain your diary / schedule, send and receive text messages, store and play music and videos, take and store photographs and store and display different files and documents.

Actual product: The handset itself; including its colour, features, design and portability.

Augmented product: Includes the brand name, guarantee, after-sales service and advice / support.

Activity 3.3

1. Visit company's website
2. Book flight and make payment
3. Arrive at airport
4. Check in at airline's desk and drop bags
5. Proceed to waiting area
6. Board aircraft and occupy seat
7. Enjoy in-flight entertainment and trolley service during flight
8. Alight from aircraft at destination
9. Proceed to baggage area and collect bags
10. Depart from the airport.

Activity 3.4

Argos is an UK-based, multi-channel retailer recognised for choice, value and convenience.

Product: Argos offers thousands of product lines including clothing, kitchen and laundry, home and furniture, garden and DIY, health & personal care, home entertainment, photography, office equipment, toys and nursery products, jewellery and gifts.

Price: Prices vary depending on the product. The company focuses on charging low prices by working closely with suppliers to keep costs down.

Place: Argos sells through its 700 stores throughout the UK and Republic of Ireland, online through its website and over the telephone. The company's website is one of the most visited in the UK.

Promotion: The company uses various forms of advertising, including television, print, outdoor and online, to appeal to its different market segments. It also uses a range of other promotional tools.

People: Argos employs about 33,000 people to perform a range of functions. The company trains its staff to ensure that they are friendly, knowledgeable and provide good customer service.

Physical evidence: The look and layout of the stores and the layout, design and usability of the company's website are all important factors in attracting customers.

Process: Over the years, the company has significantly invested in technology in order to improve the in-store and online buying experience for customers. The quick-pay system enables customers in the stores to check availability, order and pay for goods themselves without having to queue for the tills. The in-store touch screen units allow customers to check availability before ordering a product. The company also provides check and reserve services online, by phone, by text and through its iPhone app.

QUICK QUIZ ANSWERS

1 Product, Price, Promotion, Place, People, Process and Physical evidence.

2 A product is a package of benefits that satisfies a set of wants that consumers have.

3 Core, actual, augmented and potential product.

4 Idea generation, idea screening, concept development, business analysis, product development, market testing and commercialisation.

5 Cost-plus, penetration, predatory, premium and price skimming.

6 Customers, nature of goods or services, distributor characteristics, competitors' channel choice, costs and supplier's own characteristics.

7 Promotion covers all the marketing activities that are focused on letting customers know about a product or service and persuading them to buy it.

8 Advertising, sales promotion, personal selling, direct marketing, public relations, sponsorship, web marketing and point-of-sale display.

9 Physical evidence refers to 'the tangible elements that support the service delivery, and offer clues about the positioning of the service product or give the customer something solid to take away with them to symbolise the intangible benefits they have received'.

10 Personal selling is the presentation of products and persuasive communication to potential clients by sales staff employed by the supplying organisation.

CHAPTER 4

Marketing in different organisational contexts

Introduction

This chapter examines the application of marketing in different organisational contexts. The first section examines the ways in which consumers and business customers make their buying decisions.

The second section explores the nature and composition of the decision-making units for consumers and business customers.

The final section examines the different ways in which the marketing mix is used in different organisations to influence the decision-making units in FMCG (fast moving consumer goods),B2B (business-to-business), service, internet and voluntary organisations.

Topic list

Syllabus reference

4.1	Explain the different ways in which customers (Business to Business) and consumers (Business to Consumer) make their buying decisions: ▪ The buying decision-making process ▪ The buying decision-making unit
4.2	Explain the different ways in which the marketing mix is used in different organisations to influence the buying decision making units of the following: ▪ FMCGss (Fast Moving Consumer Goods) ▪ Business-to-Business organisations ▪ Service organisations ▪ Voluntary and not-for-profit organisations ▪ Internet (online) business

1 Buyer decision-making process

1.1 What is buyer behaviour?

Buyer behaviour is the decision processes and actions of people involved in buying and using products and services. To be successful marketers need to understand why consumers make the purchases that they make, what factors influence consumer purchases and how those factors change in the society.

Dibb (1996) suggests that the study of buying behaviour is important for a number of reasons.

(a) The buyer's reaction to the organisation's marketing strategy has a major impact on the survival and success of the organisation.

(b) If organisations are truly to implement the marketing concept, they must examine the main influences on what, where, when and how customers buy. Only in this way will they be able to devise a marketing mix that satisfies the needs of customers.

(c) By gaining a better understanding of the factors influencing their customers and how their customers will respond, organisations will be better able to plan effective marketing communications and activities.

However, it is important to note that not all consumers behave in the same way. Decision making and purchase patterns vary considerably within markets or product categories, between individuals – and even within individuals according to circumstances and over time. You must recognise this complexity and aim to adapt marketing communications to the needs of different target audiences.

We also need to consider the titles we use when discussing 'customers'.

1. As a customer, we would engage in a purchase transaction with a supplier of goods. In a domestic context, these would be for our own or our family's consumption.
2. As a client we would be availing ourselves of a range of professional services such as accountants, solicitors and so on.
3. As a professional, we would be exercising special skills in purchasing, often in large quantities and / or spending millions of pounds, as a part of our job on behalf of an organisation. For example, media buyers are professionals who purchase advertising space.
4. As a consumer, we are the end user of the product. A consumer may not be a customer and *vice-versa*. We do not necessarily take direct part in the purchase but, because we use up the product and gain

some satisfaction or benefit from it, we may influence its purchase and/or its re-purchase. We are the end-user of the products.

5 When we are part of a group combining our influences we are known as a Decision Making Unit (DMU), for example children influencing the purchase of breakfast cereals; the adults in a family choosing a new carpet; or a group of colleagues of differing disciplines in an organisation. The latter DMU may have a very formal structure and the former have very little.

1.2 Consumer buying – the decision-making process

▸ Key term

Consumer buyer behaviour refers to the buying behaviour of final consumers, those individuals and households who buy goods and services for personal consumption (Kotler *et al* 1999).

Customers do not buy products, they buy benefits. I do not want a packet of detergent, I want clean clothes. Accountants see price, customers want to experience value and affordability. If they do not, there is no sale. Place involves decisions such as the nature of the outlet from which the product will be sold and the physical distribution (delivery) of the product to the outlets and finally to the consumer. However, customers are not interested in the organisation's smart supply chain logistics. They wish to experience convenience with the right product, in the right place, at the right time and in the right condition for the customer's use.

The firm wants to promote products, and to persuade people to buy their products. Consumers need to experience communications to persuade them that they want these benefits, that they can afford the product which is good value and convenient to obtain.

The process of making a purchase decision consists of a number of stages (Figure 4.1), each of which is considered in detail in the following sections.

Figure 4.1 The buying decision

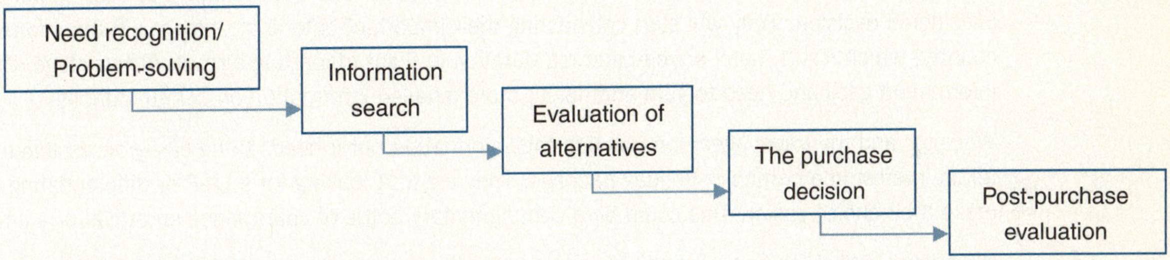

1.2.1 Need recognition / problem-solving

Recognising that, as a consumer, you need to purchase a product or service can happen for a number of reasons. It may be that you need to replace something you already own, which no longer fulfils your needs. A new father of twins may realise that his two-seater sports car is no longer the ideal car for him to own.

Other changes in your life may result in new purchases – a change of job requiring you to work from home will result in your needing office and IT facilities, or maybe you have just made a new set of friends who go skiing three times a year so you need the equipment to join them.

Outside influences also lead to us recognising a need. The knowledge that the population is ageing and today's 40-year-olds will probably not receive a sufficient State pension is prompting many to top up their personal pension plans. On a different scale, did we know that we needed a disposable toilet brush before we saw one advertised on TV? Communications can be the single most powerful influence if used well.

Needs arise for different reasons and different people will be aware of different needs, but once the need has been recognised then the consumer will be in a state of heightened attention, more likely to take notice of products / services that fulfil their needs or solve their problems.

Let us follow through an example of a couple booking their honeymoon, and see the messages and media they are exposed to as they progress through the buying process.

1.2.2 Information search

At the beginning, the information search stage can be divided into two levels.

(a) **'Heightened attention'**. The customer simply becomes more receptive to information about the particular product category.

(b) **'Active information search'**. The extent of the search will depend on the strength of the drive, the amount of information available, the ease of obtaining additional information and the satisfaction obtained from the search.

For an exotic and memorable holiday, the couple will start searching for information about their ideal honeymoon destination and itinerary.

They will search the internet, look out for newspaper and magazine articles and advertising, walk the high street to interrogate the travel agents, listen to the radio, watch TV travel programmes and ask their friends and work colleagues about their experiences. At this stage, the message needs to be about the holiday resort. The strapline needs to conjure up the feeling of being on holiday and the visual needs to feature a long white beach, turquoise sea and palm trees. The media will need to be carefully chosen to reach the target group – a bridal magazine will reach this couple but not other consumers for an exotic holiday.

1.2.3 Evaluation of alternatives

At this stage, the consumer evaluates the options that are available based on the information derived form their search at the previous stage. The customer will now try to choose between competing products or services in order to firm up the purchase decision.

Having collated a plethora of information, the couple now need to sift through that information to make a considered decision. They will start considering their important criteria in order to sift the information – which country, which resort, hotel or self-catering, duration of flight, departing airport. At this stage, they will find information gaps and need to gain additional, more detailed information on certain options.

Websites and the travel agent can provide this information but it needs to be easily accessible for them to retain interest in a particular holiday package. They are also looking for a USP or differentiating factor that will make their choice easier. This could be a complimentary bottle of champagne on arrival or a limo to the airport.

Whichever is likely to appeal to this couple is what the holiday company needs to be finding out and communicating to them. This message is unlikely to be the banner headline for the company but in all the brochures, websites and travel agents it does need to be contained within the communication from the organisation. The key objective here is to inform detail.

1.2.4 The purchase decision

Having evaluated the range of brand choices, the consumer may have formed a purchase intention to buy the most preferred brand. In most cases it is the salesperson either in a shop or on the phone that will move the consumer towards making a final purchase decision. In the case of online purchasing, the ease of access and navigability of the site will aid the purchase transaction, but a site that shows positive customer feedback and comprehensive resort guides will help the purchaser towards the final purchase.

It is important at this stage that there are no last minute hitches to put off the purchaser. A crowded travel agent, an unanswered phone or an unavailable website will mean the couple do not see the final purchase decision through and could lead to them reconsidering their decision.

Added value gained at the point of purchase can also sway a decision. A third week free could encourage people to lengthen their stay; free travel insurance can encourage them to consider another company. It is important that the messages received by the consumer at this stage help to confirm in their minds that they have made the right decision and they feel secure in their choice. The key objective here is to differentiate.

1.2.5 Post-purchase evaluation

Having purchased the brand the consumer will experience some level of satisfaction or dissatisfaction, depending on the closeness between the consumer's product expectations and the product's perceived performance. These feelings will influence whether the consumer buys the brand again, and also whether the consumer talks favourably or unfavourably about the brand to others.

There needs to be feedback devices incorporated within any communication so that problems can be detected early and acted upon. Front-line staff need to be competent in dealing with problems and complaints. The message here needs to be one of reassurance that problems will be sorted out and that there are available resources to enable that to happen. Only if this occurs can customer satisfaction arise. The key objective here is to continue the differentiation to remind the couple why they made this choice.

1.3 Business-to-Business buying decision-making process

Key term

Organisational buyer behaviour refers to the buying behaviour of organisations which buy goods and services to use in the production of other products and services that are sold, rented or supplied to others.

A number of differences between organisational and consumer markets exist which mean that a modified approach needs to be taken when considering the process of buying behaviour.

Organisational markets normally comprise fewer buyers, with those buyers often being very concentrated (a few buyers are responsible for the majority of sales). Because of this smaller customer base and the importance and power of larger customers there is generally a close relationship between buyer and seller in organisational markets, with a great degree of customisation and co-operation on product specification and other requirements. Often organisational buyers are geographically concentrated.

The specific characteristics of organisational markets may vary according to the type of organisation that comprises the market.

(a) Producer markets comprise those organisations that purchase products for the purpose of making a profit by using them to produce other products or by using them in their own operations. This may include buyers of raw materials and of semi-finished and finished items used to produce other products.

(b) Reseller markets consist of intermediaries such as retailers and wholesalers who buy the finished goods in order to resell them to make a profit. Other than minor alterations, resellers do not change the physical characteristics of the products they handle.

(c) Government markets comprise those national and local governments who buy a variety of goods and services to support their internal operations and to provide the public services that are within their remit, normally making their purchases through bids or negotiated contracts.

(d) Institutional markets comprise those organisations that seek to achieve charitable, educational, community or other non-business goals.

The stages in the process of B2B buying behaviour are:

Step 1 Recognise the problem

Step 2 Develop product specifications to solve the problem

Step 3 Search for products and suppliers

Step 4 Evaluate products relative to specifications

Step 5 Select and order the most appropriate product

Step 6 Evaluate the product and supplier performance

This process is, in outline terms, similar to that for consumer buying behaviour. It begins with the recognition that a problem exists, the stimulus for which may come either from within or outside the company. The second stage of the process requires the people participating in the buying decision to assess the problem or need, and determine what will be required to resolve or satisfy it. Here, the DMU comes into operation (see the next section).

The third stage of the process is similar to that of information search, utilising trade shows, trade publications, supplier catalogues, and soliciting proposals from known suppliers. This should result in a list of alternative products, which are then evaluated to ascertain whether they meet the product specifications. Suppliers may also be evaluated according to criteria such as price, service and ability to deliver.

2 The decision-making unit

2.1 What is the decision-making unit?

Key term

The **decision-making unit (DMU)** is a group of people who participate in or influence the purchase decision at any stage in the buying process. It comprises all stakeholders in a decision. This may involve a number of roles: gatekeeper, initiator, influencer, decider, financier, buyer and user.

Although only the buyer may appear to be the 'customer' at the point of sale, the entire decision-making unit can be identified as the target market for the marketer.

The marketing organisation needs to understand the complexity of the DMU in each market (and market segment) in which it operates. It is clearly relevant to marketers whether, for example, the woman or man in a household is the buyer / decision maker; whether a young or older person is the user; which gender or age group consumes which promotional media. This kind of information determines the product's positioning (masculine / feminine? youthful / mature?), media choices and target audience for marketing communications. It will also direct the product specifications.

With marketing communications in mind, the communication mix should leverage influence on the purchase decision: reaching and persuading the most influential role in a given purchase, using the least expenditure of effort and cost. The decider may be an obvious target, but for price sensitive decisions, for example, it may be important to target the financer (if a separate individual); if deciders are difficult to reach, it may be important to target gatekeepers; and for shared or complex decisions, it may be more cost effective to target influencers (co-opting them to share the work of promotion).

(a) Identify gatekeepers (who is most likely to be open to, or in charge of acquiring, new product information?) and the most effective information media to reach them (where do they prefer to gather product information and in what format?)

(b) Identify indicators / initiators (who is most likely to notice and draw attention to product information?) and target them with messages that arouse interest (how is the product relevant to needs, wants or interests of the DMU?)

(c) Identify influencers (whom will the decider consult or listen to?) and target them with persuasive information to arouse or reinforce desire (how does the product solve a problem, meet a need? How can it be endorsed or validated?)

(d) Identify deciders (who will have the final say?) and target them with information to arouse or reinforce intention (what are the decisive benefits of the product for meeting needs and wants? How can the perceived risks of decision be lowered – and the benefits of acting quickly be conveyed?)

(e) Identify buyers (who actually makes the purchase?) and target them with messages which facilitate action (what does the buyer need to do next? How can it be made easy?)

(f) Identify financers (who pays or authorises payment?) and target them with information to help them to justify expenditure (what benefits can be weighed against the costs?) and to complete the transaction (how can payment be made easy?)

(g) Identify users (who uses, consumes or benefits?) and target them with practical information to enable them to use the product safely and satisfyingly (what are possible areas of ignorance or difficulty? What on-going support may be required?)

The marketing organisation will also seek appropriate forms of feedback to fine-tune its marketing mix in satisfying the needs of each of the DMU roles: is product packaging effectively attracting the attention of initiators? Are promotional messages effectively persuading influencers and deciders? Is customer service effectively satisfying users? Are models effectively meeting needs and wants?

2.2 Consumer decision-making unit

The people who make up a DMU will vary according to the context in which the purchase decision is being made, and the stakeholders who will be affected by and involved in the decision. Consumers belong to a number of different groups and networks.

(a) The family is a primary group for most individuals: family norms and influences are particularly strong. Socio-cultural factors influence customary decision-making roles within the family structure: be aware that such norms vary from culture to culture. In a traditional Western or Latin family model, marketing messages may be targeted at the child (initiator / influencer) in the purchase of a toy; at the wife / mother (decider / buyer) in the case of household items; or at the husband / father (decider / buyer) in the case of the family car. Be aware, however, that gender roles and household structures are becoming more diverse.

(b) The work group can be an important influence, especially if colleagues are also part of the individual's social network. The individual's need to project status, professionalism and image at work also influence decisions: cars, clothes, office furniture and other products are often positioned accordingly.

(c) Friendship groups are an important influence on buyer behaviour: the desire to form and maintain social relationships is a basic human need. People often trust friends to advise them: marketers frequently depict product choice, in advertising, in the context of friendly sharing, advice and encouragement – and attempt to capitalise on positive word-of-mouth promotion.

(d) Interest groups (action groups, pressure groups, consumer groups and so on) may influence purchase behaviour. Membership of (or advocacy by) groups may lead to supporting or boycotting brands that do or do not conform to the group's values. Marketing messages may be targeted defensively or positively to address environmental, human rights or consumer concerns.

ACTIVITY 4.1

Think about a recent major purchase that you made.

Describe the various stages of the decision making process, explaining the role of the individuals in the decision making unit.

Exam tip

You do not need to understand the psychological factors that affect buyer behaviour in detail for your examination.

2.3 B2B decision-making unit

The DMU of a buying organisation is called its buying centre. This is not to be confused with a purchasing function or team: it is a set of buying roles exercised by different individuals and units that participate in the business decision-making process. As Kotler (1996) notes, 'the buying centre concept presents a major marketing challenge. The business marketer must learn who participates in the decision, each participant's relative influence and what evaluation criteria each decision participant uses'.

In B2B marketing, it may be relevant for an organisation to communicate not only with the purchaser but also with others who could be involved in the decision to purchase. The people involved in the purchase decision tend to have quite formal and closely defined roles; these individuals who make and influence buying decisions in a B2B environment are known as the decision-making unit, the DMU (Figure 4.2).

For example, a firm that supplies photocopiers to small businesses needs to communicate with a variety of people, including the admin assistant who will use the machine, the office manager who has encountered other machines working in other organisations, and the finance director who will be interested in how much it will cost. These are not direct customers, but may influence the decision to buy and therefore need to be communicated with.

Figure 4.2 The DMU

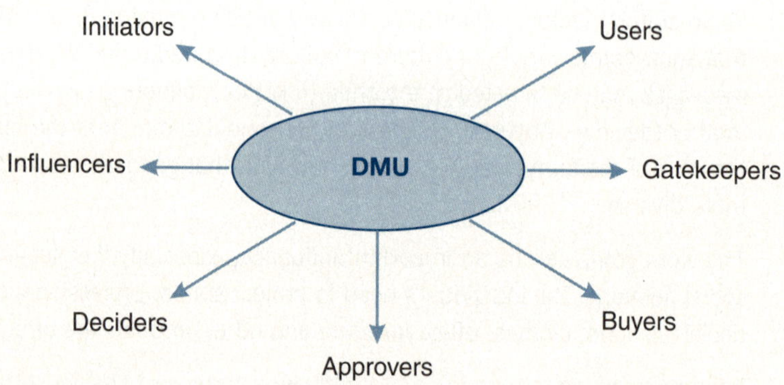

Various roles have been identified:

- In the case of a substantial organisation, the initiators might be senior management needing technology to reduce costs.
- Influencers would include technical staff such as maintenance technicians.
- Deciders in this case might well be a small committee that advise the board on the purchase decision.
- Approvers would include senior financial staff (eg financial aspects of contracts including penalty clauses for late delivery).
- The buyers in this case will be strongly influenced by the control of the deciders, with little flexibility to switch vendors or change the contract.
- Gatekeepers would include such functions as safety (compliance of equipment with local and company safety policy, eg VDU use).
- The users are the operators and the like.

The reason for this DMU analysis is that not all the DMU participants will meet sales staff and so the literature and the rest of the integrated communications must carry the company message to them. The members of the DMU are key stakeholders with whom the selling organisation needs to build strong links / relationships.

3 Using the marketing mix to influence decision-making units in different organisations

3.1 Using the marketing mix

Concentrating on any single element of the mix is pointless. The advertising campaign is not going to be effective if the product does not work, is not in the shops or costs more than people are prepared to pay for it. Moreover, the elements of the mix must be in harmony and consistent as they interact. When considering the appropriate communications mix, the marketer needs to ensure that all the other elements of the marketing mix can communicate.

The brand imagery communicated in the advertisements needs to be carried over onto the packaging, an element of product. For luxury and exclusive products, a low price would not sustain the exclusivity proposition. In the same way, if the product were available in every cut-price outlet, it would be difficult to sustain the luxury image.

In developing the detailed plans for one element such as product, it is necessary to consider issues such as point-of-sale ideas. For example, some soft drinks are sold from racks that grip a collar around the neck of the bottle; integrated design was needed for both the product and the point-of-sale promotional stand.

3.2 The marketing mix in different types of organisation

Hopefully, the business contexts within which marketing principles can be usefully applied are apparent. A few of these contexts are discussed here to give a flavour of the particular considerations including buying decisions and consumer behaviour. These contexts are:

- Fast-moving consumer goods
- Business-to-business
- Services
- Voluntary and not-for-profit (NFP) organisations
- Online businesses

3.2.1 Fast moving consumer goods organisations

Consumer goods can take two forms:

- Fast moving consumer goods are goods such as packaged food, beverages, toiletries, and tobacco.
- Consumer durables are items such as home appliances and cars.

The decision to purchase high-cost durable goods such as televisions, computers, cars and furniture and the frequency of repurchase will be influenced by changing technical features, fashions and wearing-out of the old product.

FMCGs are by comparison purchased for personal reasons and generally involve relatively low financial outlays. For FMCGs like canned foods, soft drinks and confectionery there may be habitual purchasing but products tend to have short life cycles. It follows therefore that the marketing mix will differ considerably between both types of consumer good. Understanding consumers involves appreciating the factors that affect buying decisions as well as types of buying behaviour.

Classical marketing theory was designed with consumer marketing in mind as we have discussed within this Text so far.

3.2.2 Business-to-business organisations

Business-to-business marketing (often abbreviated as B2B) is concerned with industrial goods and services, which are bought by manufacturers, distributors and other private and publicly owned institutions, such as schools and hospitals, to be used as part of their own activities.

Of course, many of the products involved in business-to-business markets are the same as those bought within the ordinary consumer markets, for example, company cars, computers, mobile phones and so on. As we'll see in a moment, however, organisational buying behaviour may be quite different from that of an ordinary consumer.

B2B market categories can be classified as follows.

(a) Capital goods include such items as buildings, machinery and motor vehicles.

(b) Components and materials include raw, partly and wholly processed materials or goods which are incorporated into the products sold by the company.

(c) Supplies are goods which assist production and distribution. This would include small but important items such as machine oil, computer disks and stationery, and cleaning products.

(d) Business services are services used by businesses, for instance employer's liability insurance.

When bought in a business-to-business context, products are distinct from consumer goods in several ways.

(a) **Conformity with standards.** Industrial products are often bound by legal or quality standards, and as a consequence, products within a particular group are often similar. Differentiation, which is such a key dimension of consumer goods, is more difficult here. At the same time, buyers lay down their own specifications, to which manufacturers must adhere.

(b) **Technical sophistication.** Many products in this area require levels of complexity and sophistication which are unheard of in consumer products. Often the industry standard gradually influences the consumer equivalent as, for instance, in the case of power tools in the DIY market. After-sales and maintenance contracts have become essential in certain areas.

(c) **High order values.** As a consequence of (a) and (b) many business goods, particularly capital equipment, are very often extremely costly items. Even in the case of supplies, where the single unit value of components and materials may be comparatively low, the quantity required frequently means that orders have a very high value.

(d) **Irregularity of purchase.** Machinery used to produce consumer goods is not bought regularly. Materials used to produce the goods certainly are, but components and materials are often bought on a contract or preferred supplier basis, so that the opportunity to get new business may not arise very often.

Although organisations are supposed to be rational in making decisions about which products to buy and which suppliers to use, there are a number of other factors they consider in making their purchase decisions; illustrated in Table 4.1.

Table 4.1 B2B buying criteria (economic factors in making purchasing decisions)

Economic factors	
Reasonable prices	The right price will not necessarily be the lowest, but must represent good value for money for the product or service.
Product specification	The product must meet or closely match the purchaser's specified needs.
Consistent quality	B2B buyers require supplier with adequate quality controls in order to minimise defects and enable them to use the product with confidence.
Reliability and continuity of supply	Buyers need to be sure that adequate supplies of the product will be available as and when required.
Customer service	Buyers need to be sure that the supplier is able to take responsibility for its product by providing fast and flexible support and assistance in case of problems.

Non–economic factors	
Career security	In making purchasing decisions, B2B buyers sometimes consider the implications in terms of risk and how favourably the selected option is viewed by top management.
Friendship and social needs	The level of trust, confidence and respect developed on a personal level between individuals in the buying and selling organisation can also influence the purchase decision.
Prestige	In making purchasing decisions about some products (like company cars), buyers might be interested in impressing their colleagues or their competitors.

Marketers must demonstrate an understanding of these factors in applying the marketing mix to the B2B market.

3.3 Service organisations

Services are distinguished from products mainly because they are generally produced at the same time as they are consumed, and cannot be stored or taken away. An enhanced marketing mix needs to be deployed.

Characteristics of services which make them distinctive from goods from a marketing perspective have been proposed. There are five major differences.

- **Intangibility:** Intangibility refers to the lack of physical substance which is involved with service delivery. Unlike a product, there is nothing to touch, feel or smell. Clearly, this creates difficulties and can inhibit the propensity to consume a service, since customers are not sure what they have.
- **Inseparability:** A service often cannot be separated from the provider of the service. The performance of a service often occurs at the same instant as its consumption. Think of having dental treatment or going on a journey. Neither exists until actually consumed by the purchaser.
- **Heterogeneity / variability:** Many services face a problem of maintaining consistency in the standard of output. Variability of quality in delivery is inevitable, because of the number of factors which may influence it. This may create problems of operations management.
- **Perishability:** Services cannot be stored. They are innately perishable. Performances at a theatre or the services of a chiropodist consist in their availability for periods of time, and if they are not occupied, the service they offer cannot be used later. This presents specific marketing problems. Meeting customer needs in these operations depends on staff being available when they are needed. This must be balanced against the need to minimise unnecessary expenditure on staff wages. Policies must seek to match demand with supply by price variations and promotions to stimulate off-peak demand.
- **Ownership:** Services do not result in the transfer of property. In the case of purchasing a product, there is permanent transfer of title and control over the use of an item. An item of service provision is often defined by the length of time it is available. This may very well lessen the perceived customer value of a service, and consequently make for unfavourable comparisons with tangible alternatives.

ACTIVITY 4.2

Think about a service that you use and consider how each of the elements below can be described.

- Intangibility
- Inseparability
- Heterogeneity/variability
- Perishability
- Ownership

Lovelock (1996) outlined eight generic differences between physical products and services:

1. The nature of the product
2. Customers' involvement in the production process
3. People as part of the product
4. Greater problems in maintaining quality
5. Harder for customers to evaluate
6. Absence of inventories
7. Relative importance of time factor
8. Structure and nature of distribution channels.

The main implication of the differences between the nature of products and services is that marketers must look beyond the traditional marketing mix (4 Ps) in trying to create effective service propositions that will meet the needs and expectation of customers. People, physical evidence and process are additional elements of the marketing mix that have become necessary to reflect the special characteristics of services marketing. The ways that marketers in service organisations use these additional elements to meet the needs of customers were discussed in the previous chapter.

THE REAL WORLD

BSkyB

BSkyB identified a new market for its services in the 13 million UK households that do not currently subscribe for any pay TV service. By developing its own package of film, entertainment and sport for a variety of platforms and deliver them without charging the contract prices associated with its more traditional model, BSkyB is also able to challenge the market share of companies like LoveFilm and Netflix.

3.4 Voluntary and not-for-profit organisations

3.4.1 What is a not-for-profit organisation?

Key term

A **not-for-profit organisation** can be defined as: '...an organisation whose attainment of its prime goal is not assessed by economic measures. However, in pursuit of that goal it may undertake profit-making activities.'

Not-for-profit refers to organisations such as private education establishments and charities that do not have profit maximising objectives. This may involve a number of different kinds of organisation with, for example, differing legal status – charities, statutory bodies offering public transport or the provision of services such as leisure, schools, health or public utilities such as water or road maintenance. Charity marketing is akin to service marketing and the extended service marketing mix is appropriate. The guiding philosophy of the charity says what it is for and how it goes about its business. Clearly, just as the components of the normal marketing mix must be in harmony with one another, so too must they be in harmony with the charity's philosophy.

ACTIVITY 4.3

What are the unique characteristics of charities and other not-for-profit organisations?

It is beyond the scope of this material to discuss the marketing implications of each type of NFP in turn but it is worthwhile perhaps highlighting the particular features associated with NFP organisations, namely:

- NFPs have multiple publics; the customers or clients who receive the product or service and the funders who provide the income to allow the organisation to do its work.
- NFPs are subject to tighter legislative requirements due to higher levels of public interest in the efficiency of their activities.
- Most NFPs deliver services rather physical products.
- Customers may be a different grouping from those paying for the service.

THE REAL WORLD

'GREAT Britain"

The UK Government has recently invested £125 million in a global advertising campaign designed to raise the status of Great Britain as one of the great tourist destinations in the world. This will then be followed up by a £100 million tactical campaign which is hoped to result in a significant increase in visitor numbers over the next four years.

The justification for the campaign is the anticipated £2.3 billion spent by tourists while in the UK, translating into the creation of 60,000 jobs. The timing is designed to build on the extra attention created by the Olympic Games and the Queen's Diamond Jubilee. The Government is working with a number of key partners such as VisitBritain to create a compelling vision of Great Britain based on its culture, history and natural beauty.

(*Marketing Week*, 2012)

3.4.2 Product

A charity's products include ideas as well as goods and services. Ideas are very important in fund-raising, pressure-group activity and communicating with the public.

(a) When a supporter provides money to a charity, the idea of what the money will be used for is a kind of product, providing satisfaction to the supporter. Often supporters give their time and skills to assist as volunteers and thereby offering a service.

(b) Pressure groups work in part by promoting new ideas into the public consciousness, so that bodies with power can be persuaded to take a desired course of action.

(c) Ideas can also be promoted to the public with the aim of changing their behaviour. Governments often take this approach, as, for instance, with energy conservation and road safety campaigns.

3.4.3 Price

Price is very important to larger charities since sales of goods and services provide their largest single source of income. Proper cost accounting techniques must be applied where appropriate. Since supporters are crucial to a charity's income, and beneficiaries are the reason why it exists, processes must be as customer-friendly as possible. This is certainly an area where philosophy is important.

3.4.4 Place

It is common for charities to have significant problems with the distribution of physical goods when they rely on volunteer labour. This is especially true of charities that operate internationally, unless they are very well established. In particular, the type of charity fund that is set up to relieve a disaster overseas is likely to have great difficulty moving the necessary supplies to where they are needed. On the other hand, charities that merely disburse funds within one country, for instance to the poor or to pay for medical research, may have very short and easily managed distribution chains.

3.4.5 Promotion

The major principles of marketing communications for non-profit organisations are the same as for consumer and business-to-business marketing. There are, however, considerable differences of emphasis. Promotion is often dominated by personal selling, with street corner and door-to-door collections or awareness campaigns. The sum of money available for organised communication may be less. Public scrutiny of policies may be higher. Almost certainly there will be a different set of communication objectives.

- Making target customers aware of a product, service or social behaviour
- Educating consumers about the offer or changes in the offer
- Changing beliefs about negative and positive consequences of taking a particular action
- Changing the relative importance of particular consequences
- Enlisting the support of a variety of individuals
- Recruiting, motivating or rewarding employees or volunteers
- Changing perceptions about the sponsoring organisation
- Influencing government bodies
- Preventing the discontinuity of support
- Proving benefits over 'competitors'
- Combating injurious rumours
- Influencing funding agencies

3.5 Online business organisations

3.5.1 What is internet marketing?

Key term

Internet marketing is the application of the internet in the selling and distribution of products and services, and a tool to disseminate information and communicate with the marketplace.

Online business has provided an opportunity for businesses to reach customers in a more streamlined way and has enabled smaller organisations and small business start-ups to compete effectively with larger players in many markets. The scope and potential of the internet are still developing. Its uses within business already embrace the following:

(a) Dissemination of information

(b) Product / service development – through almost instantaneous test marketing

(c) Transaction processing

(d) Relationship enhancement – between various groups of stakeholders, but principally between consumers and product / service suppliers

(e) Recruitment and job search – involving organisations worldwide

(f) Entertainment – including music, humour, games and some less wholesome pursuits!

(g) Social networking – business and social networks, increasing the ability to review and rate organisations and utilise word of mouth promotion on a larger scale.

3.5.2 Marketing mix for internet businesses

The development of the internet provides many new opportunities for the marketer to vary the marketing mix in order to achieve the organisation's marketing objectives. E-commerce also has major implications for the relative importance of different elements of the marketing mix for many markets regardless of whether an organisation is directly involved in it.

The product

The internet provides several opportunities for varying both the core and extended product when a company is developing its online strategy. Some companies are able to offer new digital products containing information that can be delivered over the web. Ghosh (1998) identified a number of questions that companies should ask in developing new products or adding 'digital value' for customers:

1. Can I offer additional information or transaction services to my existing customer base?
2. Can I address the needs of new customer segments by repackaging my current information assets or by creating new business propositions using the internet?
3. Can I use my ability to attract customers to generate new sources of revenue such as advertising or sales of complementary products?
4. Will my current business be significantly harmed by other companies providing some of the value I currently offer?

In some industries (eg directories), an online version of the product is more valuable to customers because it can be updated more regularly. The internet has also created options for mass customisation of products. Mass customisation or personalisation allows customers to take a more active role in the design of the product and obtain products that are much more tailored to their individual needs.

Price

The internet has had dramatic implications for pricing in many industries. First, it has led to increased price transparency and created challenges in the use of differential pricing. The increased availability of pricing information has increased customer knowledge about prices. It is also more difficult for companies to charge different prices to customers in different countries. The recent proliferation of price comparison websites has also added to this pressure and has led to the commoditisation of many products and services.

Second, price transparency has led to a general downward pressure on price for many products and services. Online companies have always been able to offer lower prices than their offline rivals because they do not have a physical presence and the high overheads associated with operating stores and a distribution network. Many online start-ups have also been known to offer significant discounts in order to achieve their growth objectives.

Third, the development of the internet has led to the use of several pricing mechanisms. These include:

- **Forward auction:** product purchased by the highest bid made in the bidding period
- **Reverse auction:** product purchased from lowest-bidding supplier in bidding period
- **Aggregated buying:** a group of buyers purchase a number of items at the same price and receive a volume discount.
- **Dynamic pricing:** prices are updated in real time according to the type of customer or current market conditions.

Place

The place element of the marketing mix involves getting the products to customers in line with demand and minimising costs of inventory, transport and storage. The development of the internet as a marketing tool has the greatest implication for place due to its global reach. With the internet, a firm's ability to reach customers is no longer limited by the location of its outlets or the regions covered by its salesforce. The growth of Amazon and lastminute.com as online businesses show just how the power of the internet can have an impact on conventional distribution channels.

Brassington & Pettitt (2006) outlined several advantages of online distribution:

- The viewer is actively searching for products and services, and every site visited could gain a potential customer if interest can be maintained.
- Print and postage costs are eliminated because no catalogue has to be produced and distributed each season.
- Order processing and handling costs are reduced with online ordering as everything is done electronically by the customer without need for physical assistance.
- Improved cost efficient and effective customer service, with IT systems that deliver real-time information flows between the customer, customer support, distribution and the supply chain.
- Better after-sales service can be provided online.
- Digital products (like music, video and magazines) are capable of being distributed via the internet, without the need to send a parcel through the post.
- Manufacturers can get closer to the customer and potentially reduce costs by cutting one or more intermediaries out of the distribution channel.

Promotion

The internet represents an additional marketing communications channel to inform customers of the benefits of a product and assist in the buying decision. During the past few years, online promotion has become more important and gained an increasing share of the marketer's budgets and efforts. From a text message that changes behaviour immediately, key words that attract more enquiries and banner adverts that change attitudes to viral marketing that makes people talk about a new product, online channels have been doing things that offline communications cannot.

Chaffey & Smith (2008) outlined a number of ways that the ten communication tools can be used to communicate or promote in the online or offline world.

1. Advertising: interactive display ads and pay per click search advertising
2. Selling: virtual sales staff and chat and affiliate marketing
3. Sales promotion: incentives, rewards and online loyalty schemes
4. PR: online editorial, e-zines, newsletters, social networks, links and virals
5. Sponsorship: sponsoring an online event, site or service
6. Direct mail: opt-in email using e-newsletters and e-blasts plus web response
7. Exhibitions: virtual exhibitions and whitepaper distribution
8. Merchandising: promotional ad serving on retail sites, personalised recommendations and e-alerts
9. Packaging: virtual tours, real packaging is displayed online
10. Word-of-mouth: Viral, affiliate marketing, e-mail a friend, links.

According to Chaffey & Smith (2008), there are six key online promotional challenges that marketers need to respond to:

1. **Mix:** marketers need to decide on the optimum mix for the different promotional tools to ensure that they are using the most cost effective techniques for acquiring target customers.
2. **Integration:** both online and offline communications must be integrated to support the overall positioning and online value proposition which the e-marketing strategy defines.
3. **Creativity:** marketers should exploit the vast untapped creative opportunities presented by the internet.
4. **Interaction:** this enhances the experience, deepens the communications impact and allows the company to collect customer data.
5. **Globalisation:** an organisation's website opens the window to a global audience.

6 **Resourcing:** marketers need resources to service online and offline customer enquiries.

THE REAL WORLD

Auto Trader launches first digital campaign

Auto Trader, the leading UK second-hand car magazine and website is to launch its first exclusively digital campaign. According to Nick Batten (*Marketing*, 7 June 2012), the campaign will tap into the close connection that owners have with their cars by featuring a collection of short films that portray some of the car stories that the company has helped people with during the past 35 years.

The adverts will be used to drive viewers to a campaign page on its website, where they will have opportunities to win memorable driving experiences.

(*Marketing*, 2012)

People

The people element of the extended marketing mix refers to how an organisation's personnel interacts with customers and other stakeholder in the process of delivering the service. Chaffey & Smith (2008) suggest that firms should consider the following tactics by which people can be replaced or automated:

1 **Auto responders:** these automatically generate a response when an email or submitted form is received.

2 **Email notification:** automatically generated by the company's system to update customers on the status of their order.

3 **Callback facility:** customers fill in their phone number on a form and specify a convenient time to be contacted.

4 **Frequently asked questions (FAQ):** compiling and categorising questions so that customers can easily find the question and a helpful answer.

5 **On-site search engines:** these help customers find what they are looking for quickly and are popular when available.

6 **Virtual assistants:** they come in varying degrees of sophistication and usually help to guide the customer through a maze of choices.

7 **Real-time live chat:** a customer support operator in a call centre can type responses to a site visitor's questions.

8 **Co-browsing:** the customer's screen can be viewed by the call centre operator in combination with callback or chat.

9 **Customer reviewers and assistants:** online social media enable organisations to recruit customers to help shape their service for other customers through reviews and comments.

Physical evidence

When buying intangible services, customers look for physical evidence such as buildings, uniforms and logos to reassure them. In the online world the evidence is digital. Thus, a typographical error or poor layout on a website will send the same worrying message as a dirty restaurant in a five-star hotel.

To create a reassuring sense of order websites should be designed in an uncluttered style with a consistent look and feel that customers feel comfortable with. Chaffey and Smith (2008) outlined a number of other important aspects of on-site reassurance, especially for retailers:

- Guarantees
- Refund policies

- Privacy policies
- Security icons
- Trade body memberships
- Awards
- Customer lists
- Customer endorsements
- Independent reviews
- News clippings

Process

The activities, transactions and communications involved in obtaining a product or service online represent a good opportunity to develop customer loyalty through deep and engaging customer services processes. Excellent processes are an important aspect of successful internet marketing. As online services and production processes are not as visible to customers, the aspects of the process that are on view through the website (like form filling, shopping baskets and follow-up emails) represent the basis on which customers will judge the service.

Chaffey & Smith (2008) outlined some events that need to happen and must be backed up by an efficient, seamless process:

- Customer wants to check availability – does the site show number in stock and when next available if out of stock?
- Product specification or price is changed – is the change seamlessly reflected in website, price lists and catalogues?
- Customer places order – is the customer notified by email that their order has been processed?
- Customer makes email enquiry – can the system cope when a wave of telephone calls and emails hit and respond promptly and accurately?
- Product dispatched – is the customer notified of this event by e-mail? Can they track their order if required?

Website optimisation involves minimising the number of people involved with responding to each event and providing them with the information required to serve the customer effectively. Proper integration of the front end and back end systems into a well managed system allow the organisation to reduce costs and stock levels.

CHAPTER ROUNDUP

- Buyer Behaviour is the decision processes and actions of people involved in buying and using products and services.
- Customers do not buy products, they buy benefits.
- The consumer buying decision-making process consists of five stages: Need recognition, information search, evaluation of alternatives, purchase decision and post-purchase evaluation.
- A number of differences between organisational and consumer markets exist which mean that a modified approach needs to be taken when considering the process of buying behaviour.
- The decision making unit (DMU) is a group of people who participate in or influence the purchase decision at any stage in the buying process.
- FMCGs are by comparison purchased for personal reasons and generally involve relatively low financial outlays.
- Business-to-business marketing (often abbreviated as B2B) is concerned with industrial goods and services, which are bought by manufacturers, distributors and other private and publicly owned institutions, such as schools and hospitals, to be used as part of their own activities.
- Services are distinguished from products mainly because they are generally produced at the same time as they are consumed, and cannot be stored or taken away.
- Not-for-profit refers to organisations such as private education establishments and charities that do not have profit maximising objectives.
- Online business has provided an opportunity for businesses to reach customers in a more streamlined way and has enabled smaller organisations and small business start-ups to compete effectively with larger players in many markets.

FURTHER READING

Chapters 3 and 11 of:

Blythe, J. (2008) Essentials of Marketing. 4th edition. Harlow, Prentice Hall.

Chapters 3, 13 and 14 of:

Brassington, F. and Pettitt, S. (2007) Essentials of Marketing. 2nd edition. Harlow, Prentice Hall.

Complete text:

Chaffey, D. and Smith, P. (2008) *EMarketing Excellence.* 3rd edition. Oxford, Butterworth Heinemann.

REFERENCES

Baker, R. (2012) Thomas Cook to use marketing to differentiate brand portfolio. *Marketing Week*, www.marketingweek.co.uk [accessed 12 June 2012].

Batten, N. (2012) Auto Trader gets personal to shift consumer perceptions. *Marketing*, www.marketingmagazine.co.uk/News/MostRead/1135276/Auto-Trader-gets-personal-shift-consumer-perceptions/ [accessed 11 June 2012].

Blythe, J. (2008) *Essentials of Marketing*. 4th edition. Harlow, Prentice Hall.

Brassington, F. and Pettitt, S. (2006). *Principles of Marketing*. 4th edition, Harlow, Prentice Hall.

Chaffey, D *et al* (2003). *Internet Marketing: Strategy, Implementation & Practice*. 2nd edition. Harlow, Pearson Education.

Chaffey, D. and Smith, P. (2008). *EMarketing Excellence*. 3rd edition. Oxford, Butterworth Heinemann.

Dibb, S., Simkin, L., and Vancini, A. (1996) 'Competition, strategy, technology and people: the challenges facing PR'. *International Journal of Advertising*, vol. 15, no. 2, pp125–136.

Harris, D. and Botten, N. (2008). *CIM Coursebook: Introduction to Marketing.* Oxford, Butterworth Heinemann.

Kotler, P. and Keller, K. (2006). *Marketing Management*. 12th edition. New Jersey, Pearson.

Lovelock, C.H. (1996) *Services Marketing*. 3rd edition. Upper Saddle River, NJ, Prentice-Hall.

O'Reilly, L. (2012) Sky takes on LoveFilm and YouView with internet TV package. *Marketing Week*, www.marketingweek.co.uk [accessed 12 June 2012].

Parsons, R. (2012) Government starts £125m 'GREAT' Britain campaign. *Marketing Week*, www.marketingweek.co.uk [accessed 12 June 2012].

QUICK QUIZ

1. Define buyer behaviour.
2. Outline the different stages in the consumer buying-decision making process.
3. What are the different types of organisations that make up the B2B market?
4. Identify the different roles in a typical B2B decision making unit.
5. Outline the ways in which B2B products differ from consumer goods.
6. What are the characteristics of services that makes them distinctive from goods?
7. What features of not-for-profit organisations make them different from other businesses?
8. Define internet marketing.
9. Identify some of the tactics that are used to replace or automate people in online businesses.
10. What factors do B2B buyers use to decide which products or services to purchase?

ACTIVITY DEBRIEFS

Activity 4.1

Much of your response will depend on the category of product you purchased.

	Buying a car
Need recognition	Car has failed an MOT test
Information search	Visit local garages View car section of local newspapers Buy and read Auto trader, Browse on Ebay
Evaluation of alternatives	Circle all relevant cars – make a shortlist to view and then go and look at the cars for sale Test drive the cars Decide between new, used or repair of existing car
Purchase decision	Confirm criteria for selection, choose between reduced shortlist
Post purchase evaluation	Thoughts about the car following the purchase, reliability, satisfaction with the drive, comments from friends

Activity 4.2

Your answer will depend on the type of service you have chosen.

Activity 4.3

They serve multiple publics (donors, clients, general public, government, etc).

They provide services rather than physical goods.

They are subject to public scrutiny and have to be transparent.

They have multiple objectives.

The recipients of the services are usually different from those that provide funding for their activities.

QUICK QUIZ ANSWERS

1. Buyer behaviour is the decision processes and actions involved in buying and using products and services.
2. Need recognition, information search, evaluation of alternatives, purchase decision and post-purchase evaluation.
3. Producers, resellers, governments and institutions.
4. Initiators, influencers, deciders, approvers, buyers, gatekeepers and users.
5. Conformity with standards, technical sophistication, high order values and irregularity of purchase.
6. Intangibility, inseparability, heterogeneity / variability, perishability and lack of ownership.
7. NFPs have multiple publics, are subject to tighter legislative requirements, deliver services rather than physical products and their customers may be a different grouping from those paying for the service.
8. Internet marketing is the application of the internet in the selling and distribution of products and services; and as a tool to disseminate information and communicate with the marketplace.
9. Auto responders, email notification, callback facility, frequently asked questions, on-site search engines, virtual assistants, real-time live chat, co-browsing and customer reviewers and assistants.
10. Reasonable prices, product specification, consistent quality, reliability and continuity of supply, customer service, career security, friendship and social needs and prestige.

Section 2:

Unit 2: Understanding Customer Relationships

CHAPTER 5

Understanding customers

Introduction

This chapter examines the importance of understanding customers, and how marketing information aids the better development of marketing activities to achieve customer satisfaction. The first section explores the need for organisations to understand the needs and wants of customers and users.

The second section discusses the importance of collecting information from a number of sources in order to gain a better understanding of customer needs.

The third section examines how the information collected from a range of sources can be stored in order to create and maintain a customer database.

The final section explores the value of customer information in developing appropriate and effective marketing mix activities to meet customer needs.

Topic list

Syllabus reference

1.1	Discuss the need for organisations to understand: ▪ The difference between the customer and user ▪ Differing needs and wants of the customer base ▪ Benefits of a marketing orientated approach
1.2	Recognise the importance of collecting information to gain a better understanding of customer needs from: ▪ Internal and external sources ▪ Secondary data sources ▪ Primary data from research ▪ Understanding some of the limitations of data collected
1.3	Explain how information collected from a range of sources can be stored in order to create and maintain a customer database: ▪ Control access to the database to stored information across the organisation ▪ Aid understanding of the organisation's customer base.
1.4	Explain how customer information can help with: ▪ Identifying differing customer needs and wants ▪ Understanding why customers purchase ▪ Developing appropriate and effective marketing mix activities to meet those needs ▪ Identifying the factors that influence decision making.

1 Customers and needs

1.1 The difference between customer and user

In the traditional sense of the word, customers are the people who buy an organisation's products and services. To communicate with them effectively, an organisation needs to know who they are, what needs the products or services are required to meet, where they are located and the most cost-effective methods of communicating with them. By doing this, it will be easier to develop effective communications, such as advertising, sales literature, packaging and product instructions, that appeal to, and are understood by, the customer. However, there are some discreet differences between customers that will have an effect on how we can communicate with them effectively.

> **Key term**
>
> A **customer** is 'an individual or organisation who buys a product or service' (Doole *et al*, 2005)

Customer

These are individuals who have no connection with an organisation, other than that they may have purchased goods or services in the past, or are purchasing at present. They can be either the traditional customer / consumer who buys a multitude of goods and services for their own use or that of their family, this category is referred to as business-to-consumer market (or B2C) or the business consumer who is buying on behalf of their organisation, known as business-to-business (B2B).

> **Key terms**
>
> A **consumer / user** is 'the person who uses the product and service or may be affected by its purchases' (Doole *et al*, 2005)

The consumer / user

While the most obvious customer is the person who purchases the product or service, the consumer is the end-user – the person who actually uses the product or service and is sometimes different from the purchaser. Therefore, although the person who pays for the product may also be the user or the consumer of the product this is not always the case. For example, a manufacturer of toys needs to communicate with both the children who will use the product, so they will exert pressure on parents, and the parents themselves, as they will be the purchaser / decision-maker. The required message therefore has a dual purpose – first, to persuade the children how exciting the toy is and second, to inform the parents of its educational value.

When the purchase becomes more important and / or more expensive, such as a car, holiday or furniture, then again more people become involved in the purchase and certain members of the family become members of the DMU. Each member of the DMU will have a different perspective and often take on similar, but less formal, roles to those identified for B2B purchases.

Customers are important to the buying decision because they are the ones who make the purchase. The distinction between customers and consumers is important to marketers because even though consumers understand what they need from a product or service, it is the customer who usually makes the actual buying decision. When customers and consumers are different people, as is usually the case in B2B marketing, the buying process becomes much more complex. Customers usually define value, while consumers define what is needed form the product or service. In situations where the people who define value and the people who specify the product or service required are different, the can disagree about priorities. This is usually because they are trying to achieve different objectives and are probably under different budgetary constraints. Often, the customer is most interested in a value-for-money proposition, whereas the consumer / user may be more concerned with product features and / or benefits.

THE REAL WORLD

Confectioner Haribo understands the distinction between their customers and consumers. Adults predominantly buy their products (sweets) while both adults and children consume them. Haribo has successfully meet both sets of expectations to be profitable. Adults may seek a simple, inexpensive but attractive treat for children (or themselves) and be attracted by price, package size, natural ingredients and convenience. Children are drawn by the appealing shapes, taste, and the approval of the peers.

ACTIVITY 5.1

How might the needs of the customer and consumer differ in the following purchases?

- Pet food, bought by the pet's owner
- A child's bicycle, bought by a parent
- A laptop PC, bought for a manager by the IT department

1.2 Types of individual customers

According to Doole *et al* (2005), not all customers will behave in a similar fashion. Customers can be differentiated by the way they purchase products and services into four different types:

(a) **The economic / rational customer:** This customer makes purchase decisions based on economic rationale alone. This customer has been able to access a complete understanding of all the other alternatives and has fully evaluated them to be able to identify the best one.

(b) **The passive customer:** This customer is basically submissive and makes irrational purchase decisions. Passive customers are usually impulsive and easily swayed by marketing promotions.

(c) **The cognitive customer:** This customer focuses on the purchasing process by seeking information and evaluating that information in the light of perceived risks in order to arrive at a decision.

(d) **The emotional customer:** This customer views making purchases to satisfy emotional needs as entirely rational and puts a lot of emphasis on the search for information. Current mood and feeling are the key determinants of the purchase decision and emotive benefits of the alternatives are much more important than rational attributes.

1.3 The benefits of a marketing oriented approach

The main benefits of a marketing orientated approach are:

(a) By making customer needs a primary focus, companies are more likely to develop products and services that meet the needs of the customers. The likelihood of repeat purchases and brand loyalty is increased as customers experience a higher level of satisfaction.

(b) Marketing orientated companies have all functions properly aligned with the strategic vision of meeting the needs of customers. This helps define the role of employees more clearly.

(c) Firms that possess a good understanding of customer needs are in a position to market more effectively to them.

(d) Consistently understanding and delivering what customers wants leads to long-term profitability. Market-oriented companies can turn one-time buyers into repeat customers, with the ultimate goal of developing many loyal customers who are more willing to pay higher prices

2 Collecting information about customer needs

2.1 The importance of information

Putting the customer at the centre of the organisation's activities and responding effectively to the changes in the external environment requires access to quality, pertinent and timely information to guide management decisions. Firms needs to acquire knowledge which comes from information collected from both within and outside the organisation. In recent years, information has become a marketing asset, which can significantly impact on the performance of the organisation. According to Doole *et al* (2005), the specific functions of information include:

- Information can be used to establish general trends in the environment
- Information can be used to scan the environment for opportunities and threats
- Information can enable the organisation to assess competitor activity
- Information can help the organisation to explore and examine consumer behaviour and help the organisation to design its approach to the customer
- Information can help the firm to gauge the extent to which its resources 'fit' with its ambitions.

Overall, marketers need information to help them to make decisions. These decisions should ultimately help the organisation to better meet the needs of customers by understanding

- Differing customer needs and wants
- Why customers purchase eg what makes them choose certain products over others
- The factors that influence customer decision-making

This information can then be used to develop an appropriate and effective marketing mix of activities to meet those needs.

Here is a list of questions that marketers might need answered.

(a) **Markets.** Who are our customers? What are they like? How are buying decisions made?

(b) **Share of the market.** What are total sales of our product? How do our sales compare with competitors' sales?

(c) **Products.** What do customers think of our product? What do they do with it? Are our products in a 'growth' or 'decline' stage of their life cycle? Should we extend our range?

(d) **Price.** How do our prices compare with others: higher, average, lower? Is the market sensitive to price?

(e) **Distribution.** Should we distribute directly, indirectly or both? What discounts are required?

(f) **Salesforce.** Do we have enough / too many salespeople? Are their territories equal to their potential? Are they contacting the right people? Should we pay commission?

(g) **Advertising.** Do we use the right media? Do we communicate the right message? Is it effective?

(h) **Customer attitudes.** What do they think of our product / firm / service / delivery?

(i) **Competitors' activities**. Who are our competitors? Are they more or less successful businesses? Why are they more or less successful?

(j) **Environmental factors.** What factors impact on marketing planning (PESTEL factors)?

2.2 Internal and external sources

Internal sources

For a company's value chain to operate normally, lots of information needs to be collected. These include the internal record keeping system (production, accounting, sales records, and so on), marketing research, salesforce field reports, customer enquiries, customer complaints, product returns, among others. All of this information must be recorded or collected, collated and managed appropriately and distributed in a timely fashion if they are to be used effectively to assist managers in making vital decisions about the organisation's marketing activities.

THE REAL WORLD

Halfords

Halfords have recently changed the way they collect information about standards of customer service in its chain of stores in order to widen its collection of data about levels of service in individual stores. Once users of secret shopper initiatives, the chain has opted instead for Empathica technology to gain feedback directly from real customers on thousands of transactions. This enables it to build incentives into store manager's contracts in order to improve the customer service around which its advertising is based: 'That's helpful, that's Halfords".

With the Empathica system customers are invited to fill in an online survey via a message at the top of the till receipt. The company is offering attractive prizes to incentivise customers to take part. Data collected on entry means the company can identify which managers and stores are performing well.

All Halfords outlets are now part of this process. In 2012 an evaluation of the scheme is being undertaken to see how this has benefitted the business and how it can take it forward.

(*Marketing Week*, 2011)

External sources

Information also comes from sources outside the organisation; including customers, suppliers, distributors, strategic alliance partners, independent third parties, commercial agencies, industry associations and the internet.

Marketing research activity can be divided into two types: primary research and secondary research.

Primary research is where you go out into the field to collect new data using appropriate research methods (eg a questionnaire).

Secondary research is where you actively research existing data, which is available from a rich variety of sources (eg government statistics).

The following diagram shows just some of the information which is available to marketers to assist in decision making. Generally it is grouped into formal primary marketing research projects, external secondary sources and internal secondary sources.

Figure 5.1 Sources of information for marketers

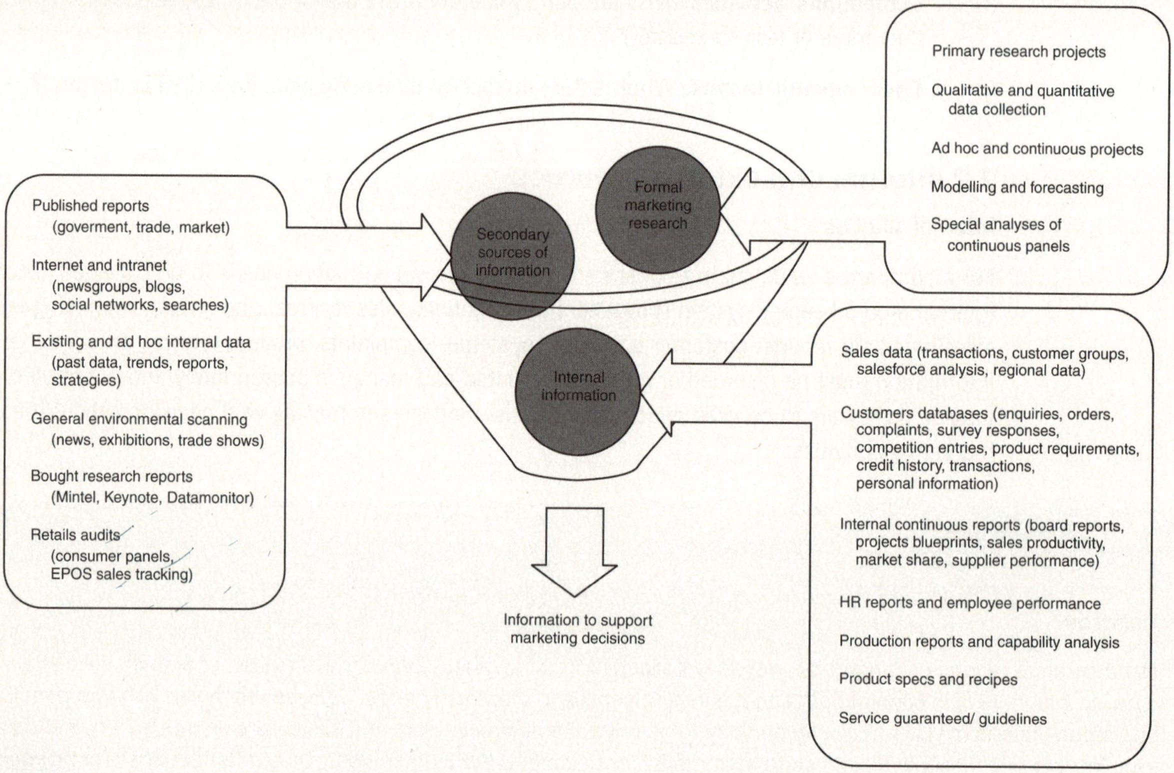

ACTIVITY 5.2

Outline the internal information sources that exist within your organisation.

2.3 Secondary data sources

> **Key term**
>
> **Secondary data** is information that has already been collected, originally for a specific purpose, but which is later used for a purpose other than that for which it was collected.

Secondary data is data that already exists in some form. Collection of secondary data is known as 'desk research'. Originally this was to distinguish it from research that involves getting out and about in the world, talking to people and watching them. In fact, a great deal of research can now be done from your desk in a literal sense, using your desktop computer and the Internet.

Secondary data is data (including internal data) not created specifically for the purpose at hand but used and analysed to provide marketing information where primary data is not (yet) available or not sufficient.

Desk research is the term used to describe a proactive search for existing data, usually as an initial, exploratory research task.

It may seem odd that we deal with 'secondary' data before we look at primary data, but it would not be sensible to embark on substantial amounts of primary research without seeing what secondary data already exists. Checking what is known already is also likely to give insights into how and what to investigate further.

Secondary information is now available in every form and on a huge scale. The problem is how to decide what information is required. The use of secondary data will generally come early in the process of marketing research. In some cases, secondary data may be sufficient in itself, but not always.

2.3.1 The uses of secondary data

It can provide a backdrop to primary research

In unfamiliar territory, it is natural that the marketer will carry out some basic research in the area, using journals, existing market reports, the press and any contacts with relevant knowledge. Such investigations will aid the marketer by providing guidance on a number of areas.

- Possible data sources
- Methods of data collection (relevant populations, sampling methods)
- The general state of the market (demand, competition and the like)

It can act as a substitute for primary research

The often substantial cost of primary research might be avoided if existing secondary data is sufficient. This data might not be perfect for the needs of the business though, and to judge whether it is enough, or whether primary research ought to be undertaken, a cost-benefit analysis should be implemented weighing up the advantages of each method.

There are some situations in which secondary data is bound to be insufficient. For instance, if your brand new version of an existing product is hugely superior to your competitors' versions because of your unique use of new technology, you have changed the entire market. Primary research will be necessary to find out the impact of your product.

It can be used as a technique in itself

Some types of information can only be acquired by examining secondary data, in particular trends over time. Historical data cannot realistically be replaced by a one-off study and an organisation's internal data would only give a limited picture.

2.4 Primary data from research

> **Key term**
>
> **Primary data** is information collected for a specific purpose and derived from a new and original source.

Primary data is information collected specifically to address a question posed by the marketer. It is used to bridge any identified gaps that might exist in a company's knowledge. Primary data may be qualitative (figures and statistics) or quantitative (attitudes and feelings) in nature.

A range of methods to collect primary data exist. The following table shows just a few as an example.

Table 5.1 Methods of collecting primary data

Qualitative data collection methods	Quantitative data collection methods
In-depth interview	Survey
Focus groups	Observation eg scanned bar code data
Analysis of online discussion forums	Online voting buttons

2.5 The limitations of data

All data collected should be evaluated using the following criteria.

(a) Is the data relevant to the purpose for which it was collected?

(b) Is it up-to-date?

(c) Is it reliable and accurate?

(d) Is the source of the data credible and objective, or unbiased? Look for the following.

Figure 5.2 The quality of data

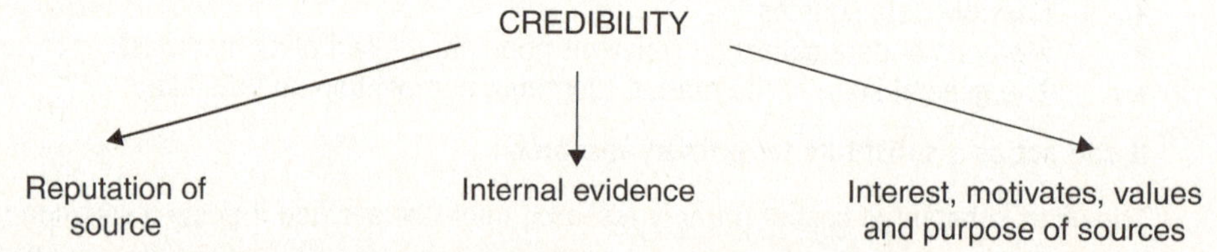

(e) Is the data subject to confirmation, or comparison with data from other sources? Are you prepared to risk basing decisions on uncorroborated data? The term triangulation refers to the ability to produce similar findings from multiple sources. If once source verifies another, the findings are viewed as more credible.

(f) Is the data based on a large and representative statistical sample of the relevant population (the group or issue under investigation)?

(g) Has the data been gathered in a way that makes it meaningful and reliable? Has the same question been put to all respondents? Were all terms consistently defined? Did researchers lead or suggest 'right' answers? Were the respondents influenced by the researcher, or each other, or the desire to be nice?

(h) Has the data collection and analysis been worthwhile? Has it fulfilled its purposes at a reasonable cost in money, time and effort?

Limitations of secondary data:

- **Relevance:** Secondary data can lack relevance because it is usually of a general nature or has been collected as another organisation's primary information.

- **Reliability:** Because secondary data was collected by another organisation, a company cannot be absolutely sure that it is accurate and reliable.

Limitations of primary data:

- It is expensive to collect because the company usually bears the full cost of its collection.
- The process of actually collecting and analysing primary data can be time-consuming and laborious.
- The research plan for collecting the required information can also be quite complex.

3 Creating a customer database

3.1 Customer databases

A marketing database can provide an organisation with much information about its customers and target groups. Every purchase a customer makes has two functions.

- Provision of sales revenue
- Provision of information as to future market opportunities

A typical customer database might include the following.

Table 5.2 Elements of a customer database

Element	Examples
Customer or company details	Account numbers, names, addresses and contact (telephone, fax, e-mail) details; basic 'mailing list' data, relationship to other customers. For business customers these fields might include sales contact, technical contact, parent company or subsidiaries, number of employees
Professional details	Company; job title; responsibilities – especially for business-to-business marketing; industry type
Personal details	Sex, age, number of people at the same address, spouse's name, children, interests, and any other relevant data known, such as newspapers read, journals subscribed to
Transaction history	What products / services are ordered, date, how often, how much is spent (turnover), payment methods
Call / contact history	Sales or after sales service calls made, complaints/queries received, meetings at shows / exhibitions, mailings sent, etc
Credit / payment history	Credit rating, amounts outstanding, aged debts
Credit transaction details	Items currently on order, dates, prices, delivery arrangements
Special account details	Membership number, loyalty or incentive points earned, discount awarded,(where customer loyalty or incentive schemes are used)

3.1.1 Sources of information and applications of the database

The sources of information in a customer database and the uses to which it can be put are outlined in the diagram below.

Figure 5.3 Sources of Information in a customer database

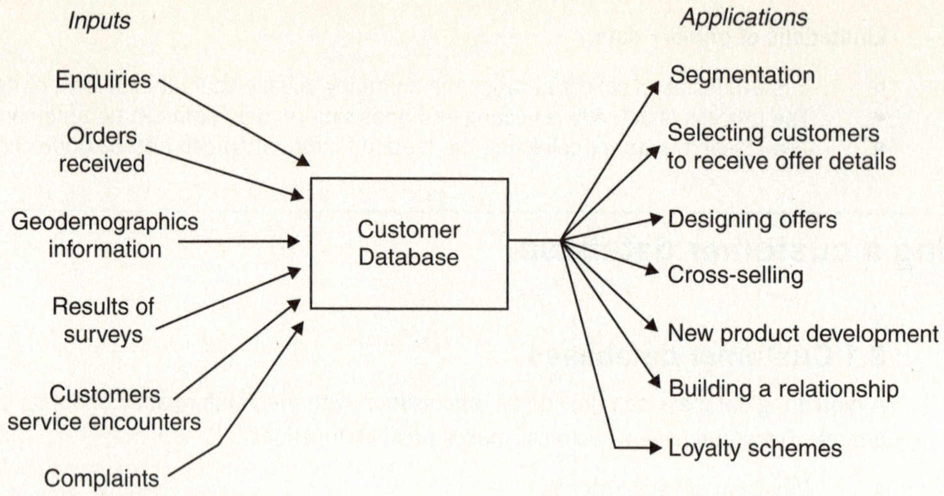

3.2 Creating a database

A database need not be computerised. A paper address book that you keep in your briefcase is a form of database and so is a card index. However, most modern business databases will be created and maintained centrally on a computer. This is obviously the most efficient method where large amounts of data are involved and for several important additional reasons.

(a) Common data for all users to share

(b) Avoidance of data duplication in files kept by different users

(c) Consistency in the organisation's use of data, and in the accuracy and up-to-dateness of data accessed by different users, because all records are centrally maintained and updated

(d) Flexibility in the way in which shared data can be queried, analysed and formatted by individual users for specific purposes, without altering the store of data itself

(e) Speed of data retrieval

3.2.1 Database formats

There are two basic kinds of computerised database.

(a) A flat file system lumps all the data into single file. A single worksheet in a spreadsheet is an example.

(b) A relational database system allows greater flexibility and storage efficiency by splitting the data up into a number of tables, which are linked and can be integrated as necessary. For example, one table may contain customer names and another customers' payment histories. A linking field such as a customer ID number would allow the user to interrogate both tables and generate an integrated report on a particular customer's purchases and payments, or a list of customers who had made multiple purchases, or a list of those with a poor payment record.

Flat systems are easy to build and maintain, and are quite adequate for applications such as mailing lists, or membership databases. Relational systems integrate a wider range of business functions, for invoicing, accounting, inventory and marketing analysis. They are, however, complicated to develop and use properly. If your organisation already operates a relational system, learn how to use it. If you are required to set up or build a relational system, get help. Use a 'wizard' or template (in the database package) or ask an expert, at least the first time.

All databases have some kind of structure, otherwise you would never be able to retrieve information from them. For instance a telephone directory stores entries in alphabetical order. Computer database packages store data as follows.

(a) Fields are the labels given to types of data. A simple customer database, for example, might include fields such as: Title, First name, Last name, Address fields, and other contact details. The fields are the columns in a tabular database.

(b) Records are the collection of fields relevant to one entry. So all the above data fields for a particular customer make up one customer record. The records are the rows in a tabular database.

Figure 5.4 Tabular database

	ID	Title	First name	Last name	Address 1	Address 2	Address 3	City	Country	Postcode	Country	Telephone	Fax	Email
	1	Mr	Kieran	Davies	25 Dill Street	Merton		London		Sw17 40F	UK	020 7884 1122		Kieran.davies@virgin.net
	2	Mrs	Shagura	Jumal	37 Nelson Road	Trafford		Manchester		M41 2BD	UK	01584 452291		sjumal@freeserve.com

(c) Tables are collections of records that describe similar data. All the customer records for a particular region or product may be stored in one table.

(d) Databases are collections of all the tables relating to a particular set of information. So your customer database may include tables for various regions, products and customer contacts.

ACTIVITY 5.3

Identify the types of data that can be included in the new database for a theatre located in a tourist city.

3.2.2 Data cleansing

A key issue in setting up a database is data cleansing: ensuring that the information is correct, up-to-date and not duplicated. Much can be done at the data entry stage, but where data is imported from other systems a good deal of preparatory work may be needed to ensure that it is in the correct format.

Data cleansing is the process of amending or removing data in a database that is incorrect, out of date, incomplete, improperly formatted, or duplicated.

▸ Assessment tip

Find out what type(s) of database your organisation (or college) uses, and for what applications. If possible, get access to the database and browse through the index, directory or switchboard to see what databases/catalogues contain what database files or tables, queries, reports and forms, with what fields.

3.3 Controlling access

Information is a vital asset for a company. To manage the future you need to be able to effectively and efficiently manage information. The company's core information will most often be under the control of IT specialists who will take care of security (both against loss and 'hacking') and legal aspects (data protection legislation) on core databases such as payroll and so on. However, with each person controlling a PC on their desk and having wide internet access, all staff need to be alert and professional. That handy personal database you have set up without any password may fall within the jurisdiction of data protection legislation and may be vulnerable to unauthorised access. For smaller organisations with no formal IT function, there is still the need for virus protection and the like. Take specialist advice when appropriate; a marketer may not always be a computer consultant.

4 The value of customer information

4.1 Identifying the factors that influence decision-making

Customers do not operate within a vacuum merely deciding what they are going to go out and buy that day. They have a range of influences and constraints imposed upon them that will affect their buying decisions.

Some are external influences, economic conditions will determine how much disposable income they have. There have been various articles expressing concern on the level of consumer spending on credit but people generally consider what they can afford rather than just go out and buy. The increasing effect of technology on the home may mean a consumer is encouraged to upgrade the family PC to enable them to access better services.

The consumer also has internal influences that will affect their buying decision. Peer group pressure is a strong influence and organisations should recognise that word-of-mouth recommendations are a powerful communications tool. We need to gain an understanding of these to fully appreciate what our communications message has to achieve.

THE REAL WORLD

Grey and youth markets

Social trends and demographic patterns mean that from time to time new markets emerge. At one end of the spectrum the grey market has proved a powerful group. Better health, longer lives, high levels of disposable income and plenty of leisure time has made the over 50's an attractive market segment for many companies.

In youth markets, teenagers have always been an important group, because of the effect of peer pressure and their desire to consume and conform to the fashions and must-haves of their age. Using their comfort with technology, their contact with their peers and how inspired they can be by the media around them, companies, like Nike and Adidas have managed to promote their teenage 'uniforms' to this impressionable group around the world.

Pre-teens are an emerging group, with girls in particular starting to show the spending characteristics once associated with older teenagers. A new pattern is the need for marketers to target both mother and daughter because of a shared interest in products, particularly evident in cosmetics.

4.2 Identifying differing needs and wants

Recognition that as a consumer you need to purchase a product or service can arise for a number of reasons. It may be that you need to replace something you already own, which no longer fulfils your needs. A new father of twins may realise that his two-seater sports car is no longer the ideal car for him to own.

Other changes in your life may result in new purchases – a change of job requiring you to work from home so that you need office and IT facilities, or maybe you have made a new set of friends who go skiing three times a year so you need the equipment to join them.

Outside influences also lead to us recognising a need. The knowledge that the population is ageing and today's 40-year-olds will probably not receive a sufficient State pension is prompting many to top up their personal pension plans. On a different scale, did we know that we needed a disposable toilet brush before we saw one advertised on TV? Communications can be the single most powerful influence if used well.

Needs arise for different reasons and different people will be aware of different needs, but once the need has been recognised then the consumer will be in a state of heightened attention, more likely to take notice of products/services that fulfil their needs or solve their problems.

Having a comprehensive customer database can help us to identify the wide range of needs that customers are trying to satisfy when they make a purchase. If we can identify a number of different reasons why customers purchase a product, integrated marketing campaigns can be designed for each.

4.3 Developing marketing mix activities to meet customer needs

In Chapters 3 and 4 we saw how the marketing mix can be used to create a series of unique 'blends' of marketing variables. Although we tend to look at how the marketing mix is used to position different products, it can also be used to position the same product for different target markets.

If we recognise that different market segments have different needs that can be satisfied by the same product, we can effectively market that product differently to each type of customer, thus persuading them that the product perfectly satisfies their needs. This is done with many products, for example, soap powders are all fairly similar, but are positioned to appeal to customers looking for whiter whites, colour-fast colours, or stain removal.

CHAPTER ROUNDUP

- While the most obvious customer is the person who purchases the product or service, the consumer is the end-user – the person who actually uses the product or service and is sometimes different from the purchaser.
- Putting the customer at the centre of the organisation's activities and responding effectively to the changes in the external environment requires access to quality, and relevant and timely information to guide management decisions.
- For a company's value chain to operate normally, lots of information needs to be collected.
- Information also comes from sources outside the organisation; including customers, suppliers, distributors, strategic alliance partners, independent third parties, commercial agencies, industry associations and the internet.
- A marketing database can provide an organisation with much information about its customers and target groups.
- All databases have some kind of structure, otherwise you would never be able to retrieve information from them.
- Information is a vital asset for a company. To manage the future you need to be able to effectively and efficiently manage information.

FURTHER READING

Chapters 3 and 5 of:

Blythe, J. (2008) Essentials of Marketing. 4th edition. Harlow, Prentice Hall.

Chapter 5 of:

Brassington, F. and Pettitt, S. (2007) Essentials of Marketing. 2nd edition. Harlow, Prentice Hall.

Whole text:

Chaffey, D. and Smith, P. (2008) *EMarketing Excellence*. 3rd edition. Oxford, Butterworth Heinemann.

Chapters 1, 2 and 4 of:

Doole, I., Lancaster, P. and Lowe, R. (2005) *Understanding and Managing Customers*. Harlow, Prentice Hall.

REFERENCES

Blythe, J. (2008) *Essentials of Marketing*. 4th edition. Harlow, Prentice Hall.

Brassington, F. and Pettitt, S. (2006) *Principles of Marketing*. 4th edition. Harlow, Prentice Hall.

Chapman, M. (2012) Halfords drops secret shoppers for customer feedback scheme. *Marketing Week*, www.marketingweek.co.uk [accessed 12 June 2012].

Cook, S. (2011) *Customer Care Excellence*. 6th edition. London, Kogan Page.

Doole, I., Lancaster, P. and Lowe, R. (2005) *Understanding and Managing Customers*. Harlow, Prentice Hall.

Harris, D. and Botten, N. (2008) *CIM Coursebook: Introduction to Marketing*. Oxford, Butterworth Heinemann.

Worthington, I. and Britton, C. (2009) *The Business Environment*. 6th edition. Harlow, Prentice Hall.

QUICK QUIZ

1 How does a 'customer' differ from a 'consumer'?

2 Outline four functions of customer information within an organisation.

3 What is secondary data?

4 What are the main uses of secondary data?

5 Identify four methods of collecting primary data.

6 What are the limitations of collecting primary data?

7 What are the different ways in which computer database packages store data?

8 Outline three sources of information for the customer database in a typical service organisation.

ACTIVITY DEBRIEFS

Activity 5.1

Pet food: The pet might prefer a particular brand with high quality ingredients, while the owner will be perfectly happy with whichever brand is available at the local supermarket.

Child's bicycle: The child might want an expensive and trendy Disney branded bicycle, while the parent wants to buy a more functional and reasonably priced model with good safety features.

Laptop PC: The manager might want a very lightweight premium model, while the IT department might prefer a standard model that is similar to those provided to other employees and have been purchased in bulk by the company.

Activity 5.2

The answer will depend on the type of organisation you work for.

Activity 5.3

(a) Analysis of theatregoers by specific **characteristics**: age, sex, home address

(b) How many **performances** each theatre customer sees in the year

(c) How many days visitors stay in the city and how they choose a day or night at the theatre

(d) **Types of production** customers like to watch

(e) **Factors** important to their decision to visit the theatre, such as price, location, play, cast, facilities

(f) Where they obtained **information** on the theatre and its productions: press, hotel, leaflets, mailings and so on

(g) **Other purchases** customers make when visiting the theatre

(h) **Other entertainment** that theatregoers choose to spend their money on

This data could then be used by the theatre management to build relationships with customers and to exploit sales and promotional opportunities.

QUICK QUIZ ANSWERS

1. A customer is an individual or organisation who buys a product or service. A consumer is the person that uses the product or service, or may be affected by its purchases.
2. Customer information can be used to establish general trends in the environment, scan the environment for opportunities and threats, enable the organisation to assess competitor activity and gauge the extent to which its resources 'fit' with its ambitions.
3. Secondary data is information that has already been collected, originally for a specific purpose, but which is later used for a purpose other than that for which it was collected.
4. Secondary data can provide a backdrop to primary research, act as a substitute for primary research and be used as a technique in itself.
5. Surveys, in-depth interviews, observation and focus groups.
6. It is expensive to collect, the process of collecting and analysing the data can be time consuming and laborious; and the research plan for collecting the required information can be quite complex.
7. Computer database packages store data as fields, records, tables and databases.
8. Your answer may have included enquiries, customer complaints, bookings / orders received, customer service encounters among many other alternatives.

CHAPTER 6

Building and maintaining customer relationships

Introduction

This chapter examines the importance of building and maintaining effective internal and external customer relationships. The first section explores the different types and characteristics of people with which an organisation develops relationships.

The second section describes the links between the marketing concept, a customer focus and the relationship marketing approach. The third section examines how marketing activities help to support relationships with external customers and aid customer retention and loyalty. The fourth section explains the importance of developing and sustaining customer, supplier and distributor relationships.

The fifth section describes approaches used to build and develop relationships both within the marketing function and across the organisation. The sixth section outlines key colleagues within the organisation with whom it is important to develop relationships. The seventh section identifies potential areas of conflict that can occur between the functions of an organisation, and the next section describes the methods that can be used to overcome these conflicts.

The final section discusses the need to take into account the views of others within the organisation when undertaking marketing activities.

Topic list

Syllabus reference

2.1	Explain the different types and characteristics of people with which an organisation develops relationships including: ▪ Customers ▪ Users ▪ Connected stakeholders ▪ Other stakeholders ▪ Differentiating between internal and external customers
2.2	Describe the links between the marketing concept, a customer focus and the relationship marketing approach including: ▪ Difference between customer acquisition and retention ▪ An understanding of the benefits of retaining customers ▪ Theoretical aspects such as Pareto and Ladder of loyalty
2.3	Explain how marketing activities help to: ▪ Support relationships with external customers ▪ Aid customer retention and loyalty
2.4	Explain the importance of developing and sustaining customer, supplier and distributor relationships through: ▪ Developing networking skills ▪ Collaboration and co-operation between intermediaries ▪ Successful negotiation between the various parties within the supply chain
2.5	Describe approaches used to build and develop relationships both within the marketing function and across the organisation in order to gain: ▪ Internal co-operation ▪ Commitment to organisational objectives ▪ Internal support for marketing initiatives
2.6	Identify key colleagues within the organisation with whom it is important to develop relationships: ▪ Other marketing team members ▪ Finance ▪ Research & Development ▪ Human resources ▪ Purchasing ▪ Manufacturing
2.7	Identify potential areas of conflict that can occur between the functions of an organisation including: ▪ The possible causes of conflict – poor, confusing, mistimed, unclear communications, different objectives, agendas and focus ▪ The potential effect of conflict on individuals and the organisation
2.8	Describe the methods that can be used to overcome conflict between organisational functions ▪ Co-operation ▪ Conciliation ▪ Internal arbitration

2.9	Discuss the need to take into account the views of others within the organisation when undertaking marketing activities including: ▪ Contributing constructive ideas with colleagues to aid plans for improving marketing activities ▪ Co-operating with others to follow plans ▪ Keeping commitments made to others ▪ Identify with others how joint efforts to follow plans can achieve improved performance

1 Customers and stakeholders

1.1 Stakeholder relationships

Key term

Stakeholders are individuals and/or groups who are affected by or affect the performance of the organisation in which they have an interest. Typically they would include employees, managers, creditors, suppliers, shareholders (if appropriate) and society at large.' (Worthington & Britton, 2006)

For any given organisation, there will be a number of individuals and groups who have some kind of a relationship with it, or have invested in it in some way, or are affected by its activities – and who therefore have a legitimate interest or 'stake' in it. These parties are called stakeholders.

There are three broad categories of stakeholder in an organisation.

(a) **Internal stakeholders**, who are members of the organisation. Key examples include the directors, managers and employees of a company – or the members of a club or association, or the volunteer workers in a charity. They may also include other functions of the organisation (eg marketing, production or finance) which have a stake in marketing activity, and/or separate units of the organisation (eg regional or product divisions) which have a stake in its plans.

(b) **Connected stakeholders** (or primary stakeholders), who have an economic or contractual relationship with the organisation. Key examples include the shareholders in a business; the customers of a business or beneficiaries of a charity; distributors and intermediaries; suppliers of goods and services; and financers / funders of the organisation.

(c) **External stakeholders** (or secondary stakeholders), who are not directly connected to the organisation, but who have an interest in its activities, or are impacted by them in some way. Examples include the government, pressure and interest groups (including professional bodies and trade unions), the news media, the local community and wider society.

The following diagram shows a quick visual snapshot of the total stakeholder environment.

Figure 6.1 Stakeholders in the marketing organisation

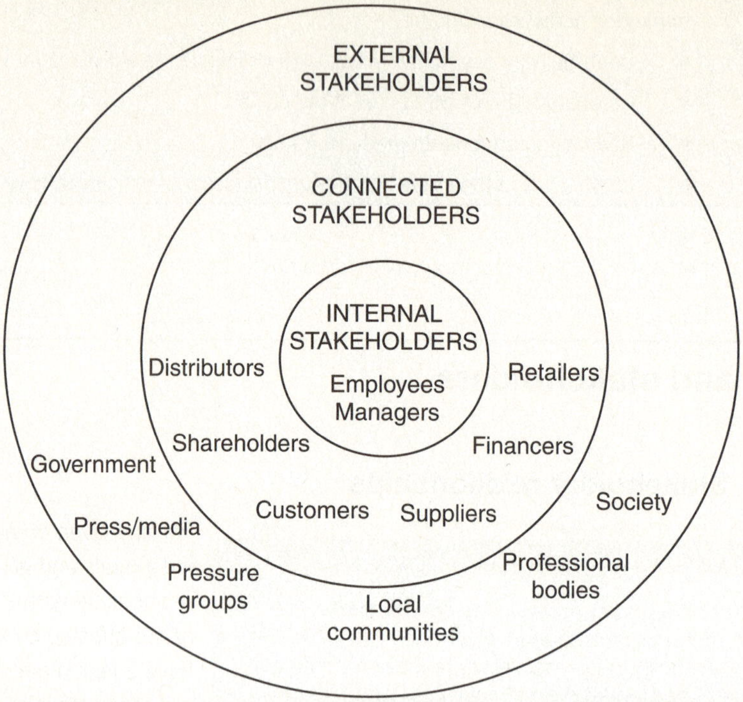

While it is useful to categorise stakeholders in this way, it would be a mistake to think of them as entirely separate groups. Customers are also members of the wider community, and may be shareholders in the company and / or members of a consumer or environmental protection group, for example. Employees of the organisation may also be customers, shareholders and perhaps members of a trade union which can bring influence to bear on their behalf with the management of the organisation. So there are always areas in which membership and interests intertwine.

The key point of stakeholder theory is that an organisation affects its environment and is affected by its environment. The boundaries of the organisation are highly permeable: influence flows from internal stakeholders outwards (eg through marketing) and from external stakeholders inwards (eg if a major customer pressures sales staff to represent its interests within the organisation, or more generally if a marketing-oriented organisation seeks to listen to its customers and meet their needs).

THE REAL WORLD

Turkey producer Bernard Matthews use communications with its external stakeholders as a way of reassuring its publics and rebuilding its reputation after the scandal over contaminated meat hit the headlines in 2007.

External stakeholders include the government, regulatory bodies, customers, suppliers the media and the community close to the company's operations. The company uses advertising, internet and social media and media and public relations to connect with all its publics. The company has four websites each focusing on different stakeholder needs: a corporate website that provides an overview of the business, a consumer site, giving information on the product range; a foodservice website, providing information to the catering trade, and a campaigning website, which supports Bernard Matthews' drive to get consumers to make turkey part of their everyday meals.

The company aims to promote its farming credentials and publicise new initiatives and the health benefits of turkey: for example, by meeting journalists to talk about what the company is doing with regards to animal welfare, sustainability, or the reduction in salt or fats in its ingredients. It uses quality marks and standards on its packaging to promote confidence in its products. It also uses public tasting sessions to promote the taste and attractiveness of fresh turkey. As the largest employer in the area it also reaches out to the local community through its youth awards schemes in Norfolk and Suffolk.

(*The Times* 100 Business Case Studies, 2012)

ACTIVITY 6.1

For your own employing organisation, or an organisation which you know well:

- Identify its major stakeholders
- Categorise them as internal, connected or external stakeholders
- Identify the major internal stakeholders of the marketing function (even if you do not have a dedicated marketing team, there will be somebody who is responsible for marketing activities)

Where possible, and where they are sufficiently significant, identify particular, named stakeholders (eg individual managers, major customers / suppliers, organisational functions or departments).

1.2 Internal and external customers

In the traditional sense of the word, customers are the people who buy an organisation's products and services. To communicate with them effectively, an organisation needs to know who they are, what needs the products or services are required to meet, where they are located and the most cost-effective methods of communicating with them. By doing this, it will be easier to develop effective communications, such as advertising, sales literature, packaging and product instructions, that appeal to, and are understood by, the customer. However, there are some discreet differences between customers that will have an effect on how we can communicate with them effectively.

Customers fall into two main categories, external and internal – each having very different needs and expectations of the organisation.

1.2.1 External customers

These are individuals who have no connection with an organisation, other than that they may have purchased goods or services in the past, or are purchasing at present. They can be either the traditional customer / consumer who buys a multitude of goods and services for their own use or that of their family – the business-to-consumer market (B2C); the business consumer who is buying on behalf of their organisation – the business-to-business (B2B), or individuals selling to one another (C2C).

1.2.2 Internal customers

Consider your internal customers and how important it is that there is good internal communication in an organisation. Think about how sometimes you are the customer and someone else is the service provider.

For example, as an employee, when you receive your pay slip from the finance department, you are the customer and expect it to be correct, to be delivered on time and the salary payment actually credited into your bank account. If there is a problem, you expect to be dealt with courteously and promptly. You do not expect to have to engage in lengthy correspondence to rectify a mistake. If you do receive information from the finance department – say, for example, about a new profit-related pay scheme – you expect it to be clearly written and well presented.

At other times, you could be the service provider to your colleagues or line manager; for instance, when you are asked to cost the production of a sales promotion item as part of a future promotional campaign. Your internal customers will expect you to have completed the task on time, accurately, and to present it clearly at the next planning meeting.

So internal marketing is about working together with colleagues and providing them with a good service so that, as a team, your organisation achieves its goals.

1.2.3 Users

The most obvious customer is the person who purchases the product or service; the enduser (or consumer) is the person who actually uses the product or service and is sometimes different from the purchaser. Therefore, although the person who pays for the product may also be the user or the consumer of the product this is not always the case.

2 Marketing and customer relationships

Increasingly, marketers are deepening their conviction that closing the sale is only one of the important milestones in an ongoing relationship. Therefore, a car dealership is not only interested in selling you a car but servicing it and, in a few years' time, supplying you with a replacement. This is building a relationship between the client, the staff at the local distributorship and the manufacturer's brand. Viewed in this context, the 18,000-mile service is not only seen to be a chance to make a sale (the income from the service), but a marketing opportunity to maintain and develop the relationship.

Thus, the reception team and the motor technicians are involved in building the relationship through their contact with the customer. Another key concept of relationship marketing is that of the 'part-time marketer' (eg any customer-facing staff). Much of the relationship building does not take part with the full-time marketers. In supermarkets, the full-time marketers may be comparatively remote. How the shopping experience feels will be greatly affected for better or worse by the interaction between customers and front-line staff at the checkout and others in customer contact roles – the 'part-time marketers'.

Although relationship marketing is important in consumer marketing, it is critical in B2B marketing. Organisations do not do business with organisations. People in one organisation do business with other people in another organisation. A key strength of an advertising agency, for example, is the quality of the relationships between the creative staff and the key personalities in the commissioning organisation. It is a very old saying that 'first you make them your friend, and then you make them your customer'.

This often involves many people interacting with many other people in the linking organisations. A network of interacting relationships is formed between the organisations, which then have to be maintained and sustained both internally (internal marketing) and externally. Thus, in considering the marketing action plan, the impact on all the relevant stakeholders is important.

Relationship management focuses on how these relationships may be positively sustained and developed. Marketing is not seen as a mechanistic set of actions, intellectual cogs in an industry machine but as an activity that depends on a network of human relationships to support the organisation's mission and objectives.

The move to relationship marketing can be seen as the leading edge in developing from a production orientation (any colour you like as long as it is black) to sales (all we need to do is push harder) to developing long-term relationships of positive benefit to both parties. In traditional sales negotiations, you could end up with winner-loser outcomes. In a relationship-marketing context, only creating and sustaining win-win outcomes will nurture and develop the relationship and future profit opportunities.

2.1 Customer acquisition and customer retention

As far as marketers are concerned, there are two different groups of customers to whom marketing messages are targeted; existing customers (for whom repeat purchase and increased purchase frequency are the objectives) and new customers (for whom a first purchase is the objective). These two groups of customers necessarily require different information, and might even be reached by different media. The organisation therefore needs two very different communications strategies to reach them.

2.1.1 The benefits of retaining customers

Everyone wants to retain their existing customers. Few companies, however, are implementing positive strategies aimed at retention. Most companies are organised for customer acquisition. Their advertising and sales programmes are designed to find and promote their products and services to new customers. The companies are organised on a product or brand basis, not on a customer segment basis. While they all have customer service departments, and most have a customer service free-phone number, they lack an integrated marketing strategy that is directed at retention, and that defines retention as the measurement of success.

You have probably heard it said that 'It's ten times cheaper to keep a customer than it is to get a new one.' Most people would agree with this statement, even though they have no way of proving it. Indeed, the majority of large organisations today are experimenting with database marketing programmes aimed, in large part, at retention. Most of these companies are not yet sure whether their experiments will be successful. Other benefits of retaining customers are described below.

(a) **Likelihood of repeat business:** Products and services that satisfy customers will make them come back again, thus giving the firm repeat business. Repeat business reduces the firm's cost of customer acquisition and also saves the customer the associated costs involved in switching suppliers.

(b) **Facilitates greater interaction between the business and customer:** As most markets move away from mass produced standard products and services to customised products and services, repeat business provides an opportunity for the firm to build a more focused relationship based on customer needs and requirements.

(c) **Reduced cost of customer acquisition:** Having a repeat customer enables the firm to save on most costs traditionally associated with customer acquisition; including advertising, sales presentations, follow-up and travel costs. It also creates the potential for the company to attract more customers through word-of-mouth advertising.

2.2 Pareto theory

The Pareto principle (also known as 'the 80/20 rule', the 'law of the vital few', or the 'principle of factor sparsity') states that, for many events, 80 per cent of the effects come from 20 per cent of the causes. Business management thinker Joseph Juran suggested the principle, and named it after Italian economist Vilfredo Pareto, who observed that 80 per cent of income in Italy went to 20 per cent of the population.

2.2.1 What is Pareto theory?

The '80/20 Rule' is a simple way of looking at your sales and profit figures and identifying the largest sources of contribution. This technique can be used for finding which of your customers are profitable, which channels to market you use are most profitable, and which products and services are profitable.

2.2.2 Why is it important?

Just as people aren't all the same, neither are your customers. Some are more important than others and some cost you more than others. Knowing which customers are the most profitable helps in a number of ways:

- You can make sure you are really looking after those customers
- You can understand what it is about them that is making them profitable
- You can then use that information to find other customers who are like them
- You can gradually build up the number of profitable customers and reduce the number of less profitable ones

2.2.3 What you need to know

The Pareto principle can be applied to many aspects of your business such as profits and sales. For example:

- 80 per cent of your profits may come from just 20 per cent of your customers
- 80 per cent of your sales may come from just 20 per cent of your products and services

This simple rule has little scientific basis but it invites you to analyse how productive your marketing effort is. It often leads to some interesting and useful insights into how you operate now and where you should be focusing your efforts in the future.

The 80 per cent and 20 per cent are not magical figures that work out exactly in all situations, nor do they need to add up to 100 per cent. Ratios such as 80/35, 80/25 or even 80/10 may equally apply, although you will be surprised to find just how close to 80/20 the relationship often is. The principle is that, in each case, we are seeking to find the source of the majority of whatever activity is being measured.

Obviously, if the 'most valuable' 20 per cent of the customer base can be identified, marketing activity can be targeted at those customers. In this way, a limited marketing budget can be spent more efficiently.

2.3 The ladder of loyalty

The ladder of loyalty is designed to illustrate how relationship marketing seeks to increase the loyalty of customer groups (including buyers, intermediaries and consumers), in order to reap the benefits of their retention, support and engagement. It can be applied in many relational settings: for example, charities and pressure groups use it to gauge the loyalty of donors, volunteers and members.

Figure 6.2 Ladder of loyalty

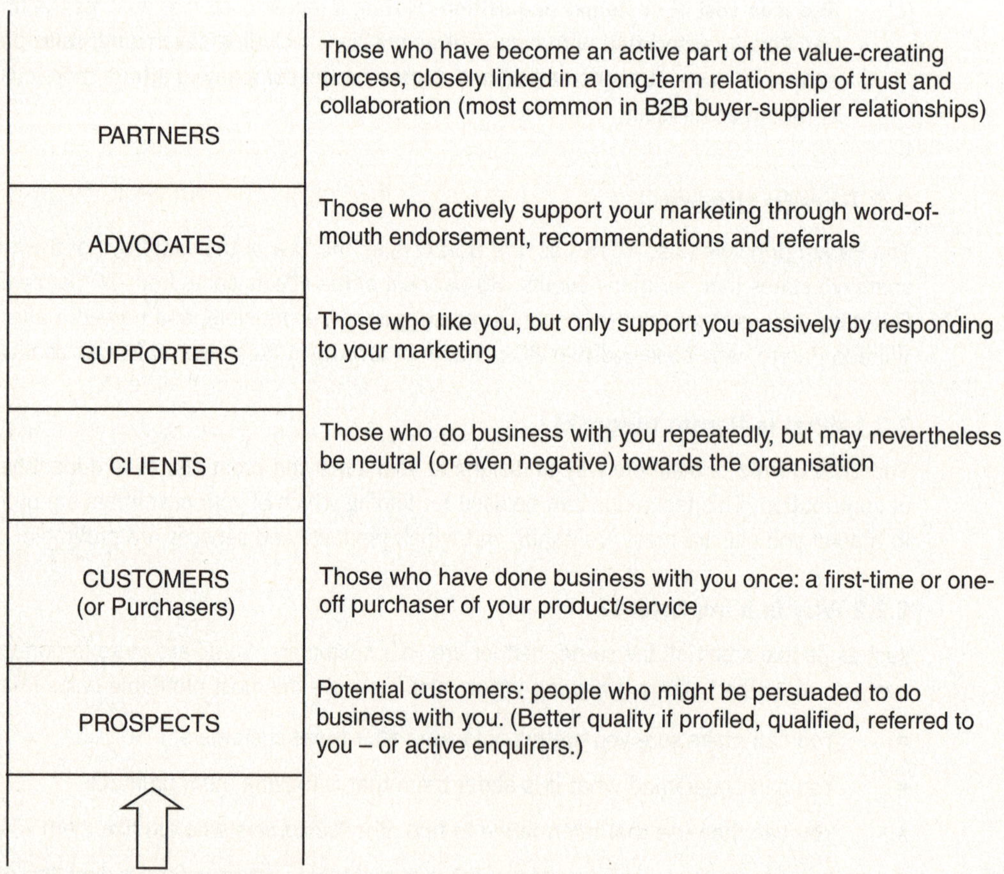

(Christopher, Payne and Ballantyne, 1991)

Finding prospects and converting them into customers (ie securing purchase) is the preoccupation of traditional or transactional marketing. Relationship marketing emphasises the conversion of new or one-off customers into repeat customers – followed by progressive conversion to each higher rung of the ladder, which represents a strengthening of the relationship over time.

Getting customers to advocate level is a particularly helpful source of leverage, as recommendations and referrals by existing customers are an easy and cost-effective way of both getting new prospects and converting them into customers and clients.

Few consumer relationships go beyond the advocate level to partnership (which is mainly a feature of B2B buyer-supplier relationships). However, some ladder models include an intermediate stage called 'membership', which implies genuine affiliation of some sort. This has long been a feature of voluntary sector relationships. Membership of political parties and charities, for example, requires commitment and cost/effort, and offers corresponding opportunities for active involvement in fund-raising and policy development. In the consumer sector, some organisations have introduced tactics to create or simulate membership-type relationships.

3 Marketing and customer loyalty

How marketing activities aid customer retention and loyalty

There are a number of techniques that can be used to move customers from 'prospect' to 'partner'. The main techniques can be summarised as follows:

(a) **Customer satisfaction:** In a competitive marketplace, customer satisfaction is the best way to ensure that buyers return repeatedly. To achieve high levels of satisfaction requires the effort of all functions within an organisation. However, there are many cases of companies that have not developed any explicit relationship marketing programme, but nevertheless achieve very high levels of customer advocacy.

Of course, many companies enjoy a high level of repeat business without providing high levels of customer satisfaction. Many customers of train companies may complain about the price and reliability of their train service, but return to it because they have no realistic alternative. Even companies which have an apparently poor standard of service can achieve high levels of repeat business by charging low prices.

(b) **Adding value to a relationship:** A relationship, to be sustainable, must add value in the eyes of customers. This value can come about in a number of ways, including:

- Making reordering of goods and services easier (for example, many hotels record guests' details and preferences so that they do not have to be re-entered each time that a guest checks in).
- Offering privileges to customers who wish to enter into some type of formal relationship (for example, many retailers hold special preview events for card holders, and send a free copy of the store's magazine).
- Developing an ability to solve problems jointly. For example, a car repair garage may diagnose problems rather than leaving it to the customer to have to specify the work that they require to be carried out. Joint problem-solving requires a considerable level of trust to have been developed between the parties.

- **Loyalty programmes:** Loyalty programmes work on the basis of providing rewards to customers in return for their continuing patronage. For the customer, a loyalty programme can add to the value of a relationships in the ways described above. For the seller, the main attractions are based on the ability to gather large amounts of information about identifiable individuals, rather than aggregate level data about the 'average' customer. A loyalty programme can also have the effect of 'tying-in' a customer, at least in the short term while the customer collects sufficient points in order to obtain a reward. For example, some coffee shops offer 'buy 10 get the 11th free' – and stamp the first two places on the card for free, to build return visits.

- **Creating barriers to exit:** Companies can try to keep their customers by making it difficult for them to defect to a competitor. Suppliers of industrial machinery create ongoing relationships where they are the sole supplier of spare parts or consumable items which the purchaser must buy if they are to continue using their equipment.

  Many companies negotiate exclusive supply agreements with a supplier in return for a promise of preferential treatment. In both cases, the customer is dependent in the short term. However, such ties can usually be broken eventually (for example, when the machinery is replaced or when an exclusive supply contract comes up for renewal), and it is at that point that the true loyalty of a customer is put to the test.

ACTIVITY 6.2

Investigate and outline the range of marketing tools used by a typical B2C organisation to encourage customer loyalty.

4 Supply chain marketing

4.1 What is supply chain marketing?

Key term

The **supply chain** – the network of suppliers, manufacturers and distributors involved in the production and delivery of a product. (CIM)

4.1.1 Developing networking skills

Good customer communication goes beyond your own immediate organisation.

The relationship your staff have with your organisation's suppliers, distributors and so on may have a critical impact on the service your customers enjoy. More efficient communication via ICT using intranets and extranets results in quicker, cheaper and more effective use of resources for all members of the distribution channel, especially when linked into quality systems such as just-in-time (JIT).

For example, the Body Shop, the retail chain that sells health and beauty products, ensures that its staff work closely with the firm it retains to distribute its merchandise to its retail network, and the distributor actually has office space within the Body Shop factory. This arrangement ensures that close relationships and good communication are achieved.

This improved communication can result in staff enjoying as close a relationship with someone working for a supplier or distributor as the person at the next desk. This is where the difficulty of deciding where the boundaries between internal and external customers arises, with some groups previously considered external now becoming part of the extended organisation.

Even end-users, although still very much categorised as external customers, are now able to order goods and services through digital, web-based or voice-activated systems requiring little, if any, human intervention.

4.1.2 Collaboration and co-ordination between intermediaries

One of the key principles of relationship management is that relationships can be co-operative rather than adversarial or competitive: buyers and suppliers, and even industry competitors, can work together to add value, to mutual benefit. It is widely acknowledged that in order to compete successfully in the global marketplace, firms cannot 'go it alone'.

They depend on the contribution of their total supply chains to enable them to deliver value to the customer better and more profitably than competitors, through: better quality materials or access to scarce materials; reliable and flexible delivery; cost savings on materials and logistics; streamlined processes enabling late customisation of products (eg Dell Computers, the specifications for which are put together by the individual buyer, from a menu of components); and the quality of service given by intermediaries to the end consumer.

A good working relationship with suppliers and other 'partners' can produce dramatic effects, such as:

- Innovation
- Improved performance
- Lower costs
- More holistic solutions to problems
- Better understanding of the needs of all parties
- New ways of working together
- More co-operation

4.2 Negotiation within the supply chain

Within a given supply chain there is often an imbalance of power. In order to ensure that the needs of all parties are met fairly, carefully and in a constructive manner, careful negotiation is required. Negotiation involves discussing issues and coming to an agreement.

Two starting points (or states of mind) exist for negotiation:

- **Distributive negotiation** – characterised by a desire to 'beat the opposition'
- **Integrative negotiation** – a friendly form with both parties looking to reach a mutually beneficial agreement

It is worth remembering that business is about appropriating value for one's own company and stakeholders and, hopefully, building a strategic position where competitors, buyers and suppliers do not pose a threat to that value position. With that in mind, we might want to consider that companies need to find a position where they are able to exercise power over other members of the supply chain. This contradicts much of what is said in the literature about 'lean' supply chain management, which should be based on equity, trust and openness. We can summarise the position in which a buyer may find themselves under four categories: buyer dominance, interdependence, independence and supplier dominance. This position will depend upon the relative utility and the relative scarcity of the goods or services that are being traded.

- **Buyer dominance** is likely to occur where there are few buyers and many suppliers and the supplier is highly dependent upon the buyer for revenue. The buyer will almost certainly have low switching costs relative to the supplier.
- **Interdependence** will occur when there are relatively few buyers and sellers and both have high switching costs.
- **Independence** will occur when there are many buyers and sellers and both buyer and seller have low switching costs.
- **Supplier dominance** occurs where there are relatively few suppliers and the buyer has high switching costs relative to the supplier.

THE REAL WORLD

Supermarkets and suppliers

Take as an example a typical supermarket such as Tesco, Sainsbury or Morrisons, each of whom have a considerable market share in the UK. There are many customers going into each of the stores and they are independent of those supermarket chains.

However, when we look at the relationships that the supermarkets have with suppliers of prepared packaged foods we have an example of buyer dominance. The relative size of the supermarket and the likelihood that the supermarket business is a significant percentage of the food supplier's revenue makes the supermarket dominant. When we consider the relationship between the food supplier and the supplier of customised plastic packaging for the product it is likely to be one of interdependence. Most probably the food supplier and the packaging firm have collaborated on the design of the packaging and may even have shared the cost of the moulds for manufacture.

5 Building and developing relationships

5.1 Internal co-operation

Just as individuals have internal customers, such as colleagues and line managers, that they have to deal with, organisations have internal customers in the form of their staff.

From an organisation's perspective, internal communication is vital to internal marketing, and the maintenance of employee motivation and company competitiveness. Simple methods of communication can be used to keep staff informed about new products/services, internal restructuring or how well (or not) the organisation is doing. In dynamic environments, where firms need to manage change effectively, communication needs to be harnessed to help staff adapt and become familiar with changes in their working environment.

According to Berry and Parasuraman (1991), who are widely credited with recognising the importance of internal marketing, 'a service company can be only as good as its people: if they aren't sold, customers won't be either.'

The point here is that most organisations provide at least some level of customer service as part of their product offering and increasingly it is seen as a way of differentiating products in an overcrowded market. Without a culture of internal marketing and effective internal customer communications, the employees within an organisation face the following problems:

- Communication problems
- Frustration and non-co-operation
- Time-wasting and inefficiency
- Stress and lack of job satisfaction
- Poor quality of work.

All of these problems eventually lead to poor service to the external customer, which eventually leads to reduced profit in the long term.

5.2 Internal support for marketing initiatives

It is important for many marketers to market their department or services internally to colleagues and other departments. Problems can be raised by other people unaware of the department's full range of services and the contribution it can make to the business.

The changing environment in which organisations operate means that it may be difficult for some to communicate with staff in the traditional way, and pressures upon staff may mean that they are less inclined to be committed to the organisation's values and culture.

The combination of downsized organisations and flatter management structures has removed layers of management and this means that employees are nearer to the decision makers and that the communication process is speeded up. However, staff that are less secure in their jobs and more pressured to work faster and harder are less likely to communicate openly with their colleagues and managers.

The trend of teleworking and home-based workers results in more people working away from the office, and this means it is more difficult to create a corporate culture and a sense of belonging where people feel happy to communicate on an informal basis.

The trend for some organisations to provide a 24/7 service often means that employees do not all meet each other and probably end up sharing personal space, such as a desk, with two others whom they have never met. This can be quite isolating.

The merging of companies across the United Kingdom and elsewhere in the world is creating global organisations that do not have local identities and which cross over into different cultures, languages and operating systems. This can make it difficult for senior managers to communicate effectively with employees.

6 Internal relationships

6.1 Within marketing

Before building relationships with others inside or outside the organisation, it is important for marketers to interact with their colleagues within the marketing function. In smaller organisations, where marketing staff might share an office or even a desk, this is unlikely to be a major problem. However, in larger ones, or those where the marketing function is decentralised, this might be a major issue.

Most marketing functions are organised along one of two lines:

- By product, service, customer or geographic location. In this case the organisation has a number of small, multi-disciplinary, marketing functions.
- By functional specialism, such as marketing research, communications, sales, etc.

In the first, where the marketing function consists of a number of small multidisciplinary departments, marketing staff must ensure that they avoid competition between departments, either for resources or for status. In the second, marketers must ensure that they understand each others' priorities and activities, and that they communicate across the functional boundaries.

6.2 Relationships with other functions

The marketing concept is designed to foster a deeper appreciation by all departments of the value and benefits of a customer orientation, but how much influence should marketing have over other departments to bring about co-ordinated effort in customer service, say, or product development? Other departments naturally stress their own special contribution to company goals, and view problems and opportunities in the light of their own expertise and culture.

ACTIVITY 6.3

Reflect on the relationships between the various departments within your organisation (or one with which you are familiar) and how each of them might adversely affect customers' perception of the organisation.

7 Sources of conflict

Conflict can be viewed as an inevitable feature of organisational life, and can result in both positive and negative outcomes.

Sometimes conflict is overt, as when it emerges in the form of a strike, or individuals refusing to communicate with each other at all. However, conflict can also be covert, with indifference and lack of cooperation occurring with no particular enthusiasm on the part of those involved. Either way, the management of conflict is likely to be easier and more effective if the symptoms of conflict can be recognised and dealt with at an earlier stage.

7.1 Causes of conflict

There are a number of factors that may play a part in creating conflict (Figure 6.3).

Figure 6.3 The causes of conflict

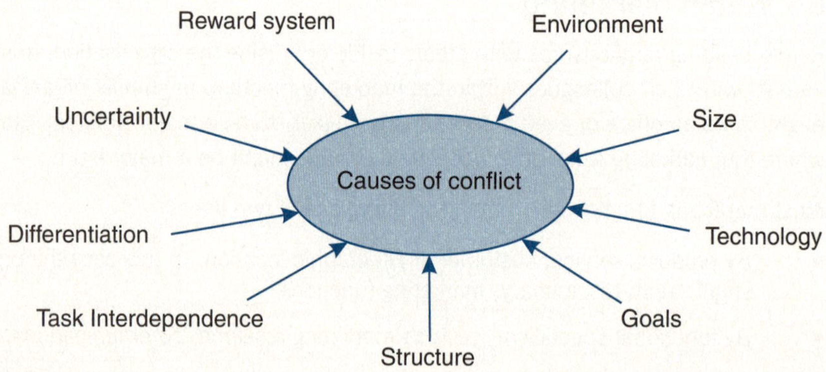

7.1.1 Environment

Departments are established to interact with major domains in the external environment.
As the uncertainty and complexity of the environment increase, greater differences in skills, attitudes, power, and operative goals develop among departments. Each department is tailored to 'fit' its environmental domain and, thus, is differentiated from other organisational groups. Moreover, increased competition, both domestically and internationally, have led to demands for lower prices, improved quality, and better service. These demands exert more intense goal pressures within an organisation and, hence, greater conflict among departments.

7.1.2 Size

As organisations increase in size, subdivision into a larger number of departments takes place. Members of departments begin to think of themselves as separate, and they erect walls between themselves and other departments. Employees feel isolated from other people in the organisation. The lengthening hierarchy also heightens power and resource differences among departments.

7.1.3 Technology

Technology determines task allocation and interdependence among departments. Groups that have interdependent tasks interact more often and must share resources. Interdependence creates frequent situations that lead to conflict.

7.1.4 Goals

The overall goals of an organisation are broken down into operative goals that guide each department. Operative goals pursued by the marketing, accounting, legal and human resources departments often seem mutually exclusive. The accomplishment of operative goals by one may block goal accomplishment by other departments and hence cause conflict. Goals of innovation also often lead to conflict because change requires co-ordination across departments. Innovation goals cause more conflict than do goals of internal efficiency.

Goal incompatibility is probably the greatest cause of intergroup conflict in organisations. The operative goals of each department reflect the specific objectives members are trying to achieve. The achievement of one department's goal often interferes with another department's goals.

A typical example of goal conflict may arise between marketing and manufacturing departments. Marketing strives to increase the breadth of the product line to meet customer tastes for variety. A broad product line means short production runs, so manufacturing has to bear higher costs. Other areas of goal conflict are quality, cost control, and new products.

Goal incompatibility exists among departments in most organisations.

7.1.5 Structure

Organisation structure reflects the division of labour as well as the systems to facilitate co-ordination and control. It defines departmental groupings and, hence, employee loyalty to the defined groups. The choice of a divisional structure, for example, means that divisions may be placed in competition for resources from headquarters, and headquarters may devise pay incentives based on competition among divisions.

7.1.6 Differentiation

This deals with the differences in cognitive and emotional orientations among managers in different functional departments. Functional specialisation requires people with specific education, skills, attitudes, and time horizons. For example, people may join a sales department because they have ability and aptitude consistent with sales work. After becoming members of the sales department, they are influenced by departmental norms and values. The underlying values and traits of personnel differ across departments, and these differences lead to horizontal conflicts.

7.1.7 Task interdependence

This refers to the dependence of one unit on another for materials, resources, or information.

- Pooled interdependence means little interaction;
- Sequential interdependence means that the output of one department goes to the next;
- Reciprocal interdependence means that departments mutually exchange materials and information.

Generally, as interdependence increases, the potential for conflict increases. In the case of pooled interdependence, units have little need to interact. Conflict is at a minimum.

Sequential and reciprocal interdependence require employees to spend time co-ordinating and sharing information. Employees must communicate frequently, and differences in goals or attitudes will surface. Conflict is especially likely to occur when agreement is not reached about the co-ordination of services to each other. Greater interdependence means departments often exert pressure for a fast response because departmental work has to wait on other departments.

7.1.8 Uncertainty

When activities are predictable, departments know where they stand. They can rely on rules or previous decisions to resolve disputes that arise. When factors in the environment are rapidly changing, or when problems arise that are poorly understood, departments may have to renegotiate their respective tasks. Managers have to sort out how new problems should be handled. The boundaries of a department's territory or jurisdiction become indistinct. Members may reach out to take on more responsibility, only to find that other groups feel invaded. In a study of hospital purchasing decisions, managers reported significantly higher levels of conflict when purchases were non-routine than when they were routine. Generally, as uncertainty about departmental relationships increases, conflict can be expected to increase.

7.1.9 Reward system

The reward system governs the degree to which subgroups co-operate or conflict with one another.

Incentives and rewards have a similar impact on conflict between organisational departments.

When departmental managers are rewarded for achieving overall organisation goals rather than departmental goals, co-operation among departments is greater.

THE REAL WORLD

Bechtel, for example, provides a bonus system to division managers based upon the achievement of Bechtel's profit goals. Regardless of how well a manager's division does, the manager is not rewarded unless the corporation performs well. This incentive system motivates division managers to co-operate with each other. If departments are rewarded only for departmental performance, managers are motivated to excel at the expense of the rest of the organisation.

Assessment tip

Think about sources of potential conflict within your own organisation. Try to determine from where these instances of conflict may have arisen.

7.2 The effects of conflict

While conflict can have negative consequences leading to dysfunctional behaviours, it can also have positive outcomes. The terms 'destructive' and 'constructive' conflict are used to differentiate between negative or positive outcomes. Daft (1989) noted that several negative consequences for organisations that may arise from conflict are as follows:

(a) **Diversion of energy.** Time and effort wasted in addressing a conflict rather than achieving organisational goals.

(b) **Altered judgement.** Judgement and perceptions become less accurate when conflict becomes more intense.

(c) **Loser effects.** The losers may deny or distort the reality of losing, withdraw, or seek scapegoats.

(d) **Poor coordination.** Under intense conflict, co-ordination does not happen. Collaboration across groups decreases – less contact, not sympathetic to other points of view – achieving departmental goals and defeating the 'enemy' take priority. There is no room for compromise.

Schmidt (1974) outlined a number of positive outcomes of conflict. They include:

- Better ideas produced;
- People forced to search for new approaches;
- Long-standing problems brought to the surface and resolved;
- Clarification of individual views;
- Stimulation of interest and creativity;
- A chance for people to test their capacities.

8 Overcoming conflict

Mullins (2010) identified some strategies for managing conflicts.

(a) Clarification of goals and objectives. The clarification and continual refinement of goals and objectives, role definitions and performance standards will help to avoid misunderstandings and conflict. Focusing attention on superordinate goals that are shared by the parties in conflict may help to defuse hostility and lead to more co-operative behaviour.

(b) Human resource management policies and procedures. Careful and detailed attention to just and equitable HRM policies and procedures may help to reduce areas of conflict.

(c) Development of interpersonal/group process skills. This may help engender a better understanding of one's own behaviour, the other person's point of view, communication processes and problem-solving. It may also assist people to work through conflict situations in a constructive manner.

(d) Group activities. Attention to the composition of groups and to factors that affect group cohesiveness may reduce dysfunctional conflict.

(e) Leadership and management. A more participative and supportive style of leadership and managerial behaviour is likely to assist in conflict management.

(f) Organisational processes. Conflict situations may be reduced by attention to such features as the nature of the authority structure; work organisation; patterns of communication and sharing of information; democratic functioning of the organisation; unnecessary adherence to bureaucratic procedures and official rules and regulations.

There are also a number of formal methods available to deal with internal conflict:

(a) **Internal arbitration** involves involving a third party within the organisation (possibly from a different function or a manager) to help resolve differences in an unbiased manner

(b) **Conciliation** involves an external third party but they are trained in conciliation and are there to establish a legally binding agreement between the parties.

THE REAL WORLD

ACAS

The Advisory, Conciliatory and Arbitration Service (Acas) is an agency intended to promote better relationships in the workplace. It is funded by the Department of Business, Innovation and Skills to give independent and impartial advice to individuals and organisations on good employment practice, and its services can be accessed freely to solve problems when things go wrong.

9 Co-operation and collaboration

> **Key term**
>
> **Total Quality Management** (TQM) is a management approach for an organization, centered on quality, based on the participation of all its members and aiming at long-term success through customer satisfaction, and benefits to all members of the organisation and to society. (ISO)

It is important for marketing staff to take into account the view of others within the organisation, and to work with them, when undertaking marketing activities.

9.1 Contributing constructive ideas

A dialogue between marketing and non-marketing staff will allow the development of marketing plans and activities that are more likely to be successful. The use of brainstorming techniques might be of benefit here.

Brainstorming is a group creativity technique designed to generate a large number of ideas for the solution to a problem. The method was first popularised in the late 1930s by Alex Faickney Osborn, an advertising executive and one of the founders of BBDO, in a book called *Applied Imagination*. Osborn (1979) proposed that groups could double their creative output by using the method of brainstorming.

9.2 Co-operating with others to follow plans

Once plans have been developed, they must be implemented. As we have already seen, marketing is a cross-functional activity, and the help and commitment of staff outside the marketing department will be needed if plans are to succeed.

The successful implementation of marketing plans might require the organisation to form one or more multidisciplinary project teams, tasked with the implementation of the plan, or parts of it. Such teams will necessarily include, and may indeed be led by, members of the marketing department.

9.3 Keeping commitments

It is very important that, whatever promises are made regarding services to be performed or information to be supplied, these promises are met. Most organisations now take a 'total quality' approach to activity.

One of the main principles of TQM is that any product or service, whether delivered within or outside the organisation, should be 'right first time'. This principle applies to marketing information and activity as it does to any other aspect of business.

CHAPTER ROUNDUP

- Stakeholders are individuals and/or groups who are affected by or affect the performance of the organisation in which they have an interest. Typically they would include employees, managers, creditors, suppliers, shareholders (if appropriate) and society at large.
- The key point of stakeholder theory is that an organisation affects its environment and is affected by its environment.
- Increasingly, marketers are deepening their conviction that closing the first sale is only one of the important milestones in an ongoing relationship.
- The ladder of loyalty is designed to illustrate how relationship marketing seeks to increase the loyalty of customer groups (including buyers, intermediaries and consumers), in order to reap the benefits of their retention, support and engagement.
- Relationship marketing emphasises the conversion of new or one-off customers into repeat customers – followed by progressive conversion to each higher rung of the ladder, which represents a strengthening of the relationship over time.
- There are a number of techniques that can be used to move customers from 'prospect' to 'partner'.
- The relationship your staff have with your organisation's suppliers, distributors and the like can have a critical impact on the service your customers enjoy.
- One of the key principles of relationship management is that relationships can be co-operative rather than adversarial or competitive: buyers and suppliers, and even industry competitors, can work together to add value, to mutual benefit.
- Within a given supply chain there is often an imbalance of power. In order to ensure that the needs of all parties are met fairly, carefully and in a constructive manner, careful negotiation is required.
- Just as individuals have internal customers, such as colleagues and line managers, that they have to deal with, organisations have internal customers in the form of their staff.
- Conflict can be viewed as an inevitable feature of organisational life, and can result in both positive and negative outcomes.

FURTHER READING

Chapter 3 of:

Blythe, J. (2008) *Essentials of Marketing.* 4th edition. Harlow, Prentice Hall.

Chapters 2, 7 and 11 of:

Doole, I., Lancaster, P. and Lowe, R. (2005) *Understanding and Managing Customers.* Harlow, Prentice Hall.

Whole texts:

Christopher, M., Payne, A. and Ballantyne, D. (1991) *Relationship Marketing: Bringing Quality, Customer Service and Marketing Together*. Oxford, Butterworth Heinemann.

Cook, S. (2011) *Customer Care Excellence*. 6th edition. London, Kogan Page.

Worthington, I. and Britton, C. (2009) *The Business Environment*. 6th edition. Harlow, Prentice Hall.

REFERENCES

Berry, L. and Parasuraman, A. (1991) *Marketing Services: Competing Through Quality*. New York, The Free Press.

Blythe, J. (2008) *Essentials of Marketing*. 4th edition. Harlow, Prentice Hall.

Brassington, F. and Pettitt, S. (2006) *Principles of Marketing*. 4th edition. Harlow, Prentice Hall.

Christopher, M., Payne, A. and Ballantyne, D. (1991) *Relationship Marketing – Bringing Quality, Customer Service and Marketing Together.* Oxford, Butterworth Heinemann.

Cook, S. (2011) *Customer Care Excellence*. 6th edition. London, Kogan Page.

Daft, R. L. (2006) *Organization Theory and Design: Understanding the theory and design of organisations.* Independence, KY, Cengage Learning South-Western Pub.

Doole, I., Lancaster, P. and Lowe, R. (2005) *Understanding & Managing Customers*. Harlow, Prentice Hall.

Harris, D. and Botten, N. (2008) *CIM Coursebook: Introduction to Marketing*. Oxford, Butterworth Heinemann.

Mullins, L. (2010) *Management and Organisational Behaviour*. 9th edition. Harlow, Prentice Hall.

Osborn, A. (1979) *Applied Imagination*. 3rd edition. New York, Charles Scribner.

The Times 100 Business Case Studies (2012) *Communicating with stakeholders: A Bernard Matthews case study. The Times*, http://businesscasestudies.co.uk/bernard-matthews/communicating-with-stakeholders [accessed 6 May 2012].

QUICK QUIZ

1 What is meant by the term 'stakeholders'?

2 Who are internal customers?

3 Outline three benefits of retaining existing customers.

4 What are the six different rungs on the ladder of loyalty?

5 Identify four different activities that marketers use to facilitate customer retention and loyalty.

6 Outline four benefits that can be derived from a good relationship with suppliers and other partners.

7 Identify five possible causes of conflicts within organisations.

8 What are the negative consequences of conflicts within organisations?

9 Outline five strategies for managing conflicts in organisations.

ACTIVITY DEBRIEFS

Activity 6.1

The answer will depend on the type of organisation you work for.

Activity 6.2

Typical tools include, loyalty cards, schemes and programmes, excellent customer service, vouchers, coupons and gifts, frequent flyer programmes and prizes.

Activity 6.3

The answer will depend on the type of organisation you work for.

QUICK QUIZ ANSWERS

1 Stakeholders are individuals or groups who are affected by or affect the performance of the organisation in which they have an interest.

2 Internal customers are other members of the organisation who obtain products or use services.

3 Likelihood of repeat business, facilitates greater interaction between the business and the customer and reduced cost of customer acquisition.

4 Prospects, customers, clients, supporters, advocates and partners.

5 Customer satisfaction, adding value to a relationship, loyalty programmes and creating barriers to exit.

6 Innovation, improved performance, lower costs and better understanding of the need of all parties.

7 Uncertainty, task dependence, differentiation, reward system and environment.

8 Diversion of energy, altered judgement, loser effects and poor co-ordination.

9 Clarification of goals and objectives, human resource management policies and procedures, development of interpersonal / group process skills, leadership and management and group activities.

CHAPTER 7

Communicating with customers

Introduction

This chapter examines the importance of communicating effectively with internal and external customers. The first section explores the importance of communication as a tool to aid the development and maintenance of long-term relationships.

The second section describes the nature and scope of the communications cycle. The third section explains the various business formats required for communicating both internally and externally with customers. The fourth section explains the importance of good verbal and non-verbal communications.

The fifth section outlines the strengths and weaknesses of different promotional activities in a range of marketing scenarios designed to aid relationship management. The sixth section describes the processes involved in undertaking a range of tactical direct marketing campaigns. The seventh section discusses how customer databases can be used to support tactical marketing communications activities, and the next section explains the process used for effectively managing a communications budget for specific communications tasks.

The final section identifies and explains the different methods available for monitoring and measuring the success of internal and external tactical communications campaigns.

Topic list

Syllabus reference

<table>
<tr><td>3.1</td><td>Explain the importance of communication as a tool to aid the development and maintenance of long-term relationships:
■ Keeping internal and external customers up to date and informed on key issues
■ A means of exchanging information relevant to the customer/ supplier relationships
■ A means of gaining Attention, Interest, Desire, Action in the context of marketing</td></tr>
<tr><td>3.2</td><td>Explain the nature and scope of the communications cycle including:
■ The Schramm Model
■ Aspects of encoding the message in relation to customer needs
■ The effect of 'noise' in the communication process</td></tr>
<tr><td>3.3</td><td>Explain the various business formats required for communicating both internally and externally with customers, including:
■ Letters
■ Memos
■ Informal reports
■ Emails</td></tr>
<tr><td>3.4</td><td>Explain the importance of good verbal and non-verbal communications:
■ Kinetics – body language such as facial expressions, eye movements and gestures
■ Meta – communications – the importance of silence in communications ie, actions speak louder than words
■ Paralanguage – the use of tone</td></tr>
<tr><td>3.5</td><td>Identify the strengths and weakness of the following promotional activities in a range of different marketing scenarios designed to aid relationship management including:
■ Sales promotions
■ Public relations
■ Intranet
■ Extranet
■ Internet / wed based promotion
■ Digital technologies
■ Personal selling from a customer perspective</td></tr>
<tr><td>3.6</td><td>Describe the processes involved in undertaking a range of tactical direct marketing campaigns including:
■ E-mail campaigns
■ E-newsletters
■ Web pages
■ Leaflet drops / direct marketing
■ Sales promotional activities
■ Tele-messaging
■ Digital messaging</td></tr>
<tr><td>3.7</td><td>Discuss how customer databases can be used to support tactical marketing communications activities targeting:
■ Internal market
■ External market
■ Connected stakeholders</td></tr>
</table>

3.8	Explain the process used for effectively managing a communications budget for specific communications tasks, including apportioning costs effectively: ▪ Identification of costs associated with the project ▪ Allocating costs accordingly ▪ Working to a set budget and planning expenditure activities ▪ Using Excel spreadsheets to record and report budget information
3.9	Identify and explain the different methods available for monitoring and measuring the success of internal and external tactical communications campaigns: ▪ Enquiry levels ▪ Sales increases ▪ Media evaluation ▪ Satisfaction surveys

1 The importance of communication

The day-to-day communications of the marketer should not be viewed as something entirely separated to the formal marketing communications of the organisation. In an integrated view of communications, advertisements and others have their place. We must also consider the formal and informal communications that take place, and even our body language and posture. We send a message with everything we do!

However, in the buying process, some stages may need other communications, for example responding by e-mail to a query on goods damaged in transit at a 'dot-com company'.

Even the communications within the organisation can be viewed not as something separate, but as internal marketing. Your internal markets (stakeholders) are key.

1.1 Exchanging information with customers and suppliers

A company letter or report is not normally written in isolation. A customer complaint may have arisen from extravagant expectations given in advertising and poor instructions on the packaging. A letter (or e-mail) attempting to resolve the issue may also draw on additional information on the company website. Additionally, the letter (or e-mail) will conform to organisational house rules (eg font used as well as headed paper or e-mail footer). The communication needs to be seen as part of two sets of integrated communications:

- The full range of communications sent out by the organisation
- The full range of communications received by the stakeholder

If you consider with whom you communicate, why, how and how often, you may be surprised at just how many people there really are, and the balance between those inside your organisation and outside it. You should also consider the people and organisations from whom you receive information. How much of that do you actually use and take in?

How effective is your communication in relaying the intended message accurately?

Communications are used in marketing for a range of specific purposes:

(a) Creating brand awareness: reaching consumers with brand messages widely and consistently enough to enable recognition and association with the right kind of images (for example, through advertising, public relations, brand identity). Like celebrities, brands need to be 'seen in all the right places' and to project their 'personality' in order to be instantly recognisable by the public.

(b) Motivating purchase: highlighting product benefits that are relevant to the needs of the target audience (for example, through advertising); offering incentives to purchase (for example, through sales promotion).

(c) Facilitating purchase: direct marketing (for example, through mail order advertising or internet marketing); informing consumers how and where to purchase ('available at...' messages, web addresses); offering sales service.

(d) Forming and maintaining customer relationships: customer contacts (for example, through personalised mailings, loyalty programmes); personal client contacts (in business markets); after-sales service (for example, through care lines and customer service).

(e) Forming and maintaining network relationships: networking with suppliers, distributors and marketing service agencies; supplying information to support transaction and decision-making.

(f) Forming and maintaining working relationships: supplying management and staff in the marketing and other departments with the information they need to integrate their marketing (especially customer-facing activities); fostering a customer-focused organisation culture through 'selling' quality values to staff.

If, for instance, you are working in the marketing department of a firm that makes and sells garden furniture, and you have responsibility for the organisation's marketing communications, then in an average working day you may communicate with a large number of people in a variety of ways (Table 7.1).

Table 7.1 Communication methods

Method	Table Title	Table Title
Post	Customers Suppliers	Complaining about an element of product or service Informing you of their services
Telephone	Suppliers Colleagues Media	Chasing or placing or negotiating terms on an order Arranging meetings Clarifying information Talking to the press about a forthcoming launch
E-mail	Suppliers Colleagues Distributors	Confirming details of an order Confirming details of a meeting Clarifying information Providing information Confirming details of their order
Fax or e-mail	Advertising agency	Confirming copy changes to a new press ad
Letters/direct mail	Customers	Informing the customer of a forthcoming price promotion
Formal meetings/ presentations	Colleagues	Presenting the last quarter's sales figures to the rest of the team
Informal ('water cooler') meetings	Colleagues	
Report	Colleagues	

1.2 Keeping customers up to date

As consumers we receive over 30 times the amount of messages we are physically able to process in any one day. Many of these are concerned with our everyday life and therefore will be accepted into our memory without problem. As marketing-focused organisations, we must ensure the messages sent to our customers are worthy of being remembered and are delivered to the recipient in the most effective and efficient manner, in order that the one chance we get maximises our opportunity.

Communication is, therefore, a core skill that marketing professionals need to use daily.

The purpose for any communication can be broken down into four main areas. Most communication will have at least one of these four factors as their main objective and it can be useful to analyse which of these are required when putting a message together. These factors can be remembered by the mnemonic DRIP.

- **Differentiate** – Identifies for the message receiver the key difference between the products / services you provide and those provided by competitor, for example 'Daz washes whiter'.
- **Remind** – Includes within the message product / service attributes they may have forgotten, for example now it's winter, it's nice to drink hot chocolate.
- **Inform** – Includes within the message details of what the product / service can provide and any action required by them, for example now that the DVLA have an improved database of car owners, you will be fined if you do not renew your car tax on time.
- **Persuade** – Usually applied to products / services we want rather than need, giving us a reason to buy, for example 'Crunchie – get that Friday feeling'.

THE REAL WORLD

Dyson manufactures a revolutionary (and premium-priced) type of vacuum cleaner and has 52 per cent of the UK market. Its communications have needed to:

- Differentiate it from conventional products – use of innovative technology.
- Remind/reassure customers that the cyclone system works better than any other and to resist the competition's attempts to gain top of mind awareness.
- Inform and educate the market about what is wrong with conventional appliances.
- Persuade potential customers to consider Dyson as the only option when next purchasing floor-cleaning appliances.

ACTIVITY 7.1

Look closely at a daily newspaper or weekly magazine and cut out at least ten different advertisements for a wide cross-section of products/services. Analyse how many of the DRIP factors you can apply to each advertisement and construct a table showing which advertisement incorporates which DRIP factors.

1.3 Communication and the AIDA model

All good marketers follow the AIDA model. The AIDA model stands for Attention, Interest, Desire, and Action (Figure 7.1).

Figure 7.1 The AIDA model

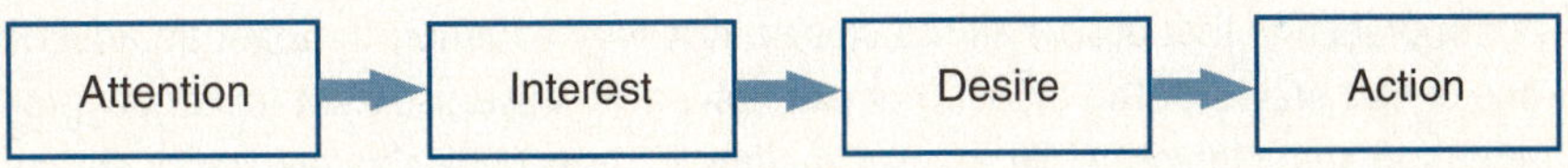

1.3.1 Attention

If you want your sales letter or advertisement to have an impact on your audience, it must first get their attention. You can do this with a hard-hitting headline or lead paragraph that hits the nail directly on the head or you can even begin your mailing with a captivating question. For instance, 'Do you want to cut your electricity cost by 45%?'

An appropriate headline for a sales letter promoting a weight loss programme might be: 'Now, you can lose 15 pounds in two weeks without having to starve; and it's easy and affordable!'

This headline not only solves a problem, but also offers a quick and easy solution that keeps in mind the price-sensitive consumer.

Your audience will be interested only in knowing 'What's in it for me?', 'Why should I invest my time in reading on, or finding out more?'

1.3.2 Interest

You must get the readers / viewers' interest by showing them why they need your product or service. You have to create a want for it. Let them know how their lives will become easier with your product or service. Show them what they are missing by not even trying it.

Here, you need to sell the key specific benefits, or differentiating features, of your product or service. You can rest your case by using testimonials or case histories. You can provide feedback from users who have benefited from your product. Always remember that you know everything there is to know about your product, so 'stale news' to you can be fresh news to the other person.

1.3.3 Desire

Now you've got the readers / viewers' attention and hooked their interest. Next, you've got to create desire. Tell the readers how exactly they'll benefit from your product. Link the benefits to their daily life. Get them to realise how your product can benefit them, how convenient it is for them to get it, and how comfortable life will be for them afterwards.

Generalities are less convincing. Specific details are far more believable. For example, when you want to sell books on lowering employee theft . . . 'By the end of this quarter, you could see your percentage of employee theft drop by more than 37%. Imagine the spectacular effect it will have on your bottom line!'.

1.3.4 Action

What do you want the reader / viewer to do next? Send in a reply card? Order the product or service? Call in asking for more information? Schedule an appointment? Notify them accordingly. It is amazing how many sales letters do not inform the reader about the subsequent step, and how many advertisements do not say where the product is available or how to contact the company.

You've worked hard so far. You have their attention, hooked interest, created desire. Isn't it appropriate to ask for action? Don't presume that your reader / viewer knows what to do next. As a support to getting the preferred action, you should always incorporate a reply card with your mailing.

1.3.5 Communications and stages

If you look at the overview of the AIDA model above, you will see that it is very difficult to create one communication that covers all the stages. It is very common to target an advertisement or direct mailing at just one or two stages of the model. For example, a TV advertisement for a new product might just seek to create attention and interest, while a direct mailing for a recognisable service might concentrate on desire and action.

▸ Assessment tip

Review some communications messages sent within your organisation. How can you see AIDA applied?

2 The communications cycle

2.1 The Schramm model

Effective communication is a two-way process, perhaps best expressed as a cycle. Signals or messages are sent by the communicator and received by the other party, who sends back some form of confirmation that the message has been received and understood ('feedback').

Wilbur Schramm (1961) developed the most commonly known model of communication (Figure 7.2), which broke the process down into five clearly defined consecutive stages or dimensions.

These are as follows:

- The sender has the need to communicate
- The need is translated into a message (encoding)
- The message is transmitted
- The receiver gets the message (decoding)
- The receiver interprets the message and provides feedback to the sender

Figure 7.2 Schramm's communications cycle

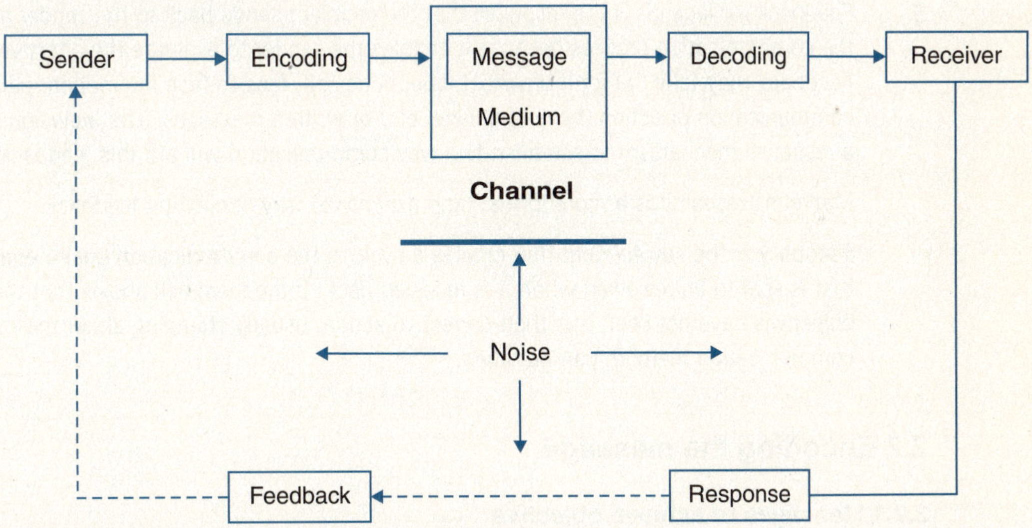

These stages can be considered in more detail, as follows.

1. The need to communicate business messages to your internal and external markets is an essential part of the marketing process. The DRIP factors help us to identify what kind of message is required at which stage of the product life cycle. In deciding to send out a message we must be clear what customer needs we are meeting and the objective behind the planned communication. Once this is clear, you can then move on to plan the message content.

2. Messages may be expressed in a number of different ways. It is usual that in any business communication the message content and method of communication is a result of careful planning rather than an off-the-cuff remark. Most promotional messages are more sophisticated than 'this product's good, so go and buy it'. In planning the message content, the sender will consider:

- The purpose of the communication
- The subject to be communicated
- The likely needs of the recipient
- The communication methods available for use.

It is imperative that we communicate to the recipient in a way they will easily understand and will arouse interest. This process is known as encoding and involves a combination of words, pictures and symbols to represent the message to be transmitted.

The first step to encoding is to decide what and how much to say; if a message contains too much information it is difficult to absorb, but if you do not include enough, it will not meet with the expectation of the recipient and may leave room for misinterpretation.

3 The medium you choose for transmission will depend on the message to be conveyed, location of the recipient, speed, convenience and degree of formality required.

The usual internal methods are memo, report, e-mail, telephone and face-to-face interaction. External methods available will be determined by the media consumption habits of the recipient. For example, one of the best ways to communicate to 16–19-year-olds is by advertising in cinemas or SMS messaging.

4 Decoding is the interpretation of the message that has been received by the recipient.

If the decoding message is the same as the encoded message then the communication will have achieved its objective. However, if the recipient decodes the message in another way, it may mean that the communication is entirely wasted.

The degree of misinterpretation will need to be established before the message content is adapted.

5 Feedback (or lack of) is the response that the recipient sends back to the sender and is a key element in the communication process because it enables the sender to evaluate the effectiveness of the message. Feedback may take the form of verbal (telephone call, face-to-face interaction, etc), non-verbal communication or action (body language, etc) or written messages. The inclusion within the message of a response mechanism to establish two-way communication will aid this feedback.

Marketing research is a more formal (and expensive) way of eliciting feedback.

Feedback is the key element that creates a cycle in the communication chain, enabling the information that is sent to be reviewed when it is received back. If the feedback shows that the communications objectives have not been met then corrective action, usually changing either the message content or communication method, can be taken.

2.2 Encoding the message

2.2.1 Messages to achieve objective

Again, there is a wide range of possibilities. Not much explicit planning is needed for: 'We have received your order'. However, a report to a client on a mix of advertising media to be used will need planning, as there may well be a range of issues needing to be addressed to get the overall desired effect: 'Place your account with us'. It is important to understand both ends of the equation. The message must not only be appropriate to our needs but also meet the stakeholder needs and expectations. The message 'Buy our product as it is cheap' may not be right for a wealthy client more interested in green issues. In constructing the message, some anticipation of stakeholder reaction is needed.

2.2.1 Format and media

Increasingly, communications at the one-to-one level are moving into electronic media. E-mails provide audit trails (you can tell if an e-mail has been received but not an ordinary letter); they are quick, cheap and, with attachments, can carry vast amounts of data (reports, images, etc, can be attached as files). It is important to provide the communication in a medium that is convenient for the receiver. Poor quality format and construction detracts from the quality of the message.

Text should be written in clear language that is appropriate for the target audience.

- Keep your sentences short
- Use active verbs
- Use 'you' and 'we'
- Choose words appropriate for the reader
- Don't be afraid to give instructions
- Avoid nominalisations
- Use positive language
- Use lists where appropriate

2.3 The effects of noise

Noise, such as distractions or the interference that occurs as the communication is being encoded, transmitted and decoded, can obstruct the transmisson of the message. There are many different types of noise that can render the message inaccurate, unclear or even mean that it is not received at all.

2.3.1 Technical noise

Technical noise can occur while the message is being transmitted; for example, when a poor telephone connection means the caller's voice cannot be heard, or when the fax machine breaks down. Now, slow broadband or not being able to pick up a mobile signal is just as problematic and frustrating and is also viewed as being a form of technical noise.

2.3.2 Physical noise

Physical noise can occur while the message is being transmitted; for example, people talking, traffic or noisy machinery could render a speaker's voice inaudible during a presentation.

2.3.3 Social noise

Social noise creates interference in the transmission and decoding of messages. It is caused when people are prejudiced against others because they are of a different age, gender or social class. For example, a young woman delivering a presentation on corporate funding to older businessmen may be perceived to lack credibility by some of the audience who are prejudiced because of her age and gender. Social noise can also be used to retain interest or differentiate the whole message.

2.3.4 Psychological noise

A person's emotional state or attitude could interfere with message transmission. A person's anger or hostile attitude can create psychological noise. For example, a customer whose goods have not been delivered may be unable to hear the reason why the goods have been delayed because he is so angry about the situation.

THE REAL WORLD

Communications barriers

A UK manufacturing company hosted a delegation from an associate company in Japan.

The marketing manager was given the task of arranging the first day's activities, which were to include a two-hour long presentation about the history, structure and objectives of the firm, a tour of the main manufacturing site and lunch followed by a brainstorming session on how the two companies could forge closer links and benefit from future joint projects. However, little consideration was given to the communication barriers that arose during the visit:

- Cultural differences in the way Japanese people greet others, their degree of formality and taste in food.
- The language barrier in that many of the delegation did not speak English and none of the host company spoke Japanese.
- The unfamiliar technical environment and organisation of the company, which meant that the jargon and abbreviations specific to the host company that were used in the presentation, made the presentation incomprehensible to most of the delegation.
- The noisy manufacturing site meant that during the tour most of the visitors could not hear what was being said to them.
- The lengthy presentation meant that the visitors who understood English had 'information overload'. Most lost concentration and could not take in the overall message that was being conveyed.
- The delegation did not feel confident or comfortable with contributing to the brainstorming session.

For future visits, the marketing manager thought of a number of ways to eliminate the communication barriers:

- Employing an interpreter.
- Researching cultural differences and using this information to provide appropriate refreshments and use appropriate greetings, seating arrangements and so on.
- Ensuring that no jargon or colloquialisms are used by speakers.
- Using small groups to tour the factory at a quiet time so that visitors could hear what the guide is saying.
- Using a shorter presentation to prevent boredom and information overload.
- Using a different presentation approach, with visual media, such as slides or video and Powerpoint software.
- Increasing interaction with the audience with question and answer techniques to check understanding.
- Providing a pack of information in English and Japanese, containing key points about the company, such as its structure, objectives and current operations.
- Avoiding the brainstorming session as it is probably too ambitious an exercise.
- Replacing it with a more social event where individual host managers can be 'partnered' with visiting managers, and interpreters used to help exchange views in a less threatening context.

ACTIVITY 7.2

Think of a recent piece of communications within your organisation and break down its components using Schramm's radio-signal model of communication.

3 Business communication formats

3.1 Letters

Despite the growth of e-mail communication, letters still play an important role in the business world.

A letter is a written (or printed) communication addressed to a person or organisation by a person or organisation and usually sent through the post.

(a) As you can see, this definition allows a great deal of scope for variations: the letter is an extremely versatile medium and format, which can be adapted to almost any purpose. At the same time, its direct person-to-person nature makes it particularly well suited to private, confidential or 'sensitive' communications.

(b) A letter is the main method of written business-to-business communication, although e-mail is swiftly replacing it.

The major sections of a typical letter are as follows:

(a) The sender's address block will contain the full contact information for the organisation (address with postcode, telephone and fax). This block may include website information or this may be printed as a 'footer' on the bottom of the headed paper.

(b) The printed heading may be customised a little with the personal contact information of the sender (eg direct telephone line and e-mail address).

(c) The reference section gives reference information to identify the document. In past days this might have been the typist and author. This is often now the location address for the letter's word-processing file.

(d) The date should be in the specific organisation's house style (eg US companies use a different format). Standard options are given in Microsoft Word and other packages.

(e) The recipient's address block should contain the recipient's correct title (Dr., Rev., etc.), name and address (including postcode or zip). Microsoft Word allows this block to be highlighted and then used to address an envelope or a label so full postal information is required.

(f) The salutation is the formal address line (eg Dear Dr Smith). The salutation and recipient's address block are almost invariably left justified.

(g) The heading block can be centred, left or right justified according to the organisation's house style. The reference and date blocks will usually be left or right justified, according to house style. The heading (if used) will often be in bold and may be left aligned or centred according to the house style.

(h) The body of the letter will generally contain a line or two of introduction and conclusion.

The main body of the letter contains the substance. The reader will not be as familiar with the context of the message as you are. Describe it briefly: it may be a response to a previous communication from the reader, or you may be making initial contact (if you are introducing yourself or advertising goods). You would usually put the following in your opening.

(a) A straightforward (brief) explanation of why you are writing. ('Thank you for your letter of 3rd March, in which you requested information about conference bookings'.)

(b) An acknowledgement of any relevant correspondence received, noting its date and nature. ('As requested [or agreed] in our telephone conversation [or meeting] of 4 September, I am sending you …'.)

(c) Important details of the circumstances leading to the letter. ('I have been asked by my colleague, George Brown, to contact you in regard to…'.)

The middle paragraph(s) should then be used to set out the letter's message, which will elaborate on or move forward from the introductory paragraph. This section will contain the substance of your response to a previous message, details of the matter in hand, or the information you wish to communicate. If you are making several points, start a new paragraph with each, so that the reader can digest each part of your message in turn.

Your letter will not be effective unless it has the desired result of creating understanding or initiating action. It is a good idea to summarise your points briefly or make clear exactly what response is required. Here are some examples.

- I look forward to meeting you to discuss the matter in more detail.
- Thank you again for your order. I trust our service will be to your satisfaction.
- If you require any further information, please [do not hesitate to] call me.
- I will be contacting you in the next few days to arrange a meeting.

The signature block will contain an ending salutation (eg Yours sincerely,) followed by a space for the sender's signature. Often handwritten signatures are illegible, so the name and qualifications (where relevant, eg FCIM, Chartered Marketer) need to be added below the signature, with the position (normally one line below), and if only general internet information is given in the heading the personal direct e-mail contact information should be given below that.

If the letter has supporting documentation (eg reports, specifications, so on) this may be listed at the foot of the page. If other people have been sent copies of the letter, the circulation list may also be given.

3.2 Reports

3.2.1 What is a report?

'Report' is a general term and one that may suggest a wide range of formats. If you give someone a verbal account, or write them a message in a letter, memo or e-mail informing them of facts, events, actions you have taken, suggestions you wish to make as a result of an investigation and so on, you are reporting. In this sense the word means simply 'telling' or 'relating': we have seen reports of this kind in memorandum form, in the visual presentation of statistics, and in the minutes of meetings.

There will be variety in the format and style of a report, according to the context.

(a) **Formal or informal.** You may think of reports as huge documents with sections, subsections, paragraphs, subparagraphs, indexes, appendices and so on. There are extensive, complex reports like this, but a single-sheet ordinary memorandum may be sufficient in many contexts.

(b) **Special reports** may be commissioned for one-off planning and decision-making, such as a market research report, or reports on a proposed project or particular issue.

(c) **Routine reports** are produced at regular intervals. Examples of routine reports are budgetary control reports, sales reports or progress reports. Occasional reports include an accident report or a disciplinary report.

3.2.2 Report writing style

Report writing involves particular requirements for objectivity, impersonality, ease of reading, precision and appropriate formality.

There are certain stylistic requirements in the writing of reports, formal or informal.

(a) **Objectivity and impersonality.** Even in a report designed to persuade as well as inform, subjective value judgements and emotions should be kept out of the content and style as far as possible: the bias, if recognised, can undermine the credibility of the report and its recommendations.

(b) **Ease of understanding.**

  (i) Avoid technical language and complex sentence structures for non-technical users.

  (ii) The material will have to be logically organised, especially if it is leading up to a conclusion or recommendation.

  (iii) Relevant themes should be signalled by appropriate headings, or highlighted for easy scanning.

  (iv) The layout of the report should display data clearly and attractively. Figures and diagrams should be used with discretion, and it might be helpful to highlight key figures which appear within large tables of numbers.

  (v) Background or supporting information may be removed to 'appendices' at the end of the report, in order to keep its main body concise and relevant at the appropriate level of detail.

(c) **Precision**

  (i) Do not use vague language. 'This option is likely to exceed expenditure budgets' is far superior to 'it would cost an awful lot of money'.

  (ii) Recommendations should be specific and firm. 'I feel more could be done...' is too vague to be helpful. Say precisely what should be done: 'customers should receive a verbal explanation in layman's terms...'.

3.2.3 Formal report structure

Reports are highly structured (especially formal reports), with sections covering: context-setting, description of methodology and findings, and conclusion or recommendations (as required).

A formal report is laid out according to certain basic guidelines. It will be split into logical sections, each referenced and headed appropriately.

TITLE

I	TERMS OF REFERENCE (or INTRODUCTION or BACKGROUND)	What was I asked to do?
II	PROCEDURE (or METHOD)	How did I go about it? [if relevant]
III	FINDINGS (or ANALYSIS or appropriate topic headings)	What did I discover?
1	Section heading	
2	Section heading	
	(a) sub heading	
	(i) sub point	
IV	CONCLUSIONS	What is the general 'thrust' of the result?
V	RECOMMENDATIONS	What particular recommendations do I wish to make? [if requested to do so]

3.2.4 Informal reports

An informal report is used for less complex and lower-level information. Its structure is less developed: it will not require elaborate referencing and layout. There will be three main sections, each of which may be headed in any way appropriate to the context in which the report is written:

- Introduction / background / situation
- Findings / analysis / information
- Summary / conclusion / recommendations

In informal reporting situations within an organisation, the 'short informal report' may well be presented in memorandum or e-mail format, which incorporates title headings and can thereafter be laid out at the writer's discretion.

3.3 E-mails

E-mails can take the role of letters, memos, notes and messages. They are less secure than they appear and also more formal than they appear. Care must be taken to ensure sensitivity to the recipients' needs, confidentiality and effective tone.

Many organisations now conduct both internal and external communications via e-mail systems. E-mail can be used for a wide variety of communication purposes, in place of letters, circulars, internal memos, notes and other brief messages. Lengthier messages (such as briefs and reports) and graphic messages (such as diagrams and maps) can be attached as file attachments.

Most organisations have guidelines for the use of e-mail.

(a) E-mail messages have a legal effect. Firms can be sued for libellous, offensive or misleading remarks made in e-mail, and e-mail messages can be cited as evidence in court.

(b) E-mail can be used excessively, to the exclusion of other forms of communication which might be more appropriate. Excessive personal use (or abuse) is also an issue for many organisations (as it has been with the telephone).

(c) E-mail is not private, and remains on the server. There are therefore dangers in using it to send confidential messages.

The most common e-mail software is Microsoft Outlook.

Most organisations also require employees to add a signature to the end of a message. This is usually set up similarly to a business card with job title and contact details. Increasingly common are branded templates which look similar to corporate letter head paper.

The following are general hints on composing e-mail messages.

Table 7.2 Composing emails

Composing emails
Do not commit to e-mail any message that is private or confidential. As mentioned above, it is not a secure medium in general: a co-worker may cover someone's e-mail while (s)he is absent, the system administrator may access messages and companies may monitor e-mail.
Do not send illegal or offensive messages. (This should not be on your agenda anyway – especially for marketing purposes – but abusive, discriminatory and harassing messages do get sent.) E-mails can be traced to their source, and systems administrators can be liable for the misdeeds of users.
Beware of informality. Writers of e-mails may dash off a friendly note, but the recipients may (quite rightly) regard it as a written (and legally valid) response which may imply contract terms.
Beware of 'tone of voice'. Sarcasm and irony do not come across well in brief, typed, computer-mediated messages. If you wish to be humorous (in an informal context), there are conventions: adding 'emoticons' such as 'smiley faces' (☺) or the typed equivalent :).
Use mixed case letters. All uppercase (ie capitals) IS INTERPRETED AS SHOUTING!
Keep the line-length reasonably short, to ensure that it displays effectively on most recipient terminals.

Composing emails
Ensure that you give the recipient's address correctly and that you state a subject. The first will avoid getting the message returned to you (remember that computers are very literal) and the second will avoid getting the message deleted by the recipient as possible junk or virus mail.
Remember that sending e-mail is instant and that you cannot usually recall a message. Check your message carefully before you click on 'send'.

Because e-mail messages can be easily personalised and sent to mass mailing lists (as well as instantly, cheaply and conveniently sent to individual recipients), they have particular advantages for marketing communications. The use of e-mail for transaction processing and relationship marketing can be extremely effective: e-mailed newsletters, product information and order confirmation from known senders is likely to be welcomed – or at least not filtered out by bulk mail avoidance tools.

3.4 Memos

Key term

A **memorandum (memo)** is the internal equivalent of a letter: it can be used for a variety of purposes. Memoranda have highly structured introductory elements, including sender, recipient, subject, date and reference: thereafter there are no formal elements required.

The memorandum or 'memo' is a very flexible form used within an organisation for communication at all levels and for many different reasons.

(a) It performs internally the same function as a letter does in external communication by an organisation, but can in effect be used for reports, briefings or instructions, brief messages or 'notes' and any kind of internal communication that is more easily or clearly conveyed in writing (rather than face-to-face or on the telephone).

(b) A memorandum may be sent upwards, downwards or sideways in the organisation. It may be sent from one individual to another, from one department to another or from one individual to a department or larger body of staff, via the internal mail system of the organisation.

(c) Nowadays, internal e-mail (using networked computers) often substitutes for hard-copy memoranda.

A memorandum may be typed onto blank sheets but many companies which generate a large volume of memoranda streamline the system and have 'memo pads' with appropriate headings already printed or memo styles set up in word processing or e-mail software.

Memorandum format will vary slightly according to the degree of formality required and the organisation's policy on matters like filing and authorisation of memoranda. Follow the conventions of 'house style' in your own organisation. A typical format, including all the required elements, is illustrated below. (You may note the similarity to e-mail message windows.)

Figure 7.3 Sample memo

Organisation's name (optional)

'MEMORANDUM' heading

To: (recipient's name or designation) Ref: (for filing)

From: (author's name or designation) Date: (in full)

Subject: (main theme of message)

The message of the memorandum is set out like that of a letter: good English in spaced paragraphs. Note, however, that no inside address, salutation or complimentary close are required.

Copies to: (recipient(s) of copies) Signed: (optional)

author signs/initials

Enc.: to indicate accompanying material

The structure and style of the message will vary according to its nature, the number of people it is addressed to, who those people are and what position they occupy. The flexibility of the medium means that some memos can be less formal than others. The same guidelines apply as with a letter.

The audience of a memo will be people within your organisation or business network.

(a) You may be writing to a fellow-specialist, and so be able to use technical language and complex ideas. Think first, however: a memo to all staff might cover a vast range of fields and abilities, from tea lady to accountant to engineer.

(b) If you are reporting to, or making a suggestion to, someone higher in the hierarchy than yourself, your tone will have to be appropriately formal, businesslike and tactful.

(c) If you are dashing off a handwritten note on a memo pad to a colleague with whom you enjoy an informal working relationship, you can be as direct, familiar and friendly as you like.

(d) If you are instructing or disciplining junior personnel, you will have to retain a certain formality for the sake of authority; a more persuasive and less formal tone might be appropriate if you are congratulating, motivating or making a request.

4 Effective communication

4.1 Verbal communication

Verbal communication means, simply, communication by speech, or 'word of mouth'. Face-to-face oral media include conversations, meetings, interviews, negotiations and public addresses, presentations or briefings. Interactive verbal communication can also take place when the sender and receiver are not physically face-to-face, through telephone calls, video conferencing or Webcasting.

The advantages and disadvantages of this form of communication may be summarised as follows.

Table 7.3 Advantages and disadvantages of verbal communication

Advantages	Disadvantages
Speed / directness: little or no time lapse between sending and receiving	Less planning time to formulate and check message and responses
Interactivity: real-time exchange of ideas, opinions, questions. Ability to respond directly to questions, make decisions	Ephemeral (passes with time): does not allow for reception at audience's own pace, repeated reference etc (as writing does)
Feedback: immediate and versatile (non-verbal messages). Ability to clarify, check, reinforce messages	Ambiguity: people's perceptions and memory of what was said may differ. (May need written checking, confirmation.)
Influence: interactivity (plus use of non-verbal messages) supports ability to persuade, motivate	Influence: strong personalities / voices can prevent others being heard
Sensitivity: interactivity and personal nature (voice, non-verbals) allows for sensitive handling of difficult messages	Technical noise: potential for interference (for example, from noise, bad phone lines)

4.2 Face-to-face communication

Face-to-face communication is particularly effective in:

(a) Allowing non-verbal cues, both audible (for example, tone of voice) and visual (body language), to be used to enhance understanding and persuasion

(b) Allowing immediate exchange and feedback

(c) Humanising the context of communication by opening the parties to each other's direct scrutiny and to personal factors

The advantages and their applications can be summarised as follows.

Table 7.4 Advantages and disadvantages of face-to-face communication

Advantages	Disadvantages
Encourages ideas generation: participants encouraging and prompting each other	Brainstorming meeting for promotion planning or customer care improvement
Encourages problem solving and conflict resolution: allows exchange and supportive communication, sensitivity to personal factors	Customer complaint handling, or employee counselling
Improves decision-making: adds different viewpoints and information in real time	Team meetings to decide strategies or allocate roles
Facilitates persuasion: use of personal charisma, logic, adjustment to feedback	Sales negotiations, pitching ideas to internal / external clients
Encourages co-operation: information sharing, participation	Team meetings
Shows the human face of an organisation, and encourages identification with it	Personal customer service

4.3 Non-verbal communication

> ▸ **Key term**
>
> **Non-verbal communication** is basically anything that conveys a message without using words or symbols. There are three forms of non-verbal communication:
>
> - Kinetics eg body language such as facial expressions, gestures, movement
> - Meta-communications eg the importance of silences, pauses in conversation for effect, slamming a door
> - Paralanguage eg tone of voice

Non-verbal communication may be linked to words (for example, a tone of voice), or it may be independent of any verbal message. Information is perceived by all the senses: tastes and smells and movements convey messages. Think what you can convey through, for example, frowning or smiling, nodding, scratching your head, putting your head in your hands, slamming a door, turning your back, screaming, being silent, keeping your office door open or closed, slouching or sitting up straight, dressing casually or turning up late to a formal meeting.

All these examples have aspects in common.

(a) They convey a message from or about the person 'doing' them.

(b) They are the kind of things done by everybody all the time: every action (or non-action) and every communication (or non-communication) conveys or adds a non-verbal message. (Remember: you cannot NOT communicate).

(c) The message conveyed is not consistent from culture to culture, person to person, or in one person over time. A nod, for example may mean agreement, non-agreement (as in India, where a shake of the head means agreement), a friendly greeting, an unfriendly greeting (if you expected a handshake or hug, say), an instruction to sit or move in the direction indicated, the easing of a stiff neck, and so on. We depend on context, expectation, perception and attitude to interpret the message – and frequently get it wrong! (If someone has her arms folded across her chest, this is not necessarily defensiveness: she may just be cold!)

(d) They may or may not be conscious or intentional. In general, we are much more aware of other people's gestures and tone of voice, and sensitive to possible meanings in them (even if we misinterpret them), than we are of the things we are doing ourselves, and the signals they convey.

(e) They may reinforce or contradict a verbal message. The words 'I'd love to stay for dinner', for example, would be reinforced by a smile, warm tone of voice, or arm around the shoulders: they would be undermined by a worried look, glance at the watch, or getting up and heading for the door.

4.3.1 Taking control of non-verbal communication

Non-verbal communication can be controlled (by the sender) and interpreted (by the receiver) to add depth and accuracy to the communication process.

You can see what a complex and involved process non-verbal communication is, and the extent of misunderstanding or misinterpretation that can occur. What can be done about this? Non-verbal communication can be controlled and used fruitfully to:

Table 7.5 Effects of controlling non-verbal communication

Effect of controlling NVC
Provide appropriate 'physical' feedback to the sender of a message (a yawn, applause, clenched fists, fidgeting)
Create a desired impression (smart dress, a smile, punctuality, a firm handshake)
Establish a desired atmosphere or conditions (a friendly smile, informal dress, attentive posture, a respectful distance)
Reinforce our spoken messages with appropriate indications of how our interest, seriousness and feelings are engaged (an emphatic gesture, sparkling eyes, a disapproving frown)

If we can learn to recognise non-verbal messages given by others, it has the benefits outlined in the table below.

Table 7.6 Additional value of non-verbal communication

Additional value of NVC
Receive non-verbal feedback from a listener and modify the message accordingly
Recognise people's real feelings when their words are constrained by formal courtesies (an excited look, a nervous tic, close affectionate proximity)
Recognise existing or potential personal problems (the angry silence, the indifferent shrug, absenteeism or lateness at work, refusal to look someone in the eye)
'Read' situations in order to modify our own communication and response strategy. Is the potential customer convinced? (Go ahead.) Is the complaining customer on the point of hysteria? (Be soothing.)

4.4 Body language

Kinetics or body language include: facial expression, eye contact, gestures, posture and personal appearance.

4.4.1 Eye contact

Eye contact – the meeting of the other person's gaze – signals interest in the West. Intermittent eye contact is usual in interpersonal communication: less might indicate disinterest or avoidance, while more implies a desire for intimacy (which may or may not be desirable to both parties and is particularly intrusive in Eastern cultures). People also tend to look away if they are thinking, or planning their message: they make contact when communicating directly, or seeking feedback. Excessive eye movement is often interpreted as avoidance, distraction or nervousness.

In a business context, avoiding eye contact can convey disinterest or shiftiness but making positive eye contact while you are delivering a presentation shows that you are relating to and connecting with your audience.

Therefore, in order for the message you are conveying to be taken as 'trustful', it is important that eye contact be maintained. In two-way communication, the fact that someone cannot meet your gaze may mean they are uncomfortable with what you are saying and you may wish to change the message content in light of this.

4.4.2 Facial expression

The eyebrows, nose, lips and mouth, jaw, musculature, skin colour and movement all contribute to the expression on someone's face. Some of these things can be controlled, making facial expression in isolation an unreliable guide to true feelings – especially since different races and cultures have different facial characteristics which make unfamiliar expressions hard to 'read'. Your facial expression and coloration can convey various meanings. A flushed face can indicate embarrassment or shyness, while the colour draining out of your face can indicate shock. Pursed lips can reveal your irritation at something, a frown can show disapproval and a smile can indicate happiness, approval or a welcome.

The expression must be appropriate to the situation. People working closely with customers are often told to 'keep smiling'. However, if the customer is in the process of making a serious complaint, a fixed smile will only infuriate them further.

4.4.3 Gestures

People make gestures unconsciously: jabbing a finger in the air for emphasis, or tapping the fingers when impatient. They also make conscious gestures (and not only impolite ones): finger against the lips for silence, jerk of the head to indicate a direction, shrug to indicate indifference. Like any other form of non-verbal communication, there is a wide variety of possible interpretations of any given gesture. Some gestures take on an 'agreed' common meaning within a culture, but you should bear in mind that these meanings can be lost or changed – like words – and that other cultures may not share them. Indeed, some cultures use gestures more or less than others: a level of gesticulation that would seem natural to an Italian, for example, might suggest impending nervous breakdown to a native American.

4.4.4 Posture

Posture is positioning. It includes conscious or unconscious decisions about whether you sit, stand, walk or lie down, and how: lounging, hunching and sitting up straight, for example, may convey relaxation, negativity or alertness respectively.

If you adopt an upright posture, it can show that you are attentive and the opposite can show that you are disinterested. If you were lounging in your seat when your managing director walks past, it could indicate that you do not respect the individual and you are probably not working hard either.

It is important to adopt an open posture when dealing with customers, folded arms will put people off whereas leaning towards them will indicate listening. Other postures and gestures can be used to send out non-verbal messages – consider how you would feel if the person you are speaking to started drumming their fingers.

We now know from a series of studies on human and animal behaviour that we tend to mirror the body language of the person we are communicating with if we feel empathy with that person and their point of view.

4.4.5 Physical space

Physical space also refers to the invisible line that surrounds people and is referred to as personal space. By breaching someone's personal space you can intimidate him or her and be perceived as overbearing and insensitive.

An accepted move into someone's physical space in Britain is the friendly handshake. In Europe and other countries, kissing on the cheek may be acceptable. Different countries and cultures have different norms. In China, the size of acceptable physical space is much smaller than in Britain because their population density is much greater.

Physical space can also be about how people are seated while communicating. Sitting on a big chair behind a big desk so that people who enter your office have to sit on a lower chair opposite you, with the desk as a barrier, can communicate your authority and the level of formality you expect from others. Alternatively, you can achieve informality in meetings by using a horseshoe-shape layout.

4.5 Paralanguage

This is not 'what is said', but 'the way that it is said'. For example, the speaker's tone of voice (is he angry or relaxed) or the way emphasis is placed on particular words or parts of a statement.

Interpersonal communication studies indicate that the non-content or non-verbal aspects of a message are at least as important as the actual content. While verbal statements can convey states of being, listeners use paralinguistic cues, such as vocal pitch, loudness or amplitude, pitch variation, pauses, and fluency, to perceive the exact state of being.

For example, a communicator might use a verbal statement to convey confidence (eg 'I am positively sure that...'), but listeners will consciously and unconsciously interpret the paralanguage to assess the communicator's degree of confidence. It is also known that, in any situation where people meet for the first time, listeners pay more attention to the paralanguage of a conversation, than they do to the actual content.

In service situations where it is appropriate (and perhaps even expected) for service providers to be particularly kind, warm, and friendly (eg in health and beautycare, hotel, restaurant, transportation, and counselling services), service providers need to use more paralinguistic cues associated with a conversational style. Such cues are likely to facilitate employees to portray an image that they are people-oriented rather than task-oriented. On the other hand, in service situations where consumers are likely to expect the provider to be more business- or task-oriented, (eg in the financial, legal, and advertising fields), service providers might place more weight on using a public speaking style. For example, an attorney who wants to present a competent and yet friendly image might use a public speaking style to portray competence and dynamism – but also the kinesic non-verbal cues of nodding, frequent eye contact, and occasional smiling to convey warmth and friendliness.

4.6 Meta-communications

This is 'communications about communications', or the feelings and emotions exchanged between participants to a conversation about how well (or badly) that communication is going. According to Shimojima *et al*. (1997):

There are two different kinds of communications going on in a human conversation:

(a) Base-communications, namely, exchanges of information about the topic situation of a dialogue, and

(b) Meta-communications, namely, exchanges of information about the progress of the conversation itself. Meta-communications can be done by verbal means (texts, rhythms, pitches, powers, and speeds of speech) and non-verbal means (gestures, gesticulations, gaze directions, and inhalations), and they are often unintentional. Nevertheless, meta-communications play crucial roles in our joint-managements of conversation, for, without them, we cannot share the information about the progress of base-communications, problems occurring in them, turn exchanges, topic changes, and background knowledge of each participant.

ACTIVITY 7.3

If you have access to video recording, perhaps by means of a mobile phone, record a conversation between two of your friends. Analyse the conversation for evidence of kinesics, paralanguage and meta-communications.

5 Promotional activities

Having identified the various segments that 'customers' can fall into, we have to consider the best methods of communicating with those groups. We must also realise that as ICT developments, such as e-mail and mobile phones, have made communication cheaper, faster and more frequent, customers are expecting to establish a dialogue as part of the buying decision-making process, to ensure the planned purchase will meet their needs.

To communicate with external customers, organisations use a range of activities that can be described as the external communications mix. These activities range from advertising, direct marketing and selling to public relations and the creation of a strong corporate identity. These activities are used to create brands, to inform customers about product improvements and to promote sales, and because most organisations are not interested in a one-off sale, communications are used to build an ongoing relationship with the customer.

When combining the promotional tools to produce a customised communications package which meets the needs of our own organisation, it is important to consider how each of the tools used will complement and support each other in achieving the organisation's promotional objectives.

5.1 Sales promotions

> **Key term**
>
> **Sales promotion** is a short-term tactical marketing tool that gives customers additional reasons or incentives to purchase (CIM)

Sales promotion activity is aimed at the customer (intermediary or consumer) market, typically in order to increase short-term sales volume, by encouraging first time, repeat or multiple purchase within a stated time frame ('offer closes on such-and-such a date'). It seeks to do this by adding value to the product or service: customers are offered something extra – or the chance to obtain something extra – if they purchase, purchase more or purchase again.

Sales promotions can be used as a dual-purpose tool by targeting two different customer groups. Consumer promotions to encourage consumers to go and buy, these are referred to as pull strategies because the customer by demanding the product is pulling it through the distribution chain. Trade promotions targeting the intermediaries in the distribution chain are used to encourage the intermediaries (often wholesalers or retailers) to stock or recommend the product. This is known as a push strategy as the organisation seeks to push the product through the chain towards the end-user. By using a combination of push and pull it should be possible to have the product in store at the precise moment the customer demands it.

The objectives of sales promotion, stated in broad terms, may be:

(a) To increase awareness and interest among target audiences: the incentive or added value element may increase engagement, and competition-style promotions may require customers to research the product to provide answers, say

(b) To motivate customers to try a product or switch from competing brands

(c) To smooth seasonal fluctuations in demand, via incentives to purchase in off-peak periods, say

(d) To foster customer retention, by encouraging repeat or multiple purchase; offering opportunities to try related products (supporting cross-selling); and capturing customer data (supporting relationship marketing)

Consumer sales promotion techniques include:

(a) Price promotions: eg discounted selling price or additional product on current purchase, or coupons (on packs or advertisements) offering discounts on next purchase

(b) 'Gift with purchase' or 'premium' promotions: the consumer receives a bonus, gift or refund on purchase or repeat purchase, or on sending in tokens or proofs of multiple purchases

(c) Competitions and prizes: eg entry in prize draws or 'lucky purchase' prizes, often used both to stimulate purchase (more chances to win) and to capture customer data

(d) Frequent user (loyalty) incentives: eg air miles programmes or points-for-prizes reward cards

Trade promotions are directed at trade customers (intermediaries), to encourage them to stock or sell more of a product or service (sometimes called a 'push' marketing strategy). Techniques include:

(a) Monetary incentives such as increased trade discounts, extended credit or 'baker's dozen' packs (13 items / packs for the price of 12)

(b) Collaborative advertising and promotion: sharing costs with the dealer or retailer to promote both the brand and the stockist

(c) Point-of-sale support: supplying display materials, information and merchandising

(d) Competitions and awards for the most successful dealers or sales people

(e) Business gifts: linked to sales or purely relational (eg diaries, calendars and other Christmas gifts – although these may be subject to ethical guidelines)

(f) Consumer promotions demonstrating an aggressive 'pull' strategy which offers the intermediary good sales

Sales promotion is limited in its scope, aims and target audiences (intermediary and consumer customers). For these uses, its advantages and disadvantages can be summarised as follows.

Table 7.7 Advantages and disadvantages of sales promotions

Advantages	Disadvantages
Short-term measurable boost in sales	May pose fulfilment challenges (if over-subscribed)
Push tactic to gain distributor and POS support	May suggest incentive required for purchase to be worthwhile
Flexible for collaborative promotions and creative synergy	Does not necessarily create brand loyalty (if consumers switch from promotion to promotion)
Potential source of customer data (eg through competition entry)	Product given away or discounted: impact on bottom line profit

Sales promotions have great value in relationship management, if used wisely. Consumer promotions may trigger the first step in the relationship – a customer switching to 'our' brand. Many of the sales promotion tools also concentrate on encouraging loyalty – a key component of relationship management.

Similarly, trade promotions are used at every stage of the supplier-customer relationship.

Once again, they can encourage switching or loyalty. Sales promotions are used widely in modern supply-chain management approaches, where organisations form long-term relationships for mutual benefit.

5.2 Public relations

Key term

Public relations is 'the planned and sustained effort to establish and maintain goodwill and mutual understanding between an organisation and its publics' (Institute of Public Relations)

Public relations are essentially concerned with developing a corporate personality that communicates the general philosophies of that organisation to its publics. PR activities therefore fall into three main categories:

1 Development of the corporate image – the face of the company
2 Communication of that image and all that falls within it
3 Specific related activities where the image is used

The spectrum of public relations is increasing all the time in an era where there is little discernible difference between products and services. It is often the customer's perception of the corporate personality which PR seeks to create that offers the differentiation point.

Public relations can convey greater credibility than an advertising message as it is perceived to have originated from a more independent source. The credibility of the newspaper that is reporting on the organisation will be considered rather than the organisation itself.

The scope of PR is very broad, but some frequently used techniques are as follows.

Table 7.8 Widely-used PR techniques

Consumer marketing support	▪ Publicity: generating editorial coverage in the press ▪ Consumer and trade press releases (to secure coverage) ▪ Sending product samples for media (or consumer) trial and review ▪ Product placement (in TV, movies) ▪ Product / service literature (including brochures, video and CD-ROM) ▪ Special events (eg celebrity store openings, product launch events, in-store competitions) ▪ Consumer exhibitions and shows ▪ Customer magazines, e-zines, newsletters, blogs ▪ Sport, arts and community sponsorship ▪ Publicity 'stunts' (attention-grabbing events to gain media coverage)
B2B communication	▪ Corporate identity (logos, liveries, house style of communications) ▪ Corporate literature, website, videos ▪ Trade exhibitions and conferences ▪ Trade and general press relations ▪ Corporate hospitality and gifts
Internal/employee communication	▪ In-house magazines, employee newsletters and corporate intranet (internal-access website) ▪ Recruitment exhibitions and conferences ▪ Direct employee communications: briefings, consultation meetings, works councils and so on
Corporate, external and public affairs	▪ Corporate literature and website ▪ Corporate social responsibility and community involvement programmes: liaison with pressure groups, community representatives, local chambers of commerce ▪ Sponsorship of arts, sporting and community organisations and events (often as part of a CSR profile) ▪ Media relations: networking and image management through trade, local, national (and possibly international) press ▪ Offering spokespeople and 'experts' for media interviews, consultation or authorship of articles ▪ Local / central government and industry/trade lobbying, to protect or promote corporate / industry interests ▪ Crisis and issues management: minimising the negative impacts of problems and bad publicity by managing media and public relations
Financial public relations	▪ Financial media relations ▪ Design of annual and interim financial reports for shareholders ▪ Facility visits for analysts, brokers, fund managers etc ▪ Shareholder meetings and communications

The advantages and disadvantages of PR as a promotional tool can be summarised as follows.

Table 7.9 Advantages and disadvantages of PR as a promotional tool

Advantages	Disadvantages
Raises awareness of wider audiences	The organisation can't control editorial content or guarantee coverage when desired (unlike advertising)
Builds corporate identity, supporting relationship with stakeholders (internal and external)	Media have their own agenda (circulation / ratings, public information) which may not always support positive publicity for the organisation
Relatively low cost (no media costs)	Difficult to measure effectiveness / impact
Can add legitimacy (implication of endorsement or recommendation), word-of-mouth promotion and goodwill (support in times of difficulty)	There is a risk of poor publicity and negative associations – as well as positive ones. (Yes, there is such a thing as bad publicity!)
Supports advertising, sales promotion and personal selling	

Public relations often suffers the same drawbacks in relationship management as advertising – much PR activity is aimed at a broad market, rather than individual customers.

5.3 Digital and web-based technologies

Technological developments in communications are making massive changes to our personal and working lives. They are changing the way we shop, find out information, communicate with others inside and outside our organisation; they are affecting the way organisations promote their products and services and how they do business with suppliers and distributors.

The introduction of computers has transformed the way information is handled and communicated.

Data in a digital format means that when a document is typed any mistakes can be quickly corrected before it is printed out and information such as invoices, forms and previous letters can be indexed and retrieved easily.

Electronic point of sale (EPOS) systems allow retailers to record and monitor sales data.

Linked to 'smart' card purchases, EPOS data provides organisations with detailed profiles of customer preferences and purchasing habits. Databases can be used to store information about customer purchase history so that mail-merged documents can be sent to customers with offers tailored to their needs.

Even the way you use the telephone has changed. Mobile telephones mean you can be constantly in touch with colleagues and customers even when you are away from the office.

People can leave voice mail and fax messages at any time, without having to rely on others to take the information down correctly. Businesses can deal speedily with massive telephone response through voice mail and automated processes.

We are now seeing the general use of videophone technology combined with mobile phones, which will change the way you communicate on the telephone, because your body language and facial expressions can be observed.

Internet technology can be used strategically to enable communication with particular audiences.

- The internet itself enables public access to an organisation's website.
- An **intranet** refers to a private internal network which is normally used to enable communication with employees.
- **Extranets** allow particular external audiences such as distributors, suppliers and certain customers access to an organisation's facilities.

The internet offers two main marketing opportunities, namely distribution and communication. The ability to reach customers directly and so avoid many channel intermediaries reduces transaction costs and is a prime goal for most organisations.

The use of the internet as a communications medium is equally attractive. It is more than a medium as it facilitates interactivity and a two-way dialogue that no other method of communication can support. Unlike other forms of communication, dialogue is induced by the customer, the speed and duration of the communication is customer controlled and the intensity of the relationship (with the online brand), is again customer managed. All the traditional tools of the promotional mix can be deployed over the internet, with varying degrees of success. E-mail campaigns and e-newsletters are cost effective means of communicating with stakeholders who have expressed an interest in receiving these communications.

(a) Interactive catalogues and newsletters can be emailed, downloaded or viewed on-line, to convey information to target audiences on topics of interest to them (new products, industry developments, exhibitions, sales promotions, training opportunities for employees and so on) with links to related website pages if stakeholders want to follow up on particular items. These approaches allow complex data to be made available to stakeholders, with the element of choice reinforcing their interest and motivation at the follow-up stage.

(b) SMS text messaging is a huge advertising growth area, and the integration of digital mobile phone networks with the internet has also facilitated a range of m-commerce (mobile commerce) applications. SMS is low-cost, easy-to-use and highly personal and compelling (especially in the always-connected youth market). It is used for relational marketing by brands including Cadbury, Smirnoff, Avon, British Airways, Nestlé, Pepsi, Häagen-Dazs and even Liverpool FC.

(c) Web advertising. The internet is a major advertising medium, through dedicated corporate and brand websites; pop-up and banner / button advertising (giving a click-through link to a website); and ranking on internet search engines (to increase site exposure). The forecast global penetration of the internet over the next few years would give it a significantly larger (international, 24/7) audience than any of the TV networks, print media outlets or other advertising vehicles. Studies have shown that brand awareness increases some five per cent after using banner advertising. The other plus point for web advertising is the ability to monitor traffic, gathering information on users' interests and browsing habits, and placing 'cookies' on their computers to enable customisation of future contacts.

The internet, like other web-based media, is a powerful relationship management tool. All methods and media allow us to be very targeted or quite general in our target, dependent upon the linked site or portal chosen to carry the advertising. Content can be personalised, so each user receives information and messages that are relevant to them specifically. All uses are very measurable in that we are able to monitor the degree of 'click through'. A high level of interaction can also be built in to engage the viewer, and the content is flexible and can be updated regularly – at a cost.

5.4 Intranet / extranet

An intranet is an information system that is used to communicate internally within an organisation.

This allows all employees within an organisation, regardless of how many sites they are located at or the geographical location of those sites, to communicate almost instantaneously. This effectively negates the need for memos as we highlighted earlier, but also allows for electronic transfer of any electronically held information such as reports, letters and data to be transmitted as attachments. The organisational address book allows users to select by name without putting in the whole e-mail address.

An extranet extends the intranet capacity to suppliers and distributors. Along with other approaches detailed in this chapter, this can replace time-consuming and costly invoice raising and sending out cheques, by fully automating these processes alongside many others.

Different media forms can be accommodated with photographs, videos and artwork being transferable.

Intranets and extranets are powerful tools in relationship management, as they are only open to current relationship 'partners'. Like all digital media, the content viewed can be tailored or personalised by means of cookies (packets of data identifying the user) so each viewer receives a personal communication.

5.5 Personal selling

If the organisation relies on consumer advertising to draw customers into stores to ask for its brands, the role of the salesforce may primarily be servicing: ensuring that retailers carry sufficient stock, negotiating adequate shelf space and so on. In high-value consumer goods or services' markets (such as car or insurance sales), where personal information and persuasion may be required to close the sale, the selling role may be paramount. In business-to-business (B2B) markets, the relationship between client and sales representative (or account handler) is more complex, important and on-going.

Personal selling is part of the co-ordinated promotional mix. It will need to be supported by a range of other marketing communication activities:

(a) **Product advertising**, public relations and sales promotion, drawing consumer attention and interest to the product and its sources and motivating retailers to stock and sell the product

(b) **'Leads'** (interested prospective customers) generated by contacts and enquiries made through exhibitions, promotional competitions, enquiry coupons and other methods

(c) **Informational tools** such as brochures and presentation kits. These can add interest and variety to sales presentations, and leave customers with helpful reminders and information

(d) **Sales support information:** customer / segment profiling; competitor intelligence; access to customer contact / transaction histories and product data and so on. (This is an important aspect of customer relationship management, enabling field sales teams to facilitate immediate response and transactions – without time-lags to obtain the information required.)

Personal selling is an effective tool for relationship development, since it deepens personal contacts between individual sellers and buyers. It is highly interactive and flexible, enabling the salesperson to customise the message to the audience's immediate and individual interests, needs and concerns. The two-way nature of the process allows dialogue, question-and-answer and feedback. Personal selling enables more of a collaborative approach to defining and creating customer value, and is therefore most appropriate for high-value consumer purchases, and for B2B relationships.

The main disadvantage is that this is labour intensive, and therefore costly. A salesperson can only interact with one customer at a time. The organisation will have to make a value judgement between the effectiveness of relationship development and persuasion – and the relative expense.

Personal selling is often appropriate in B2B markets, where there are fewer, higher-value customers who are looking for a more complex total offering tailored to a more specific set of requirements. Personal selling allows a partnership relationship to be established which:

- Adds value by allowing customer needs to be met more flexibly;
- Allows salesforce effort to be targeted at high-return relationships; and
- Reinforces the 'inertia' of industrial markets, making it hard for buyers to switch suppliers, and creating loyalty and inter-dependency over time.

It should also be noted that although 'selling' will not be relevant to all stakeholder relationships, there may be elements of negotiation and / or persuasion involved in forming relationships and exercising influence in relation to non-customer stakeholder groups. A one-to-one discussion approach, similar to personal selling, may be used for:

- Clarification and discussion of issues eg with representatives of pressure groups
- Supplier relationships: eg negotiation of requirements and terms, contract and relationship management, or dispute resolution. (This is really personal selling seen from the customer's side.)
- Internal marketing: eg one-to-one interviews with employees or their representatives, for motivation, consultation, briefings, change management, conflict resolution and so on

5.6 Advertising

When combining the promotional tools to produce a customised communications package which meets the needs of our own organisation, it is important to consider how each of the tools used will complement and support each other in achieving the organisation's promotional objectives. Some methods more naturally slot into the role of primary media, enabling mass communication and building awareness on a large scale. These tend to be above-the-line media. The promotional toolbox contains the following above-the-line media.

- Television
- Press
- Radio
- Outdoor
- Cinema
- Internet
- Branding.

Much of the inter-media decisions taken will depend not only on the budget available but also the media characteristics that the brand/service requires in order that it be communicated in the best possible way. In looking at each of the following media we must also consider their ability to communicate:

- At a visual level;
- At an audio level; and
- At the right level of detail.

While advertising is commonly used, it is relatively ineffective in the context of relationship management. Advertising tends to be an impersonal tool, whereas relationships are individual. While advertising has the potential to reach very large target markets, relationship management concentrates on one-to-one communication.

6 Direct marketing

Direct marketing encompasses a wide range of media and distribution opportunities.

- Television
- Radio
- Direct mail
- Direct response advertising
- Telemarketing
- Statement stuffers
- Inserts
- Take-ones
- Electronic media
- Door to door
- Mail order
- Computerised home shopping
- Home shopping networks

In developing a comprehensive direct marketing strategy, organisations will often utilise a range of different yet complementary techniques.

Direct mail tends to be the main medium of direct response advertising. It has become the synonym for it. The reasons for this is that other major media, newspapers and magazines, are familiar to people in advertising in other contexts. Newspaper ads can include coupons to fill out and return, and radio and TV can give a phone number to ring (DRTV is now very common). However, direct mail has a number of strengths as a direct response medium.

- The advertiser can target down to individual level.
- The communication can be personalised. Known data about the individual can be used, while modern printing techniques mean that parts of a letter can be altered to accommodate this.
- The medium is good for reinforcing interest stimulated by other media such as TV. It can supply the response mechanism (a coupon) that is not yet available in that medium.
- The opportunity to use different creative formats is almost unlimited.
- Testing potential is sophisticated: a limited number of items can be sent out to a 'test' cell and the results can be evaluated. As success is achieved, so the mailing campaign can be rolled out.

The cornerstone upon which the direct mailing is based, however, is the mailing list. It is far and away the most important element in the list of variables, which also include the offer, timing and creative content.

A comprehensive customer database is an essential element to direct marketing because it is an efficient means of maintaining a mailing list with the most up to date information about specific customers. A database is a collection of available information on past and current customers together with future prospects, structured to allow for the implementation of effective marketing strategies. Database marketing is a customer-oriented approach to marketing, and its special power lies in the techniques it uses to harness the capabilities of computer and telecommunications technology. Building accurate and up-to-date profiles of existing customers enables the company to:

- Extend help to a company's target audience
- Stimulate further demand
- Stay close to them: recording and keeping an electronic database memory of customers and prospects and of all communications and commercial contacts helps to improve all future contacts

THE REAL WORLD

From mass marketing to mass customisation

The ability to capture data on a huge scale and to analyse it quickly and cost effectively has changed the face of marketing irrevocably. Companies are now able to store thousands of data about individual customer transactions, building up profiles and reinforcing relationships that was not possible previously on a mass scale. This process has been called mass customisation and companies are starting to use it to their competitive advantage: Levi Strauss for example now record customer statistics to produce jeans tailored to exact body measurements. At Ritz hotels customer preferences are recorded so that if you ask for an extra pillow at their hotel in Paris, you will almost certainly be asked if you would like one when you arrive in Naples.

6.1 E-mail and e-newsletters

E-mail can be used in the same way as direct mail with the communication adapted to be screen size and easy to print off. Attachments or hyperlinks to websites can further enhance the message although after many virus scares concerning unsolicited attachments, consumers are choosing to delete 'Spam' in droves without even opening the e-mail. However, the significant cost and time benefits of e-mail over postal methods especially on a global scale will continue to secure its future use.

6.2 Web pages

Other methods are not personalised and rely on the message recipient responding to the initial communication. Technology has widened the scope of the messages that can be sent. Mail order used to be totally dependent upon the postal and telephone system, now mail order is changing significantly with the use of websites and online ordering (e-commerce). The inclusion of website addresses on all forms of communication is encouraging people to contact the organisation for either more information or to order the product. For these methods to work, websites must be kept up to date and relevant. Ease of use and navigation is also important online. Security and speed of fulfilment are important when ordering online.

6.3 Interactive TV

Direct response TV gives the customer two ways of communicating with the organisation. Digital viewers can use the 'Red Button' option if advertisers in-build this function into their television advertising. Renault used this with the launch of the re-styled Megane. The red button led the viewer to more detailed information, lists of local dealers and an invitation to test drive. Non-digital viewers are offered a telephone hotline number to gain more information.

6.4 Leaflets and direct marketing

Direct mail can be a powerful communication tool but where it is sent indiscriminately it can irritate people and be judged as 'junk mail'. Wastage can be reduced if the mail shots are targeted at the right people. For example, it is very annoying for existing customers to be sent details of an 'introductory' offer that they cannot take up because they are not a new customer.

Although the style of a letter is personal there are some techniques that you can use when writing direct mail letters:

(a) Say what you mean clearly – be clear what your key message is.

(b) Sound enthusiastic – if you are writing with an offer, make it sound worth taking up.

(c) Write personally – where possible use computer software that enables you to personalise letters with names and even inserting the address or a reference to the customer's current product package in the text of the letter. So, for example, a breakdown recovery service could write to its existing customers and in the text of the letter say, 'Now Mrs Wood, if your car wouldn't start outside 10 Acacia Avenue, wouldn't it be convenient if you had the 'home start' service added to your current breakdown cover?'

(d) Questions can be used to good effect when you are trying to get your recipients to desire or want your product or service.

(e) You can go into detail in a direct mail letter in a way that you cannot in an advertisement.

(f) In most circumstances you should use a friendly tone – but it does depend on the situation. So, if you were writing about a critical illness cover, your tone would be more serious.

If you want a response or some form of action from the recipient, make it very clear what it is; perhaps mention it more than once. The P.S. at the end of a direct mail letter can be used to good effect to remind the customer what they need to do and by when. For example, you could say 'P.S. Don't forget that if you want the two free books when you join our book club you need to complete the attached post card and return it before 31 May...'.

6.5 Tele-messaging

Telemarketing is becoming a less acceptable way of communicating with customers, as the misuse of this medium by certain product categories (eg double-glazing) has led to customers feeling intruded upon and response rates are minimal. Legislation has led to this practice being illegal during certain times of the day. The continued misuse can only mean that reputable organisations should avoid this method and use others such as email or mail shots.

6.6 Digital messaging

Text messaging is most widely used by airtime providers to try to get their customers to utilise more-paid-for services (such as latest football scores). It is probably the most immediate personalised method of direct mail, especially to the ever-evasive youth market.

The issue at present is that this form of communication is seen as intrusive, and more creative ways of producing tailor-made messages are required for the consumer to see the benefit.

7 Customer databases and tactical marketing

To communicate with customers effectively, we need to know who they are, what needs the products or services are required to meet, where they are located and the most cost-effective methods of communicating with them. In the next chapter we will look at the detailed content and use of customer databases.

7.1 Internal market

We all keep a database of internal customers, whether we intend to or not. Most e-mail systems (such as Microsoft's Outlook) allow us to access address books or contact lists, and these can be used to build mailing lists for internal direct marketing. Most users, however, do not use these tools to their full capabilities. A typical address book function will store details of name, job title, physical address, e-mail address, department, location and much more. This information can be used to build distribution lists of potential e-mail recipients that share common characteristics, such as 'all managers', 'all head office staff' and so on.

A corporate intranet can also be used to target direct marketing in the same way as any website. Staff can be sent RSS feeds, summaries of information with links should they wish to find out more, based on their stated interests or even on their historic viewing profiles.

In this way, recipients should only be mailed about things they are interested in, and should receive less internal junk mail.

7.2 External market

Communicating with external customers and prospects is more important, and more complex, than with internal customers. We need to know who these individuals or organisations are, and much more. A database of external customers is not something that should be trusted to an individual employee in any but the smallest organisation. It would be too easy, for example, for two employees to send the same customer conflicting or confusing communications, or even to overload them with direct marketing messages. As we shall see in the next chapter, an organisation needs a structured and controlled approach to the management of both a customer database and customer communications.

7.3 Connected stakeholders

There are big ethical and legal issues related to passing customer data to third parties. However, an organisation can extract certain data, or summarise it, and pass this anonymous data to other interested parties. For example, a retailer might analyse the buying patterns of customers and pass this data to its suppliers so they can make changes or improvements to their products. Similarly, an organisation supplying financial services might realise that customers need a particular service that is outside the organisation's area of expertise. This information could be 'sold' to a third party organisation in return for commission on any resultant sales to the target market.

8 Managing a communications budget

8.1 Establishing a budget

A budget is a consolidated statement of the resources required to achieve desired objectives, or to implement planned activities. It is a planning and control tool relevant to all aspects of management activities. A forecast is an estimate of what might happen in the future.

In terms of measuring marketing effectiveness, budgeted results often comprise:

- Targets for the overall financial objectives and other strategy objectives such as productivity targets
- Subsidiary financial targets, including the sales budget and marketing expenditure budget
- Product-market strategy targets
- Targets for each element of the marketing mix

Analysis of marketing costs can be a highly detailed process and it may be difficult to allocate costs to specific marketing activities (especially staff costs, when staff may be working on several different areas at the same time). It is, however, important that for the purposes of avoiding escalating marketing spend a careful check of actual spend against budget is kept. Generally, marketers use simple Microsoft Excel spreadsheets for such purposes with the budget split into specific marketing activities.

There are several methods of setting the communications budget that have been identified.

Table 7.10 Methods for setting a communications budget

Competitive parity	Fixing promotional expenditure in relation to the expenditure incurred by competitors. (This is unsatisfactory because it presupposes that the competitor's decision must be a good one.)
The task method (or objective and task method)	The marketing task for the organisation is set and a promotional budget is prepared which will help to ensure that this objective is achieved. A problem occurs if the objective is achieved only by paying out more on promotion than the extra profits obtained would justify.
Communication stage models	These are based on the idea that the link between promotion and sales cannot be measured directly, but can be measured by means of intermediate stages (for example, increase in awareness, comprehension, and then intention to buy).
All you can afford	Crude and unscientific, but commonly used. The firm simply takes a view on what it thinks it can afford to spend on promotion, given that it would like to spend as much as it can.
Investment	The advertising and promotions budget can be designed around the amount felt necessary to maintain a certain brand value.
Rule-of-thumb, non-scientific methods	These include setting expenditure at a certain percentage of sales or profits.

8.2 Identifying costs

The costs of any communications activity can be broken down into two distinct types:

(a) **Direct costs** – which are those incurred as a direct consequence of the activity. These would typically include the cost of any sub-contracted services (such as agency work), any direct labour costs (that could be avoided if the activity were not undertaken), and any materials and other costs such as printing and postage.

(b) **Indirect costs** – such as overheads (heat, light, rent, depreciation etc) that are incurred in supporting the general activity of the organisation but must be recovered from the organisation's revenues. Many of these costs will be incurred whether a particular communications activity is undertaken or not, but a share of such costs should be apportioned to the activity to reflect the true cost of carrying it out.

8.3 Allocating costs

As seen above, there is a clear difference between direct and indirect costs. It is much easier to identify which communications activity has given rise to which direct costs. Individual invoices from sub-contractors can be allocated to the activity to which they relate, or split according to some pre-agreed formula if they relate to more than one activity.

Indirect costs are more difficult to allocate, and most organisations use a simple system of cost recovery to ensure that all indirect costs are allocated fairly to different activities.

The total budgeted indirect cost for the function is calculated (say, £50,000), as is the total budgeted direct cost (say £100,000). The relationship between the two levels of budgeted expenditure (1 : 2) is then used as a basis for cost recovery. If a communications activity incurs direct costs of £30,000 it is charged with £15,000 of indirect costs.

8.4 Working to budget

It is useful to pause for a moment, to consider why organisations budget for their activities.

A budget has five key roles in organisational management:

1 The budget is a target for the level of expenditure the organisation expects will not be exceeded in the period, provided the level of activity is in line with the budget assumptions.

2 The budget is a communications tool, to allow the organisation to let all relevant parties know what is expected of them.

3 The budget is a co-ordination tool, to ensure that each part of the organisation understands how their activity relates to that of other parts.

4 The budget is a control tool, so managers can tell whether activity (and the associated costs) is happening in line with the targets set.

5 The budget is an evaluation tool, so the performance of individuals and departments can be appraised to see how well (or badly) they are doing.

Working to budget is therefore important, as long as the underlying assumptions used to establish the budget are still valid. Such assumptions would include activity levels, the organisation's strategy, and external factors such as inflation or competition. Many organisations now use 'flexible budgeting', to allow the budget to be adjusted (or 'flexed') to take into account the impact of any changes from the original assumptions (such as, for example, a major customer going out of business).

8.5 Using spreadsheets

The most common software tool for budgetary control is the spreadsheet. A budgetary control spreadsheet can be prepared for an individual communications activity, a department, or the whole of the marketing function.

Typically, budgetary control spreadsheets divide the year into accounting periods, and spread the budget across these time periods against the different direct and indirect cost headings. Actual expenditure can then be shown alongside the budget for each time period (as the year progresses), and any differences or 'variances' between actual and budget highlighted. Such variances are often identified, by colour, or simply by 'sign' (ie positive or negative) as 'favourable' or 'adverse'. A favourable variance is where expenditure is less than budget, or income is higher than budget. An adverse variance is obviously the opposite.

9 Measuring the success of communications campaigns

9.1 How can success be measured?

In considering which media to use within a communications campaign one of the factors that influences our choice is 'what has worked well in the past', so it is important that we can effectively evaluate what each medium has contributed towards the overall campaign results.

Accountants and marketers have long argued about the measurability and accountability of spending what is probably the single biggest expenditure that the organisation makes.

Television is perhaps the most audited of the above-the-line tools. Day-by-day, minute-by minute audience figures tell us who is watching at any time during the 24-hour day. Digital television has introduced two-way communication, so for the first time we can actually measure the audience's response by the number of 'red buttons' clicked. The inclusion of website addresses and direct response telephone numbers has also introduced a measurable aspect into television advertising.

Overall marketing effectiveness can be difficult to measure. Audits, financial measures, targets and information gathering (such as customer feedback) can help. Where possible, performance should be measured in quantitative terms because these are less subjective and less liable to bias. The following are some possible techniques that relate to promotional measurement.

- Personal selling – Sales increases
- Public relations – Editorial coverage
- Direct marketing – Enquiries generated
- Advertising – Brand awareness
- Sales promotion – Coupons redeemed
- Exhibitions – Contacts made

9.1.1 Inquiry/response levels

To measure the response to a sales promotion campaign that used a '20p off' coupon you could set up a system with retailers to count the number of redeemed vouchers. By media coding the coupon you will know which magazine produced the most responses.

Similarly, the response rates from direct marketing campaigns should be evaluated and, if appropriate, a further check made to calculate how much response is actually converted to sales. This way the cost of a campaign can be measured against the monetary gain from sales.

9.1.2 Sales increases

It is not appropriate to only look at sales when you are measuring the success of an advertisement or a campaign because other factors in the marketing mix or the external environment could affect sales (in either a negative or a positive way). For example, if there was media coverage of a research report suggesting that chocolate improved your IQ and reduced stress at the same time as the 'Chocco' advertising campaign, then this could be the reason for a sales increase and not the effect of the advertising campaign. Or, perhaps weather conditions could affect cocoa production adversely, which could cause price rises and reduce demand for 'Chocco', no matter how effective the advertising campaign.

9.1.3 Media evaluation

Within the promotional message the evaluation has two elements to consider, the content of the message itself and how well that worked at communicating, and the efficiency of the media chosen in transmitting the message.

The message content can be evaluated either by commissioning marketing research or by looking at the accuracy in the feedback we are getting from the consumer. If they are entering retail stores asking for the product or lots of people are walking round singing our jingle, we can assume the message is getting through.

The effectiveness of the media can also be measured by marketing research but although we may be aware that awareness has risen to 80 per cent how can we judge which media helped to achieve that the most.

9.1.4 Satisfaction surveys

Good customer service is the lifeblood of any business. Although new customers are important, good customer service will help generate customer loyalty and repeat business.

With each satisfied customer a business is likely to win many more customers through recommendations. Remember, if you are not taking care of your customers, your competition will.

A customer satisfaction survey will help an organisation not only to see how effective its efforts have been, but also to identify problem areas for further action. It will also demonstrate to customers that the organisation cares and is proactively looking for ways to improve the service that it provides.

As well as obtaining valuable market research data, customer surveys are also a good way to publicise aspects of an organisation's service of which its customers may not be aware.

It is important to read through a survey from a market research view point, to check that it asks the right questions in the right way and that the feedback information will make informed decisions possible. Then, read through the survey from a marketing viewpoint, checking that each question is phrased in such a way that every opportunity has been taken to promote the business.

To benefit most from a customer survey, the organisation needs to be prepared to accept the worst. A customer satisfaction survey should be designed to highlight problems so that they can be addressed; undertaken regularly, such surveys will prevent complacency and will also give early warning on where competitors' initiatives may be losing the organisation business.

> **▸ Assessment tip**
>
> Find out what monitoring and control activities are in operation within your own organisation. Evaluate whether or not these are appropriate. How would you make improvements?

CHAPTER ROUNDUP

- The day-to-day communications of the marketer should not be viewed as something entirely separated to the formal marketing communications of the organisation.
- All good marketers follow the AIDA model. The AIDA model stands for Attention, Interest, Desire, and Action.
- Effective communication is a two-way process, perhaps best expressed as a cycle. Signals or messages are sent by the communicator and received by the other party, who sends back some form of confirmation that the message has been received and understood ('feedback').
- 'Report' is a general term and one that may suggest a wide range of formats.
- Report writing involves particular requirements for objectivity, impersonality, ease of reading, precision and appropriate formality.
- E-mails can take the role of letters, memos, notes and messages. They are less secure than they appear and also more formal than they appear.
- A memorandum is the internal equivalent of a letter: it can be used for a variety of purposes.
- Face-to-face oral media include conversations, meetings, interviews, negotiations and public addresses, presentations or briefings.
- Non-verbal communication is basically anything that conveys a message without using words or symbols.
- Sales promotion activity is aimed at the customer (intermediary or consumer) market, typically in order to increase short-term sales volume, by encouraging first time, repeat or multiple purchase within a stated time frame ('offer closes on such-and-such a date').
- Personal selling is part of the co-ordinated promotional mix.
- A budget is a consolidated statement of the resources required to achieve desired objectives, or to implement planned activities.

FURTHER READING

Chapter 9 of:

Blythe, J. (2008). *Essentials of Marketing*. 4th edition. Harlow, Prentice Hall.

Chapters 9, 10 and 11 of:

Brassington, F. and Pettitt, S. (2007). *Essentials of Marketing*. 2nd edition. Harlow, Prentice Hall.

Whole text:

Cook, S. (2011) *Customer Care Excellence*. 6th edition. London, Kogan Page.

Chapters 4 and 10 of:

Doole, I., Lancaster, P. and Lowe, R. (2005) *Understanding and Managing Customers*. Harlow, Prentice Hall.

REFERENCES

Blythe, J. (2008) *Essentials of Marketing*. 4th edition. Harlow, Prentice Hall.

Brassington, F. and Pettitt, S. (2006) *Principles of Marketing*. 4th edition. Harlow, Prentice Hall.

Cook, S. (2011) *Customer Care Excellence*. 6th edition. London, Kogan Page.

Doole, I., Lancaster, P. and Lowe, R. (2005) *Understanding and Managing Customers*. Harlow, Prentice Hall.

Harris, D. and Botten, N. (2008) *CIM Coursebook: Introduction to Marketing*. Oxford, Butterworth Heinemann.

Schramm, W. (1961) 'How communication works.' *In:* W. Schramm (ed) *The process and effects of mass communication*. Urbana, IL, University of Illinois Press.

QUICK QUIZ

1. What are the main functions of communications in marketing?
2. What does the AIDA acronym stand for?
3. Outline four business communication formats.
4. What are the different forms of non-verbal communication?
5. What are the typical objectives of sales promotion activities?
6. What is 'public relations'?
7. Outline the main strengths of direct marketing as a direct response medium.
8. What are the main methods of setting communications budget?
9. What are some possible techniques for measuring promotional activities?

Activity 7.1

Differentiate can be used in two ways, first to bring attention to a unique attribute that the product/service can offer such as the Dyson bag-less vacuum system, and second, to try to provide a point of difference between products where very little difference actually exists. For example, Daz washes whiter, Persil cares and Ariel digests stains but they all clean clothes.

Remind is often used for products in the maturity stage of the product life cycle. Well known and probably used by all at some time, people need to be reminded to use again or to use more frequently, for example Kellogg's cereals, Lemsips, Horlicks, After Eight mints and so on.

Inform is often used where the potential customers need to make an informed decision about the product/service choice they are about to make, because their personal circumstances will mean they need a slightly different product to the next person. Financial products such as pensions, insurance and mortgages fall into this category as well as mobile phones and related airtime packages.

Persuade is often used for luxury items or again products that have very little real difference between them. Think of the strap line attached to the L'Oreal range 'Because you're worth it'. Often used for chocolate and other nice things to eat, for example Mr Kipling's 'exceedingly good' cakes.

Activity 7.2

The answer will depend on the type of organisation you work for and the recent communication selected.

Activity 7.3

This is a practical exercise.

QUICK QUIZ ANSWERS

1 Creating brand awareness, motivating purchase, facilitating purchase, forming and maintaining customer relationships, forming and maintaining network relationships and forming and maintaining working relationships.

2 Awareness, interest, desire and action.

3 Letters, reports, e-mails and memos.

4 Body language (facial expression, eye contact, gestures, posture and appearance), paralanguage and meta-communications.

5 To increase awareness and interest, to motivate customers to try a product, to smooth seasonal fluctuations in demand and to foster customer retention.

6 It is the planned and sustained effort to establish and maintain goodwill and mutual understanding between an organisation and its publics.

7 The advertiser can target down to individual level, the communication can be personalised, medium is good for reinforcing interests stimulated by other media, the opportunity to use different creative formats and testing potential is sophisticated.

8 Competitive parity, task method, communication stage models, all you can afford, investment and rule of thumb.

9 Sales increases, editorial coverage, enquiries generated, brand awareness, coupons redeemed and contacts made.

CHAPTER 8

Providing effective customer service

Introduction

This chapter examines the importance of providing effective customer service for internal and external customers. The first section explores the concept of customer care and customer service and its importance in different sectors.

The second section explains the relationship between customer care, customer focus and relationship marketing. The third section describes the different stages of a customer care programme and discusses why these programmes are important to delivering a consistent level of customer service and customer support. The fourth section explains the importance of obtaining formal and informal customer feedback and identifies a range of methods for collecting information.

The fifth section describes the measures that can be used to monitor the success of customer service support activities. The sixth section explains how an understanding of information technology and databases is essential to managing customer care and customer service activities.

The final section explains the process for managing yourself in a disciplined, time orderly and customer conscious way.

Topic list

Syllabus reference

4.1	Describe the concept of customer care and customer service and its importance in different sectors including: ▪ Consumer (FMCG markets) ▪ Business-to-business markets ▪ Not-for-profit and public sector organisations
4.2	Explain the relationship between customer care, customer focus, and relationship marketing: ▪ Customer satisfaction being a marketing objective of a market oriented organisation ▪ Customer service as an element of the marketing mix ▪ The link between quality, marketing and customer service being the key to successful relationship marketing
4.3	Describe the different stages of a customer care programme and discuss why these programmes are important to delivering a consistent level of customer service and customer support: ▪ Identify customer needs and perceptions ▪ Establish a mission statement ▪ Set service level standards ▪ Establish a management process and communicate it to staff ▪ Establish a complaints system ▪ Develop control systems
4.4	Explain the importance of obtaining formal and informal customer feedback and identify a range of methods for collecting information including: ▪ Questionnaires ▪ Feedback cards ▪ Telephone surveys ▪ Suggestion boxes ▪ Online forums ▪ Informal methods ie discussions, questions at point of sale
4.5	Describe the measures that can be used to monitor the success of customer service support activities: ▪ Number of complaints ▪ Measuring / recording service standards for customer responses ▪ Level of sales growth and decline (new business from existing customers) ▪ Customer retention ▪ Existing customer data
4.6	Explain how an understanding of information technology and databases are essential to managing customer care and customer service activities: ▪ The importance of a database and its potential applications ▪ Data components that may be included within a customer / prospect database (including geographic, demographic, psychographic and buying pattern data) ▪ Ensuring the database is up to date ▪ Meeting the legal and ethical requirements regarding collection, storage and use of information

4.7	Explain the process for managing own self in a disciplined, time orderly and customer conscious way: ▪ Working to achieve your personal objectives ▪ Utilising resources effectively ▪ Completing tasks on time ▪ Seeing through what you have started and closing customer enquiries ▪ Delivering on promises ▪ Monitoring personal achievement and success

1 Customer care and customer service

1.1 What is customer care?

> **Key term**
>
> **Customer care** is 'a fundamental approach to the standards of service quality' which 'covers every aspect of a company's operations from the design of a product or service to how it is packaged, delivered and serviced' (Clutterbuck, 2001)

Customers want to feel valued by the employees they encounter. They want their questions answered in a confident and courteous way, not using jargon, and not assuming they have a high level of subject knowledge. How many times have you gone into your local electrical retailer to make a relatively simple purchase to be blinded by jargon and science when you get in there, leaving fairly hastily because you are frightened to reveal your ignorance?

What you really wanted was someone to listen to your needs and then advise you on which one of the plethora of products available will meet those needs.

Customer care aims to close the gap between customers' expectations and their experience in every aspect of the customer-supplier relationship. It is an important source of product and service differentiation, competitive advantage and customer retention and loyalty.

The term 'customer care' is often used interchangeably with 'customer service'. The latter term, however, originally had a much narrower focus on order-cycle related activities: it is only comparatively recently, with the recognition of customer focus at the strategic level, that it has been extended to cover activities throughout the organisation at pre-, during- and post-transaction stages.

1.2 Customer service

Customer service is the point of contact between the customer and the organisation at each point of the transaction process.

Ultimately, all systems will impact on the customer and so should be evaluated in order to establish how these can add to the customer experience rather than become a source of complaints.

Figure 8.1 Customer service systems

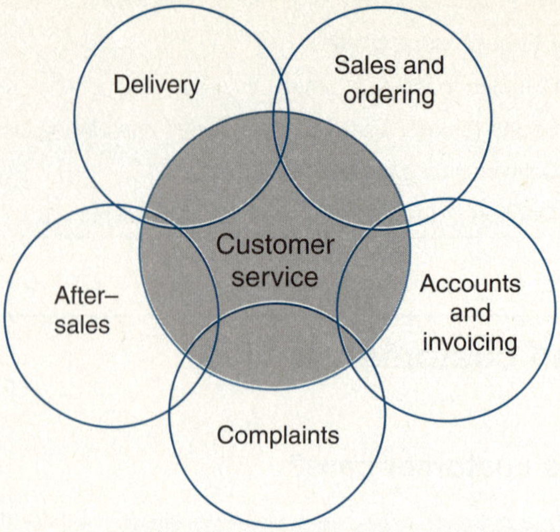

The five key areas where systems exist are as follows:

1 **Sales and ordering** – consider the speed of processing orders. Is the customer updated regularly?

2 **Accounts and invoicing** – accuracy and a variety of payment methods are key here.

Is affordable credit required?

3 **Delivery** – is delivery time specific, when the customer wants? Are the goods delivered intact?

4 **After-sales** – dealing with customer questions. How easy is it for customers to contact you?

5 **Complaints** – how easy is it to complain? Do complaints get resolved?

Staff will be able to respond effectively to customers if they follow some simple guidelines. (You might like to think of the mnemonic 'failure' to recall the following points.)

Table 8.1 'FAILURE' mnemonic for responding effectively to customers

Element	Points to consider
First contact	▪ Immediate focus of attention (even if in the middle of something: an acknowledgement of the customer's presence and a promise to attend to him or her as soon as possible) ▪ Greeting ('Good morning') ▪ Engagement in the conversation ('Can I help you?')
Attention	▪ Concentration (single focus) ▪ Eye contact (in cultures where this is a sign of attention and not, as in China – for example, – an intrusion)
Information	▪ Not leaving the customer mid-contact for any reason, without informing him or her of what you need to do and how long it will take ▪ Giving the customer the information (s)he requires, or making arrangements to do so, or offering other options
Language	▪ Avoiding technical jargon ▪ Listening for what the problem / request / query really is
Understanding	▪ Show willing ▪ Offer options, solutions, win-win approaches ▪ Look for feedback that suggests satisfaction has not yet been achieved

Element	Points to consider
Responsiveness	■ Treat each customer as a special case: every contact matters ■ Respond to the customer – not the pressure of work problems or distraction (s)he represents ■ Dialogue – not monologue
Ending	■ Confirm, sum-up, repeat back conclusions ■ Close with positive relationship-building ('Thank you')

THE REAL WORLD

Marks & Spencers

Marks & Spencers, long time favourite of the British public, fell out of favour at the Christmas gift buying season when its returns policy lagged behind the more customer focused approach of other high street retailers.

M & S's high street presence in every town reassured customers that unwanted or unsuitable goods bought as presents could be quickly and conveniently exchanged.

However, M & S dug in when items returned were being sold at a sale price; only the current sale price would be refunded for goods bought at the full cost. Customers felt cheated and sales and loyalty to this once respected high street giant declined dramatically.

Other high street retailers were using gift receipts – this bore no price on it but recorded the value of the original transaction meaning the customer could exchange goods for other goods of the same value.

1.3 Customer care and service in different sectors

The satisfaction of external customers is the result of a range of satisfying internal relationships and transactions between colleagues and departments. Encouraging staff to consider the needs of their internal customers ('the next person to handle your work') will help to foster quality and service at the interface with external customers. Key factors in managing the quality of internal service operations include:

- The recruitment of skilled customer-facing people
- The supply of appropriate (and sufficient) training
- The empowerment of staff to take decisions that will attract and keep customers
- The reward and recognition of staff who deliver outstanding service

The delivery of customer care depends on:

- Gathering, analysing, communicating and acting upon customer feedback. Feedback enables an organisation to remain customer focused and to use the customer's experiences to trigger and drive necessary changes and improvements.
- Establishing a partnership approach to relationships with customers (and suppliers) in order to identify and meet needs more effectively at all links in the value-delivery chain.
- Reinforcing customer loyalty with incentives and rewards, to show that the organisation values its 'valued customers'.
- Establishing efficient customer-friendly systems. It is no good expecting staff to give great service to customers if the systems, procedures, technology and information flows do not support their efforts.

ACTIVITY 8.1

Why do supermarkets have express checkouts?

1.3.1 Business-to-business markets

Within a B2B environment, the organisations within the supply chain expect all parties to be focused on the needs of the consumer at the end of the chain. They will expect empathy between parties with a recognition that by pulling together the consumer will benefit. There may not be so many documented processes to enable this as in a B2C environment but the end aim is the same. The inertia that characterises industrial markets may work in the supplier's favour, but in the face of increasing global competition there is no room for complacency: once lost, a customer will not easily be regained.

1.3.2 Not-for-profit markets

Schools, universities, museums and charitable and volunteer organisations still have 'customers', and operate under more or less competitive conditions. A charity, for example, may be competing for volunteer labour and funding not only with other charitable causes but with a host of other uses for people's time and money. Customer service is integral to the mission and objectives of non-profit organisations, and delivering effective customer care may be essential to building and maintaining their image, staffing, public funding and ability to attract and retain paying customers (where relevant).

1.3.3 Public sector markets

Despite traditionally operating under monopolistic or near-monopolistic conditions, the public sector is also subject to pressures for better customer care. Some activities will have to compete with the private sector (for example, in the case of local authority leisure and sports centres). They are often subject to external regulation and benchmarking, which impose standards of effectiveness and efficiency. In the UK, the public sector is going through a period of rapid change – from the old-established 'public servant' role to a more dynamic 'competitive' style in line with government policy.

2 Customer care and relationship marketing

From the organisation's point of view, customer care is all of the following.

(a) Part of the overall package of purchase benefits that its product / service offers, and therefore an important part of the marketing mix in attracting customers.

(b) A source of differentiation from competing products (particularly where globalisation has diluted the significance of product features and functionality), which may also attract customers.

(c) A mechanism of customer retention, by creating 'pull' factors and minimising 'push' factors to make it more likely that customers will stay with the brand than go elsewhere.

(d) A way of creating customer loyalty: engaging customers' emotional involvement with the brand, making them feel valued and making on-going contact from the organisation (as part of a relationship marketing strategy) more welcome.

(e) A way of maximising positive (and minimising negative) 'word of mouth' promotion by customers on the basis of their experience.

(f) A source of vital feedback information on customers' expectations and experience, to support more effective and efficient marketing in future. (We discuss this further below.)

(g) A source of employee satisfaction that enhances performance and enables the organisation to retain valuable human resources.

(h) A source of positive employer branding that enhances the organisation's ability to attract high-quality, customer-focused staff.

2.1 Customer satisfaction as an objective

Satisfying customers is at the heart of marketing. Who then assumes responsibility for this important function? Possibly the marketing department or the salesforce? True, both can have an influence on customer satisfaction, but marketing as a philosophy is wider than this narrow group of employees. Employees outside the marketing department or salesforce can also play an important role in determining customer satisfaction.

Marketing is more than just a range of techniques that enables the company to determine customer requirements; rather it is a shared business ethos. The marketing concept (as discussed earlier in this Study Text) is a philosophy that places customers central to all organisational activities. The long-term strategies of an organisation might be centred on profit maximisation, market share growth, or growth in real terms but none of this can be achieved without satisfying customers. Without customers there would be no business.

2.2 Customer service in the marketing mix

An organisation's people come into contact with customers and can have a massive impact on customer satisfaction levels. In the customers' eyes, staff are generally inseparable from the total service. This implies the need for well trained, motivated staff mindful of the adage 'the customer is always right'. It is important therefore that every member of staff contributes to the marketing philosophy and support the firm's external marketing activities.

As organisations introduce streamlined hierarchies and more flexible working practices, marketing offers the opportunity for their employees to operate in interdisciplinary teams furthering an overall marketing philosophy. Corporate investment in their most valuable asset, employees, through training and development supports the processes of creating and defending competitive advantages gained from successful marketing.

A customer focus implies that the company focuses its activities and products on customer needs. In the customer-driven approach, customer needs are the drivers of all strategic marketing decisions. No strategy is pursued until it passes the test of customer research.

Every aspect of a market offering, including the nature of the product itself, is driven by the needs of potential customers.

The three 'additional' Ps of the marketing mix were added to reflect the service content of a purchase.

2.3 Relationship marketing

Relationship marketing is the devoting of marketing resources to maintaining and exploiting the firm's existing customer base rather than using the resources solely to attract new customers. Successful relationship marketing requires the integration of customer service, quality and marketing (Christopher *et al*, 1992) which is the concept of customer care.

We introduced relationship marketing in previous chapters as an approach to marketing that aims at keeping customers – rather than merely attracting them. Relationship marketing involves:

- Customer / supplier partnership: entering into dialogue with customers to create mutually beneficial (win-win) exchanges
- Personalisation of contact: making customers feel that their business is valued and that their individual needs are being recognised and catered for

- Continual deepening and improving of the relationship: making sure that every contact with the brand satisfies – or delights – the customer.

Customer care is linked to quality – not just of customer service, but of the total offering marketed to, and experienced by, the customer. A customer care orientation is akin to the quality management orientation which has been called 'total quality management' or TQM.

3 Designing a customer care programme

Customer care is an organisation-wide orientation, which requires vision, leadership and cultural reinforcement – not just 'rules for customer service'. Nevertheless, a customer care programme may provide a framework for planning, monitoring and evaluating customer service quality.

The following are the stages involved in designing a customer care programme:

Figure 8.2 Designing a customer care programme

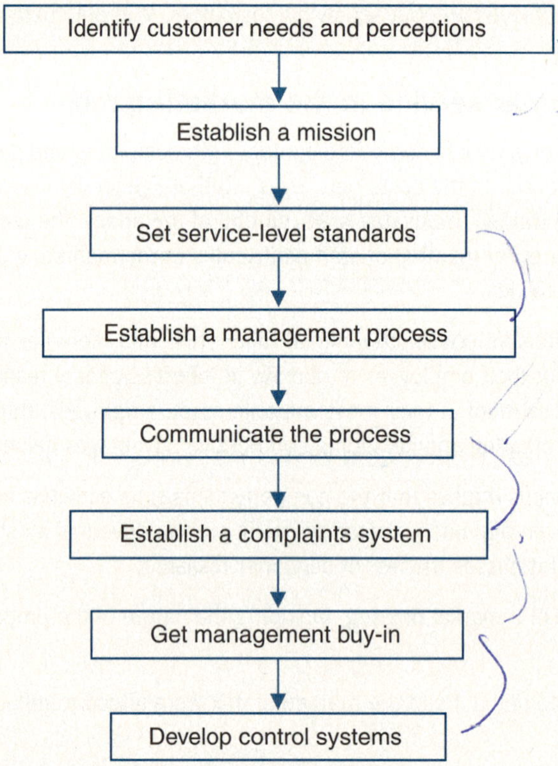

3.1 Identifying customer needs and perceptions

The work carried out in establishing the level of customer service required will feed into this start point. The aim of the customer care programme will be to continue the provision of what we have established as a base level standard. This area will, as shown earlier, focus not just on the product or services provided but also the systems used and staff skills available. Research will be needed to ensure this base standard is current and this could include an element of 'benchmarking' against not just competitive products but also other industries that are considered best in their provision of customer service. UPS parcel systems and Singapore Airlines have excellent service standards, which are recognised across the world. Some of the elements of the service could be transferred into other industry sectors.

3.2 Establishing a mission

Obviously, the organisation's approach to customer service must be echoed within this mission statement, as essentially it is the means of communication to both the customer and the employees of the organisation. The mission statement gives direction and purpose, also expressing the cultural glue that determines how the organisation will interact with their customers. The provision of a mission statement also implies top-level commitment within the organisation, which is essential to the success and ease of implementation of the programme.

3.3 Setting service-level standards

Standards covering all aspects of the service in terms of staff behaviour, appearance and courtesy and responsiveness are required. These should be prescriptive where necessary, that is answer the phone within four rings, but also be sufficiently flexible for the staff member to feel empowered to deal with the situation. Situations which should be referred to a senior person should clearly be highlighted.

The complaints procedure should be clearly documented with time scales and supporting paperwork necessary for the smooth running of the system. There should also be a customer-friendly version for communicating in store, on website, or within a telephone conversation. Follow-up procedures also need to be put in place to follow up complaints and to ensure they are all resolved.

Service standards for systems and processes also need to be considered and deadlines set. 'Delivery within 24 hours' or 'You won't find it cheaper anywhere else' are statements that systems need to monitor and highlight where corrective action may be required.

3.4 Establishing a management process

This is the area which should define who does what, by what and when. Responsibility needs to be allocated and timescales set. Information flow needs to be enabling rather than disabling for the system to work well.

3.5 Communicating the process

Internal communication, in terms of training and objective setting, should be done to ensure everyone knows how they should be completing tasks and how they will be measured.

Feedback from staff should be encouraged to ensure procedures that are unworkable are not imposed on the very people who have most experience.

Communication systems may need to be implemented, these could include team meetings, intranet systems and training away days.

3.6 Establishing a complaints system

The customer needs to be able to complain. Those 44 per cent of people who did not complain, but wanted to, are still remembering and repeating their negative experience, but without giving us the chance to put it right. Therefore, we need to ensure the process of complaining is not a painful one. This can be achieved in several ways:

- Ensure staff are trained and have empathy with the cause of complaint.
- Ensure there are systems and procedures in place to record reoccurring faults/bad service to ensure rectifying action can be taken.
- Ensure the complaints procedure is fully documented and the essence communicated to the customer, for example, refunds on faulty goods are only given on production of a receipt.

- Ensure that the customer knows what action is to be taken and the timescales that are appropriate to the situation, for example 'We will write to you with a response in the next seven days.'
- Make it easy – a customer service desk, a 'contact us' section on the website, a helpline number.

It is important to remember that complaints are emotive issues that have many causes.

Sometimes the staff member may be at a loss to see why a certain aspect is such a problem.

But there are always opportunities – to rectify faults for the future and to demonstrate how well we as an organisation deal with them because we care.

Satisfied customers take up less time, cause less stress and deliver job satisfaction. Word of mouth is the most effective promotional tool. Customer service is essential for survival and growth.

3.7 Having management commitment

This is necessary to gain access to the resources in terms of recruitment, skills and systems that may need to be put in place for the system to work. It is also necessary to echo the cultural push towards delighting the consumer. Consumers quickly pick up on insincere messages and empty promises.

3.8 Developing control systems

The programme must be developed in such a way that measurable objectives can be developed and performance measured against those objectives. Systems need to have defaults that highlight reoccurring problem areas and upcoming deadlines.

Performance towards objectives should be communicated and hopefully celebrated. A system of continuous improvement needs to be maintained in order that the service received by the customer continues to evolve and change to meet their needs.

4 Obtaining customer feedback

4.1 The importance of feedback

Organisations must gather systematic, specific and meaningful feedback in order to learn and grow.

Feedback, in this context, is part of a control system which reports back the results of a process or action, in order to compare them against the planned or intended outcome.

The gathering of feedback by customer-facing staff is important primarily so that:

- The organisation will have customer-generated data about customer needs and wants, in order to fine-tune the marketing mix, marketing communications (promotion) and customer care.
- Customers will feel that they have been listened to – and heard; that their satisfaction or dissatisfaction, and the reasons for it, are taken seriously by the organisation.
- Staff called upon to deal with customers have the ability to influence organisational policy (and even strategy) in areas that affect their work.
- Information keeps flowing into the organisation and through the organisation (particularly in an upward direction), creating opportunities for learning, innovation and adaptation.

Organisations which do not gather and utilise feedback become rigid and unable to adapt their behaviour to changing environments and customer demands. Crozier (1967) suggests that in large, hierarchical, bureaucratic organisations, the control mechanism – whereby feedback on errors is used to initiate corrective action – is hampered: bureaucracies cannot learn from their mistakes!

Complacent organisations may measure customer service performance in a vague or misguided fashion. The following are classic examples.

(a) The use of vague, generalised statements like 'quite good', 'getting better', 'world class'

(b) The counting of customer complaints in the belief that the incidence of complaints is a direct measure of customer satisfaction (without realising that, in most cases, only between 10 and 20 per cent of customers actually complain: the rest simply take their business elsewhere)

(c) Reliance on infrequent survey data about customer perceptions – and the selective application of the data thus acquired

(d) So-called 'improvements' that only address front-line 'customer care' features like answering the telephone within three rings – when what really matters is how customers are handled once the telephone has been picked up.

Organisations must gather systematic, specific and meaningful feedback in order to adapt, learn and grow.

- **Positive feedback** – satisfied responses – is useful to confirm organisational plans and strategies. It is also helpful in encouraging staff and reinforcing positive customer service behaviours through customer recognition and appreciation.
- **Negative feedback** – dissatisfied responses – is, however, even more useful in defining what it is that the organisation needs to do in order to gain and retain customers.

Feedback is not always negative, some customers actively seek ways to praise organisations that excel in customer service. The following table summarises the ways that information can be gathered to assess the level of customer service.

Table 8.2 Formal and informal methods of data collections

Formal feedback collection	Informal feedback methods
▪ Surveys, telephone, web based, questionnaire ▪ Online forums (on organisation's website) ▪ Suggestion boxes ▪ Analysis of formal complaints data ▪ Review customer retention figures ▪ Sales figure analysis	▪ Front line staff-customer discussions ▪ Online forums and review sites set up by third parties ▪ Press monitoring

4.2 Encouraging customer complaints

Customer service staff are gatherers of customer feedback, both formally and informally. They can be supported by training; feedback reporting systems; and culture and resources for encouraging feedback (and implementing solutions).

In other words, customers should be encouraged to complain! The following guidelines are given by Johns (1994).

- Make it easy for people to complain: eg by establishing free-call or local-call rate telephone numbers or complaint / feedback / review forms.
- Ask for feedback by selecting and approaching customers at random.
- Use random customer visits to sample the service first hand.
- Train staff to listen to complaints positively, as a learning opportunity, without becoming defensive.
- Act quickly and with goodwill to solve any problem identified, so complaints will be perceived to be worthwhile and positive. (This may mean replacing products or repeating services.)
- Communicate the intention to prevent recurrence of the problem.

- Reward customer feedback with appropriate incentives: discount vouchers, entry into Prize Draws and so on. Where feedback leads to change, customers should be thanked for their important contribution.

In addition, customer-facing staff have extensive opportunities to gather informal direct and indirect feedback by observing and talking to customers. They need to listen intentionally for explicit or implied complaints or suggestions for improvement. Returned products, for example, should be interpreted as non-verbal forms of complaint, as should returned mailings – or indeed, customer failure to recall company advertisements when asked.

THE REAL WORLD

Switching suppliers

Organisations relying on customer inertia to retain their customer base run a great risk. Customers are more savvy, expect value for their money and to be listened to more than ever before. The Accenture Global Consumer Survey analysed customers who switched their suppliers for wireless phone, cable or utility services between 2010 and 2011 and found the highest ever number of defections – that is customers either moving totally to a new supplier or mixing and matching services (a growing trend known as partial switching). The main reason behind the switch: companies failing to deliver on their initial promises.

(*Destination CRM*, 2012)

Assessment tip

Draft a similar noticeboard (or staff web page) notice, with simple guidelines for staff in your organisation for dealing with awkward customers.

Use your own experience and common sense to suggest the content of your guidelines – or check the customer service manual (or similar) of your organisation.

4.3 Methods of collecting feedback

4.3.1 Mail surveys

The mail survey has to do everything you would do if you were with the customer. It has to be visually appealing, have a pleasant tone, and be clear. The survey instrument is under the direct control of the customer. Its physical look will affect the customer's willingness to respond; the clarity of the instructions and questions will affect the customer's ability to interpret their meaning correctly.

Single-page questionnaires and comment cards should be attractive and easy to read.

Longer questionnaires should be printed in booklet form, on A4 paper that is folded in half and stapled in the middle to produce a standard A5 page. The cover should be visually appealing to interest the customer, and no questions should appear on the cover. The cover should give the title of the survey activity and indicate who is conducting the work.

Survey questions should be presented in a logical sequence. Many survey experts believe that the first question on the survey, more than any other, will determine whether your customer completes or discards the questionnaire. Starting with a fairly simple question is a good idea because it suggests to the customer that completing the survey will be neither difficult nor time-consuming. It is also advisable to ask a fairly interesting question to gain the customer's interest.

The next set of questions should focus on matters that the customer is most likely to consider useful or salient. This continues the process of attracting the customer's attention so that he or she becomes engaged with thinking about the questions being asked and becomes interested in completing the survey.

Grouping questions together that share common themes makes sense because the customer then focuses on that particular area of enquiry. To the extent practical, you should group questions that have similar types of response options. For example, questions that have yes/no responses should be together and questions that have scale responses should be together.

4.3.2 Telephone surveys

As customers have no questionnaire in front of them during a telephone survey, concerns about visual appeal are not applicable. Issues regarding ordering and clarity of questions are important, and the same principles apply as with mail surveys.

In-person and telephone surveys involve spoken language, which can be very different from written language, and customers must be able to respond to questions based only on the information they hear. So it is critical that your interviewers be well trained and speak clearly. Also, the interviewers act as an intermediary between the customer and the questions posed.

The following principles apply to telephone surveys:

(a) The introduction the customer hears will probably determine whether the interview is conducted or the customer hangs up. The introduction should be concise, state the purpose of the call, estimate the length of the call, and assure confidentiality.

(b) Because customers will rely on verbal cues and instructions, rather than written ones, questions should have a limited number of responses (about three or four).

(c) Each question should be relatively short.

(d) Avoid questions that ask customers to look up information or check with others.

(e) In constructing the questionnaire, be sure to read the questions aloud to others to see if they sound clear and understandable. Remember, what works for the written word does not always work for the spoken word.

(f) When changing subjects, telephone surveys should cue the customer with transitional statements such as, 'Now, I'd like to turn to your experiences with…'

(g) Instructions for the interviewer must be perfectly clear, and the same format should be used throughout the survey. For example, interviewer instructions are typically written inside brackets, in all capital letters.

4.3.3 Suggestion boxes

High tech isn't always the way to go. The original customer feedback device, the suggestion box, is still effective and easily administered. Check it daily and regularly replenish pencils and forms. The normal customer follow-up procedures apply.

4.3.4 Online surveys

Internet surveys use a web-based form that the user completes online at a designated web address. You should only consider this method of data collection if the potential respondents have access to the internet.

To administer an internet survey, you must have a method of contacting the people selected for the sample. After compiling the sample list, send an e-mail alert that will lead potential respondents to the survey website. Upon entering the website, respondents can then log in and take the survey. Internet surveys have several advantages:

- They are interactive, like telephone surveys, allowing programmed skip patterns and links to more detailed survey instructions. Unlike a telephone survey, respondents can see the questions.
- Respondents can complete the questionnaire at a time convenient to them.
- There are no calling or mailing costs.

- E-mail surveys are one of the fastest and least intrusive means for gathering customer feedback. Up to 50 per cent of the responses are received within 24 hours.
- They are also cheaper to conduct since you pay no interviewers or printing and distribution costs.
- In addition, the survey will definitely get to the right individual; they will usually not be intercepted and routed to another person.

However, there are also some disadvantages. For example, it is likely that respondents will have no perception of anonymity. Also, as e-mail use increases, people are becoming less patient with the many unsolicited messages they receive.

4.3.5 Focus groups

The focus group is a popular technique in marketing circles, and one that is frequently used in the early stages of product design or specification. Typically a group of between six and ten people are invited to discuss potential products or services, usually prompted by a series of carefully worded questions or statements. In this way a group enables potential users to voice their wants and discuss the features that they might like to see in new products or services.

The disadvantage of the focus group is that it depends entirely on what potential users say about their preferences and wants, rather than what they actually need in reality. These two things are often not the same at all, and if the group becomes dominated by one or two people it is possible to find that many stated opinions are merely the results of group dynamics rather than the real needs and wants of users.

In some instances this might be appropriate. These effects can be used to predict the response of the public at large to image changes, for example.

Online focus group research offers exciting new possibilities for on-line conferencing.

Traditional focus groups require:

- The rental of a physical facility, transportation for participants, refreshments, recording facilities for transcription purposes, and time set-up and cleanup
- The recruitment of participants from the immediate local area
- Travel costs for moderators who must be located at the same site as the participants.

Online focus groups overcome many of these limitations.

Features of online focus groups include:

- The ability to restrict access to pre-authorised participants
- Automatic production of instant word-for-word transcripts
- Use of online survey forms without leaving the focus group
- Use of online participant profiles filled out in advance (reducing the need for 'get acquainted' activities)
- Elaborate electronic moderator discussion controls
- Display (with no action needed by participants) of discussion materials such as PowerPoint slides, Excel charts and spreadsheets and other text materials, photographs and other visuals, live websites and their contents, live pictures from web cameras, and even streaming audio and video
- The ability to continue discussion on a split screen while viewing materials such as those described above.

4.3.6 Feedback cards

Feedback cards are paper cards containing one or more survey questions, designed to gather customer feedback after a service encounter. The cards are typically completed by customers immediately after an interaction, but can also be completed later and mailed back, or visitors can provide additional information via a web survey. They can give you feedback on a specific customer experience, or provide general feedback about your organisation. They are a good way to reach customers or clients for whom you do not have contact information, or who do not interact with your company through other channels. Feedback cards can also help you collect customer contact information for future interactions and can usually elicit feedback from customers who do not feel comfortable sharing feedback directly with a representative.

4.3.7 Informal methods

If your business relies on customers coming to you, dedicate a percentage of your day to mingling with them.

- Treat each customer exchange individually.
- Avoid the generic: 'Is everything okay?' Instead try 'If you were to suggest one thing we could improve, what would it be?'
- Carry a notebook to capture customers comments, logging them in their presence.

5 Monitoring the success of customer service

5.1 Why monitor success?

Continuous improvement, through the adoption of such initiatives as total quality management (TQM), business process re-engineering (BPR) and Kaizen (the Japanese philosophy of continuous improvement), has been one of the core themes of business management during the past decade.

The goal of modern business is no longer just 'to be good' but 'to be better than our competitors'.

Organisations cannot stand still, or they run the risk of being overtaken by competitors that change and improve their products and service standards.

Regardless of the product or service that an organisation supplies, that product or service is surrounded or 'augmented' by an overall service package, which the customer experiences from the first moment they come into contact with the organisation. In a world where the core products and services offered by competitors are very similar, it is often only the customer service package that differentiates one organisation from another.

5.2 Number of complaints

Is it the case that a fall in the number of customer complaints means that our customer service levels are improving? Or are our customers no longer complaining to us (because they realise it does no good) and are now complaining to each other (or, even worse, to our competitors)?

While the number of customer complaints can give an indication of how they perceive our service levels, we cannot rely on it as an accurate measure. Perhaps more customers are complaining because we have changed our systems to make it easier for them to do so.

Or maybe the level of customer complaints has fallen because they are now using an open forum on the internet rather than coming to us.

In a 'steady state', or in the short term, customer complaints can give us an indication whether service levels are improving or worsening. In the longer term, however, we must supplement data about complaints with other measures.

5.3 Measuring service standards

The only people who can accurately judge our service levels are our customers. In the previous section we looked at ways to gather customer feedback, and all of these can give us data about how our service levels are perceived. This data, together with that relating to complaint levels, must be combined with data from other sources if we are to really understand our service level performance.

5.3.1 Sales records

The 'bottom line' of customer service is the level of revenues we earn. If sales are rising, we must be doing something right. The problem with using sales data as an indicator of customer service levels is that it is affected by so many other variables. Have we just launched a new advertising or promotional campaign? Has one of our competitors done the same? What about changes in the global environment? Are customer disposable incomes up? What is happening to the rest of our industry?

5.3.2 Customer retention

It is very true that 'a happy customer comes back for more'. Looking at the conversion rate from 'new customer' to 'repeat purchase' can give us an indication of how customers perceive our service levels, but no more than that. Once again, this data is dependent on a wide variety of variables from elsewhere in the marketing mix (product quality, pricing strategy, brand perception, promotional activity) and the business environment (competition, economy, social factors) that it is almost impossible to identify what component part of any change is due to service levels.

5.3.3 Existing customer data

If a happy customer comes back for more, then a very happy customer probably comes back more frequently, and for ever-greater quantities. Once again, data relating to purchase frequency and volumes can be affected by myriad influences, but it may be possible to identify some impact of service levels. Of course, the best way to find out how customers feel about our service levels is still to ask them!

5.3.4 Mystery shoppers

The point-of-sale is the critical moment of truth in determining whether a customer is satisfied, the sale is made, or if a customer ever buys from you again. Evaluation of this interaction is important in understanding the type of service your customer is receiving and whether sales associates or team members are following your prescribed procedures and protocols. In essence, on-site mystery shoppers look at sales and service efforts from two perspectives – the customer's as well as the company's. It doesn't matter if the evaluation is for a retail store, restaurant, car dealership, apartment development, or fun park.

On-site mystery shoppers also have the advantage of being able to assess the physical aspects of the location including: the cleanliness and upkeep of the facility, the proper use of merchandising and marketing materials, the appearance of the staff and their attire (including uniforms), product presentation and demonstration, and so on.

Provided the identity of mystery shoppers is kept confidential, this is one of the best ways of getting direct feedback about service levels, from three perspectives:

1. At a point in time – how are we doing?
2. Over time – are we improving?
3. In comparison to our competitors – are we better than them?

6 Using IT in customer service activities

6.1 The range of IT systems

Relationship marketing requires the storage and manipulation and analysis of huge amounts of customer information in order that the relationship can deliver added value to the customer. The use of customer databases to store and manipulate this data has led to the term 'database marketing'.

Loyalty schemes work on a similar principle: the large supermarkets can use their EPOS not only for stock control purposes but also to target offers that are relevant to customers.

For example, a customer who regularly buys dog food would not be sent money-off vouchers to keep the customer 'loyal' for cat food.

Customer relationship management systems work on a similar principle. The key idea is that each customer is treated as an individual, and in particular, organisations can use computer software to identify the customers with the highest customer lifetime value (CLV). For example, basic current account holders are not particularly profitable customers for banks compared to those with (or wanting) loans, mortgages, insurance business and pensions are much more profitable. The idea behind CLV is to spend marketing time and effort on those customers who are likely to be the most valuable over their lifetime.

The length of 'lifetime' will vary by industry. Manufacturers of baby products will know that families will probably be in that market sector for about eight years – the average time between the oldest and the youngest child moving into the five years plus bracket. However, these organisations will also have products in other sectors such as household cleaning materials and hair care, where the positive experiences gained from the baby care products will result in the customer entering a relationship for a longer lifetime with different products. Hence, it is possible to have a relationship and retain loyalty for a 'lifetime'.

6.1.1 Insight: Data mining

Key term

Data mining is when sophisticated systems are used to track customer or client files to identify products or services that could be targeted in the future.

The high-street retailer Next uses this technique with their mail order catalogue noting when customers make key life-cycle purchases. A sudden change in purchasing, for example homewares, will mean the customer may have just purchased their first home, so Next will send more information concerning their range of furniture or someone ordering maternity wear will shortly be interested in baby wear. Being first to communicate with the customer is a widely accepted mission statement for the approach to customer care itself.

Internet and database technologies offer some key advantages for gathering customer data. The key to their value is keeping the data up to date and relevant.

(a) Market research into customers' 'stated intentions' and perceptions can be replaced or augmented by actual customer behaviour and demonstrated preferences: websites allow the tracking and storage of customer browsing (identifying areas of interest) and transaction/purchase history.

(b) Market research and customer feedback gathering can be carried out via such methods as:

- Online or e-mail-distributed questionnaires and feedback forms
- 'Message boards' on the website, allowing visitors to communicate with the company (and each other)
- Site monitoring to record hits, browsing and purchase patterns of users
- Inviting e-mailed comments and suggestions

Such methods are more convenient for the customer than face-to-face interviews and writing/mailing: they require less effort and allow 24-7 flexibility. From the company's point of view, they also facilitate the immediate analysis and integration of results, automatic 'thank you' messages and so on.

(c) Companies can also access external online databases compiled and managed by specialist data providers: market research publishers (for example, Mintel and Keynote), producers of statistical data (for example, the UK Central Statistical Office and Eurostat) and others.

6.2 Database applications

> **Key term**
>
> **Database marketing** is an interactive approach to marketing which uses individually addressable marketing media and channels to extend help to a company's target audience, stimulate their demand and stay close to them by recording and keeping an electronic database memory of customer, prospect and all communication and commercial contacts, to help them improve all future contacts and ensure more realistic planning of all marketing.

Database marketing involves using computers to capture and store data relating to customers' past purchase history. For instance, if a mail order company sells clothing in its catalogue, each customer file is computerised so that contact (name, address, postcode) and purchase details (type of item, size, colour preference, price, etc.) are stored. All the departments in the firm can access this information quickly and cheaply. For example, the accounts department may need to access it to chase payment and the marketing department could use it to target offers to customers. So customers who buy clothes for people under a certain height would only be sent information relating to the 'petite' range of clothing based on their past purchase behaviour.

Customer data held in computerised databases can be interrogated and manipulated in various ways through the process of data mining.

Allen *et al* (2001) suggest the following projects which can be conducted using database marketing techniques.

(a) Identify the best customers (recency of the latest purchase, frequency of purchases and monetary value of all purchases) to determine which customers are most profitable to market to.

(b) Develop new customers. Collect lists of potential customers to incorporate in the database.

(c) Tailor messages based on customer usage. Target mail and e-mail based on the types and frequency of purchases indicated by the customer's purchase profile.

(d) Recognise customers after purchase. Reinforce the purchase decision by appropriate follow-up.

(e) Cross-sell related and complementary products. Use the customer purchase database to identify opportunities to suggest additional products during the buying session.

(f) Personalise customer service. Online purchase data can prompt customer service representatives to show that the customer is recognised, his needs known, and his time (eg in giving details) valued.

(g) Eliminate conflicting or confusing communications. Present a coherent image over time to individual customers – however different the message to different customer groups. (For example, don't keep sending 'dear first-time customer' messages to long-standing customers!)

Database marketing supports customer service by targeting and personalising communications.

The two key points of this for adding value to customer service may be described as follows.

Table 8.3 Benefits of targeted and personalised communications

Targeting communications (mailing list management): greater relevance to the customer	■ Targeting customers in particular geographic areas with information (suppliers, services, events) relevant to their local area ■ Targeting customers with relevant offerings, message content, and style, according to lifestyle, age group and other demographic and personal factors ■ Targeting customers with their preferred communication purposes (new product information, newsletters, special offers) and media (e-mail, phone, mail)
Personalising communications: greater relevance and sense of recognition for the customer	■ Personally addressed mailed or e-mailed communications ■ Individual customer information made available in real time to call centre staff to personalise telephone contacts and streamline transactions (no need for the customer to supply details each time) ■ Contacts and product recommendations based on preferences and contact or transaction history: ('Since you enquired about...', 'As a regular purchaser of...', 'Since we haven't heard from you for some time...') ■ Relational use of personal information (for example, birthday cards)

Postma (1999) suggests that such techniques:

(a) **Build relationships.** 'Reacting to the personal behaviour of customers or prospects by responding to their obvious interests with an electronic message, a letter, a brochure or an offer actually fosters clients' feeling that you are becoming acquainted with their tastes and preferences and are taking them into consideration.'

(b) **Reinforce loyalty.** 'Loyal customers will value being recognised as such and receiving direct communications.'

(c) **Out-perform human beings!** 'An assistant in a fashion store may very well recognise a client's face after half a year, but will not instantly remember the client's measurements and tastes. A database, on the other hand, has no problem whatsoever retaining these facts or other information about the customer's average expenditure, quality standards or preferred brand. We won't even mention the fact that the employee who served the customer last time has moved on to a different job and been replaced.'

6.3 Data components

The type of data held in a typical customer database might include the following:

- Geographic – Where do our customers live? How far do they travel (if at all, they might buy from home)?
- Demographic – What socio-economic group do our customers belong to? How old are they? What occupations or professions are represented? What life stage are our customers at?
- Psychographic – Attributes relating to personality, values, attitudes, interests, or lifestyles. They are also called IAO variables (for Interests, Attitudes, and Opinions).
- Buying pattern – How frequently do our customers buy? What do they buy, and in what quantities?
- Other – The basic data such as name, address, telephone number, loyalty scheme membership.

6.4 Ensuring the data is up-to-date

One of the major issues in managing any database application is that of 'data redundancy' – what proportion of the data is no longer fulfilling the purpose for which it was collected and held? Data can be redundant for three reasons:

1 **It is obsolete.** Much of the data in any customer database relates to ex-customers – those that used to purchase from us, but no longer do. This may be because we have lost the customer to a rival, or simply because they have moved from the area.

2 **It is duplicated.** This is a very common issue with customer data. How many organisations send you multiple copies of their direct mail or catalogue, because you appear more than once on their database? Do you have two or more loyalty cards for the same retailer?

3 **It could have changed.** Data that is not updated rapidly becomes of little value.

If you have used direct mail, you will know just how many items are 'returned to sender'. How many of you receive direct mail items addressed to people who lived at your address many years ago?

On-line application processing (OLAP) information systems can improve data redundancy levels by automatically capturing data, but the sheer volume of data held on a typical customer database means that a level of data redundancy of 10 to 20 per cent is not uncommon.

6.5 Meeting legal and ethical requirements

Legislation and regulations exist in many countries to protect consumers from the misuse of personal details held on computer, unsolicited mail and invasion of privacy.

In the UK, controls on data usage include the following.

(a) The **Data Protection Act 1998** (and related Codes of Practice) provide that data controllers (organisations or individuals who control the contents of files of personal data and the use of personal data) must register with the Data Protection Registrar. They must limit their use of personal data (defined as any information about an identifiable living individual) to the uses registered, and not disclose data to third parties (including e-mail addresses sent in a 'cc' reference) without permission.

(b) The **Criminal Justice and Public Order Act 1994** makes it illegal to procure the disclosure of computer-held information, and to sell or offer to sell computer-held information.

(c) The **Mailing Preference Service** allows customers to state whether they would (and more often would not) be willing to receive direct mail on a range of specific areas. (This is the way to get taken off (or, if you are a Marketing Student, put on) mailing databases.)

(d) The **UK Privacy and Electronic Communications Regulations 2003**, requires proactive agreement (eg ticking an 'opt-in' box) to receive electronic communications such as e-mail marketing.

(e) Various countries have **'Do Not Call' registers** enabling people to opt out of telemarketing call lists. (Australia for example, implemented such a register in May 2007.)

6.5.1 Data Protection Act 1998

The Data Protection Act 1998 (DPA) defines a legal basis for the handling in the UK of information relating to living people. It is the main piece of legislation that governs protection of personal data in the UK. Although the Act does not mention privacy, in practice it provides a way in which individuals can enforce the control of information about them.

The Act covers any data that can be used to identify a living person, and applies to all customer databases. This includes names, birthday and anniversary dates, addresses, telephone numbers, fax numbers, e-mail addresses and so on. It only applies to that data which is held, or intended to be held, on computers ('equipment operating automatically in response to instructions given for that purpose'), or held in a 'relevant filing system'.

The Act defines eight principles of information-handling practice:

1 Personal data shall be processed fairly and lawfully.

2 Personal data shall be obtained only for one or more specified and lawful purposes, and shall not be further processed in any manner incompatible with that purpose or those purposes.

3 Personal data shall be adequate, relevant and not excessive in relation to the purpose or purposes for which they are processed.

4 Personal data shall be accurate and, where necessary, kept up to date.

5 Personal data processed for any purpose or purposes shall not be kept for longer than is necessary for that purpose or those purposes.

6 Personal data shall be processed in accordance with the rights of data subjects under this Act.

7 Appropriate technical and organisational measures shall be taken against unauthorised or unlawful processing of personal data and against accidental loss or destruction of, or damage to, personal data.

8 Personal data shall not be transferred to a country or territory outside the European Economic Area unless that country or territory ensures an adequate level of protection for the rights and freedoms of data subjects in relation to the processing of personal data.

It is clear, therefore, that organisations have a legal duty to comply with the DPA, in addition to any ethical 'duty of care' to their customers. This makes the management of customer databases a professional issue, and it should not therefore be trusted to any and every individual within the organisation.

7 Managing yourself

The performance management cycle is a simple process by which your personal performance is managed within an organisation. It consists of a series of appraisal meetings (which may be formal or informal) at which past performance is reviewed and future performance is planned. Work is then carried out, and a further meeting held to review performance, and so on.

A typical appraisal meeting will therefore have three component parts:

1 Reviewing past performance

2 Setting objectives for the coming period

3 Planning personal development activities, and any other support the organisation can give to ensure the individual performs as required.

7.1 Setting personal objectives

Everyone should know what the organisation expects of them. Some objectives may be set by managers during the appraisal process, and others may be set by the individual themselves.

Personal objectives generally fall into two categories:

- **Objectives related to value**, such as improving processes, reducing costs, or increasing customer service levels.
- **Objectives related to outputs**, such as sales levels or quantities produced.

Objectives should be 'SMART' (Figure 8.3):

Figure 8.3 SMART objectives

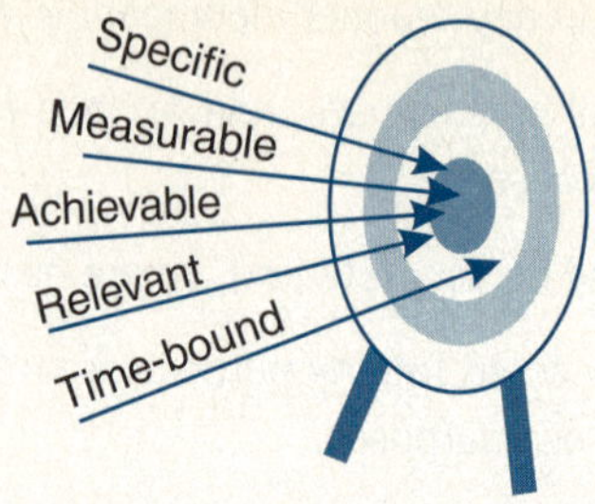

- **Specific**. The objective should be expressed in terms that are clearly defined and understood. This is easy with quantitative objectives (such as 'increase sales by 5%) but less straightforward with qualitative objectives (such as 'increase customer satisfaction levels'). Making the objective measurable can help in the latter case.
- **Measurable**. For an objective to be valid, you have to know when you have achieved it. This may be a quantified level of performance, or may be a specific deliverable (a report, for example).
- **Achievable**. This aspect of the objective is about ownership. The individual to whom the objective is applied must perceive achievement as being attainable. Good objectives are in the form of 'stretch targets' – only achievable with a high degree of effort. This not only improves performance significantly, but also motivates the individual.
- **Relevant**. The variable being measured must be within the sphere of influence of the individual to which it applies. There is no point, for example, asking a member of the accounts department to improve the time taken for customers to pay, if the only person who can influence this is the sales representative who visits the customer.
- **Time-bound**. By when? If performance is to be reviewed on, for example, a six monthly basis, then an objective should be set at such a level that it could be achieved in that timescale. If the objective is long term, then progress measures must be identified so regular reviews can be held.

ACTIVITY 8.2

Identify three objectives that relate to your personal performance, either at work or at college. Put each into 'SMART' form.

7.2 Working to achieve objectives

Once your personal objectives have been agreed, you need to work out how to achieve them. This involves a series of steps, as shown in Figure 8.4:

Step 1 Break each objective down into a series of achievable and time-bound short-term goals. Not only will this allow you to measure your progress towards achieving your objectives, it will motivate you as you 'tick off' the goals. Identify the tasks that need to be performed in order to achieve each goal. These tasks might be such things as processes to perform, documents to create, or meetings to attend.

Step 2 Identify the time required for each task. In summation, these times will allow you to check that all your objectives really are achievable within the constraint of the total time you have available.

Step 3 Identify the resources you need in order to achieve each goal within the time specified.

These resources may be financial, material (such as a PC), or human (such as the help of colleagues).

Step 4 Prioritise your objectives and goals, so you can recognise the relative urgency of each and work out which should take precedence over the others.

Step 5 Produce a detailed time and resource plan for the period between now and your next review meeting. Show which tasks you will perform, what resources are required, and when you expect to achieve each goal and objective.

Step 6 Perform the tasks, and compare performance to the plan.

Step 7 Revise the plan as you go, and don't be afraid to recognise that some goals and objectives might become unachievable due to your own poor performance or external influences. Report such instances to your manager, so they are aware in advance.

Figure 8.4 Working through objectives

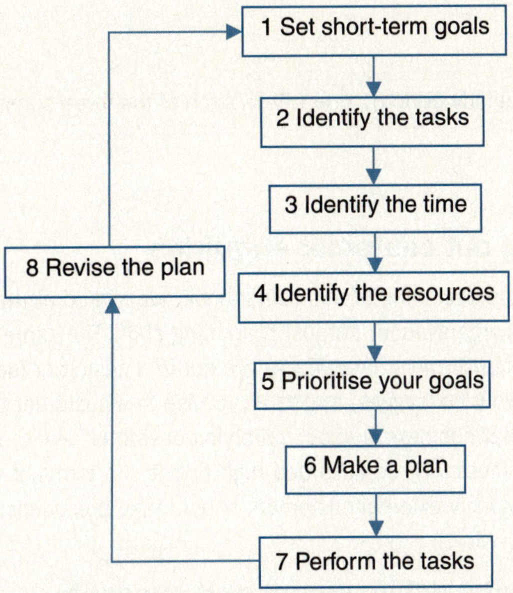

For any one of the objectives you identified in the previous activity, produce a detailed progress plan in line with the first six steps outlined above.

7.3 Effective resource utilisation

In step 4 of the process outlined in Figure 8.4 above, we looked at identifying the resources needed to perform each task. In all organisations, resources are scarce, and demand often exceeds supply. It is therefore essential that resource utilisation is planned in such a way that the organisation's objectives are achieved. If it is not possible to achieve all the objectives, resources must be allocated to those tasks that support the objectives that are perceived as higher priority.

Mediating in discussion relating to resource allocation between conflicting objectives is a key role of managers.

7.4 Completing tasks on time

Most objectives, and therefore the tasks performed in moving towards their achievement, have three dimensions:

The scope and quality of the task.

That is, what needs to be done, and what level of achievement or quality of output is expected.

- The cost of the task. How much resource is required, and how much that resource costs the organisation.
- The time taken to perform the task.
- The deadline for completion.

These three dimensions are in conflict, each with the other. If, for example, we need to reduce the cost of a task, this can often be achieved by using less resource (and quality falls) or by working only when 'spare' time is available (and the task takes longer to complete).

Similarly, a task can be performed more quickly by allocating more resources (increasing cost) or by sacrificing quality.

In many instances, one of the three constraints is likely to be most important. Often, 'time is of the essence', and cost and quality must come second to meeting a deadline.

ACTIVITY 8.3

Identify three tasks that you regularly perform, one where each of the three constraints (cost, quality and time) is more important.

7.5 Closing out customer enquiries

Right back at the beginning of this coursebook, we looked at the idea that marketing is the responsibility of everyone in the organisation, not just marketing staff. The same is true of customer service, particularly if you include internal customers. Even if you are not in a customer-facing role, there will be many occasions when you, or one of your colleagues, makes a promise to a customer that you have a hand in meeting. If you 'buy into' the idea that business is about satisfying customer needs, any task or objective with a customer service aspect must, necessarily, be accorded high priority. In terms of which customer promises should take preference, obviously external customers should take precedence over internal customers.

7.6 Monitoring achievement and success

In order to get the greatest benefit from any performance review process, it is essential that you record and monitor all progress that you make towards the achievement of your objectives. This will allow you, in conjunction with your manager, to review your effectiveness.

Keeping a record of your achievements is not just important for performance review, but also adds value to your curriculum vitae (CV).

CHAPTER ROUNDUP

- Customer care aims to close the gap between customers' expectations and their experience in every aspect of the customer/supplier relationship.
- Customer service is the point of contact between the customer and the organisation at each point of the transaction process.
- The satisfaction of external customers is the result of a range of satisfying internal relationships and transactions between colleagues and departments.
- Despite traditionally operating under monopolistic or near-monopolistic conditions, the public sector is also subject to pressures for better customer care.
- Satisfying customers is at the heart of marketing.
- Relationship marketing is the devoting of marketing resources to maintaining and exploiting the firm's existing customer base rather than using the resources solely to attract new customers.
- A customer care programme may provide a framework for planning, monitoring and evaluating customer service quality.
- Organisations must gather systematic, specific and meaningful feedback in order to learn and grow.
- Continuous improvement, through the adoption of such initiatives as total quality management
- (TQM), business process re-engineering (BPR) and Kaizen, has been one of the core themes of business management during the past decade.
- Relationship marketing requires the storage and manipulation and analysis of huge amounts of customer information in order that the relationship can deliver added value to the customer.
- Legislation and regulations exist in many countries to protect consumers from the misuse of personal details held on computer, unsolicited mail and invasion of privacy.
- The Data Protection Act 1998 (DPA) defines a legal basis for the handling in the UK of information relating to living people. It is the main piece of legislation that governs protection of personal data in the UK.
- The performance management cycle is a simple process by which your personal performance is managed within an organisation.

FURTHER READING

Whole texts:

Blythe, J. (2008) *Essentials of Marketing*. 4th edition. Harlow, Prentice Hall.

Brassington, F. and Pettitt, S. (2007) *Essentials of Marketing*. 2nd edition. Harlow, Prentice Hall.

Cook, S. (2011) *Customer Care Excellence*. 6th edition. London, Kogan Page.

Chapters 7–9 and 11 of:

Doole, I., Lancaster, P. and Lowe, R. (2005) *Understanding and Managing Customers*. Harlow, Prentice Hall.

REFERENCES

Blythe, J. (2008) *Essentials of Marketing*. 4th edition. Harlow, Prentice Hall.

Brassington, F. and Pettitt, S. (2006) *Principles of Marketing*. 4th edition. Harlow, Prentice Hall.

Christopher, M., Payne, A. and Ballantyne, D. (1992) *Relationship Marketing*. Oxford, Butterworth Heinneman.

Clutterbuck, D. (2001) *Communication Competence and Business Success: A Comparative Review of Communication Programs.* San Francisco, International Association of Business Communicators.

Cook, S. (2011) *Customer Care Excellence*. 6th edition. London, Kogan Page.

Crozier, M. (1967) *The Bureaucratic Phenomenon*. Chicago, University of Chicago Press.

Doole, I., Lancaster, P. and Lowe, R. (2005) *Understanding and Managing Customers*. Harlow, Prentice Hall.

Harris, D. and Botten, N. (2008) *CIM Coursebook: Introduction to Marketing*. Oxford, Butterworth Heinemann.

Johns, E. (1994) *The Essential Marketing Sourcebook*. 2nd edition. London, FT/Fitman.

Klie, L. (2011) Despite improvements in service, two out of three consumers switched companies in 2011. *Destination CRM*, http://www.destinationcrm.com/Articles/PrintArticle.aspx?ArticleID=80565 [accessed 14 February 2012].

Postma, P. (1999) *The New Marketing Era.* New York, McGraw-Hill.

QUICK QUIZ

1 What is customer care?

2 What are the five key areas where customer service systems exist?

3 What are the key factors in managing the quality of internal service operations?

4 What are the stages involved in designing a customer care programme?

5 What are the formal methods for collecting customer feedback?

6 What are the main methods of measuring the success of customer service activities?

7 What is database marketing?

8 What are the eight principles of information handling practice contained in the Data Protection Act 1998?

9 What does the acronym 'SMART' stand for?

ACTIVITY DEBRIEFS

Activity 8.1

A supermarket express checkout is a cashier checkout designed for customers with a limited number of items. The purpose is to allow those with a few grocery items (usually 10 items or less) to receive faster checkout service and be able to leave the store quickly. It usually saves time waiting in line at the supermarket.

Activity 8.2

The answer will depend on your personal and work situation. Examples of SMART objectives include:

- To complete my Introductory Certificate in Marketing project by 31 March 2013.
- To respond to all customer queries within 48 hours of receipt.
- To complete my CIM examinations and obtain a CIM Professional Diploma in Marketing by December 2015.

Activity 8.3

The answer will depend on your personal and work situation. Examples might include:

- Weekly shopping at the local supermarket (cost)
- Delivering presentations to prospective clients (quality)
- Travelling to work by bus (time)

QUICK QUIZ ANSWERS

1 Customer care is 'a fundamental approach to the standards of service quality' which 'covers every aspect of a company's operations from the design of a product or service to how it is packaged, delivered and serviced'. (Clutterbuck, 2001).

2 Sales and ordering, accounts and invoicing, delivery, after-sales and complaints.

3 The recruitment of skilled customer-facing people, the supply of appropriate (and sufficient) training, the empowerment of staff to take decisions that will attract and keep customers and the reward and recognition of staff who deliver outstanding service.

4 Identify customer needs and perception, establish a mission, set service-level standards, establish a management process, communicate the process, establish a complaints system, get management buy-in and develop control systems.

5 Mail surveys, telephone surveys, suggestion boxes, feedback cards, online surveys and focus groups.

6 Sales records, customer retention, existing customer data and mystery shoppers.

7 Database marketing is an interactive approach to marketing which uses individually addressable marketing media and channels to extend help to a company's target audience, stimulate their demand and stay close to them by recording and keeping an electronic database memory of customer, prospect and all communication and commercial contacts, to help them improve all future contacts and ensure more realistic planning of all marketing.

8 They are:

   1 Personal data shall be processed fairly and lawfully.

   2 Personal data shall be obtained only for one or more specified and lawful purposes, and shall not be further processed in any manner incompatible with that purpose or those purposes. Personal data shall be adequate,

   3 Personal data shall be relevant and not excessive in relation to the purpose or purposes for which they are processed.

   4 Personal data shall be accurate and, where necessary, kept up to date.

   5 Personal data processed for any purpose or purposes shall not be kept for longer than is necessary for that purpose or those purposes.

   6 Personal data shall be processed in accordance with the rights of data subjects under this Act.

   7 Appropriate technical and organisational measures shall be taken against unauthorised or unlawful processing of personal data and against accidental loss or destruction of, or damage to, personal data.

   8 Personal data shall not be transferred to a country or territory outside the European Economic Area unless that country or territory ensures an adequate level of protection for the rights and freedoms of data subjects in relation to the processing of personal data.

9 Specific, measurable, achievable, relevant and time-bound.

Index

Notes

Notes

Notes

Review form

Please help us to ensure that the CIM learning materials we produce remain as accurate and user-friendly as possible. We cannot promise to answer every submission we receive, but we do promise that it will be read and taken into account when we update this Study Text.

Name: ______________________ **Address:** ______________________

____

____

1. How have you used this Text?
(Tick one box only)

- ☐ Self study (book only)
- ☐ On a course: college______________
- ☐ Other ______________

2. During the past six months do you recall seeing/receiving any of the following?
(Tick as many boxes as are relevant)

- ☐ Our advertisement in *The Marketer*
- ☐ Our brochure with a letter through the post
- ☐ Our website www.bpp.com

3. Why did you decide to purchase this Text?
(Tick one box only)

- ☐ Have used companion Assessment workbook
- ☐ Have used BPP Texts in the past
- ☐ Recommendation by friend/colleague
- ☐ Recommendation by a lecturer at college
- ☐ Saw advertising in journals
- ☐ Saw information on BPP website
- ☐ Other ______________

4. Which (if any) aspects of our advertising do you find useful?
(Tick as many boxes as are relevant)

- ☐ Prices and publication dates of new editions
- ☐ Information on product content
- ☐ Facility to order books off-the-page
- ☐ None of the above

5. Have you used the companion Assessment Workbook? Yes ☐ No ☐

6. Have you used the companion Passcards? Yes ☐ No ☐

7. Your ratings, comments and suggestions would be appreciated on the following areas.

	Very useful	*Useful*	*Not useful*
Introductory section (How to use this text, study checklist, etc)	☐	☐	☐
Chapter introductions	☐	☐	☐
Syllabus learning outcomes	☐	☐	☐
Activities	☐	☐	☐
The Real World examples	☐	☐	☐
Quick quizzes	☐	☐	☐
Quality of explanations			
Index	☐	☐	☐
Structure and presentation	☐	☐	☐

	Excellent	*Good*	*Adequate*	*Poor*
Overall opinion of this Text	☐	☐	☐	☐

8. Do you intend to continue using BPP CIM products? ☐ Yes ☐ No

On the reverse of this page is space for you to write your comments about our Study Text. We welcome your feedback.

Please return to: CIM Publishing Manager, BPP Learning Media, FREEPOST, London, W12 8BR.

TELL US WHAT YOU THINK

Please note any further comments and suggestions/errors below. For example, was the text accurate, readable, concise, user-friendly and comprehensive?